Sexual Cultures in Aotearoa/New Zealand Education

# SEXUAL CULTURES IN AOTEAROA/NEW ZEALAND EDUCATION

EDITED BY **ALEXANDRA C. GUNN**
AND **LEE A. SMITH**

Published by Otago University Press
Level 1, 398 Cumberland Street
Dunedin, New Zealand
university.press@otago.ac.nz
www.otago.ac.nz/press

First published 2015
Copyright © the authors as named.
Volume copyright © Otago University Press

The moral rights of the authors have been asserted.

ISBN 978-1-877578-68-7

A catalogue record for this book is available from the National Library of New Zealand. This book is copyright. Except for the purpose of fair review, no part may be stored or transmitted in any form or by any means, electronic or mechanical, including recording or storage in any information retrieval system, without permission in writing from the publishers. No reproduction may be made, whether by photocopying or by any other means, unless a licence has been obtained from the publisher.

Cover design: Sam Orchard
Editor: Imogen Coxhead
Index: Diane Lowther

Printed in New Zealand by Printing.com, Wellington

# Contents

**Foreword**
Prof. Kerry H. Robinson, Western Sydney University ... 7

1. **Introduction**
   Alexandra C. Gunn & Lee A. Smith ... 9

2. **The potential of queer theorising in early childhood education:** *Disrupting heteronormativity and practising for inclusion*
   Alexandra C. Gunn ... 21

3. **Conversations with potential:** *Teaching for inclusion*
   Ann Hardie ... 35

4. **'I like my beer cold, my TV loud and my homosexuals f-laming':** *Using critical literacy to draw attention to heteronormative hegemony in texts of popular culture*
   Susan Sandretto ... 49

5. **How are teenage male students redefining masculinity and heterosexuality?**
   Steven S. Sexton ... 67

6. **Queer students and same-sex partners at the school formal**
   Lee A. Smith ... 82

7. **'Picturing' heteronormativity in secondary schools**
   Louisa Allen ... 99

8. **Sexuality, education and diversity**
   Katie Fitzpatrick ... 117

9. **Acknowledging and working double binds:** *The im/possible work of a high school Queer–Straight Alliance*
   Kathleen Quinlivan — 135

10. **(Trans)gender diversity, cisnormativity and New Zealand education cultures:** *A dialogue*
    James Burford, Joey MacDonald, Sam Orchard & Philip Wills — 150

11. **'I feel proud of what I've achieved while having a baby so young':** *Teenage mothers contest normative constructions of their sexual, social and educational identities*
    Jenny Hindin-Miller & Rebeccah Hibbert — 173

12. **A queer lens on initial teacher education**
    Vicki M. Carpenter & Debora Lee — 189

13. **Pulling the monstrosity of (hetero)normativity out of the closet:** *Teacher education as a problem and an answer*
    lisahunter, Debi Futter-Puati & Janette Kelly — 209

14. **Challenging the pervasiveness of heteronormativity**
    Lee A. Smith & Alexandra C. Gunn — 226

    **Appendix:** Additional resources — 240

    **Author biographies** — 242

    **Index** — 247

# Foreword

### Kerry H. Robinson

Alex Gunn and Lee Smith are to be congratulated for bringing together this groundbreaking collection of papers exploring sexual cultures in Aotearoa/New Zealand. The book is timely and will make an invaluable contribution to the body of knowledge and debate about gender and sexuality diversity in education, not just in New Zealand but internationally.

This collection brings together a dynamic mix of papers, by significant New Zealand researchers and educators, that explore the multiple manifestations, pervasiveness and impact of heteronormativity across different educational sectors, from early childhood, primary and secondary schooling, through to teacher education. Taking an eclectic approach to theory of gender and sexuality, knowledge and power, and around the tensions of educational institutions as sites of potential change, this book addresses the contradictory, challenging and complex issues associated with heteronormativity in education. The contributors make the critical point that heteronormativity does not just negatively impact children and young people who are sexuality and gender diverse, it also and narrows the options of all children and young people (and adults) in terms of how they can safely and supportively explore and express their gender and sexual identities and desires.

This is not a new area of research; indeed, many of these authors have made noteworthy and inspiring contributions over many years to working for change in this area through research and as educators. Collectively, this work makes a difference.

Still, the authors demonstrate the need for educators and policymakers to effectively intervene in heteronormative discourses and practices that are pervasive in schools and other educational sites. Schooling continues to be identified as the major site of young people's experiences of homophobia and transphobia, mainly from their peers, but also from teachers. The heteronormativity that prevails in the curricula – for example, the failure of sexuality education to appropriately reflect the experiences and include the specific needs of sexuality- and gender-diverse young people – can have significant consequences on their health and wellbeing. The urgency and significance of this is highlighted in the recent Australian study *Growing Up Queer* (Robinson et al. 2014). Of the 1032 18–27-year-olds who completed the survey in this research, 41 per cent had thought about self-harm and/or suicide; 33 per cent had harmed themselves; and 16 per cent had attempted suicide, the youngest at the age of 10. These are disturbing figures. The discussions in this book are foundational to counteracting the heteronormativity that contributes to many young people's feelings of exclusion and despair.

The importance of addressing heteronormativity early in life, including in early childhood education settings, cannot be overstated. It is essential to provide young children with positive narratives of gender and sexuality diversity, to allow them to explore their gender without the expectations and pressure to conform to heternormative gender binaries, and to start building positive ethical and respectful relationships around gender and sexuality diversity early in their lives. These are all critical aspects of building children's sexual citizenship. This book makes an important contribution to opening up the spaces required to begin to have new and different discussions with young children about gender and sexuality; and to challenging the discourses that underpin the misconception that gender and sexuality issues are irrelevant to young children.

Children are active agents in the process of gender construction, not only regulating their own expressions of gender within binary norms but also actively policing the gender performances of other children. This process of gender construction is inextricably constituted within and normalised through the process of 'heterosexualisation' that is an integral part of children's everyday educational experiences, reflected through mock weddings, chase and kiss, mummies and daddies. This play-acting, or rehearsing of heternormative narratives, is frequently encouraged and celebrated in family and early childhood educational settings. It remains to be seen if new same-sex marriage laws will provide a counter social discourse.

This is an exciting book in that each author encourages readers to critically reflect on the research and on the arguments; readers are both invited and challenged to begin to think differently about sexual cultures in education. As Michel Foucault reminds us: 'There are times in life when the question of knowing if one can think differently than one thinks, and perceive differently than one sees, is absolutely necessary if one is to go on looking and reflecting at all.'

# 1.
# Introduction

## Alexandra C. Gunn & Lee A. Smith

Aotearoa/New Zealand is a small country located in the South Pacific with a population of four million. In 2014 the *Lonely Planet* travel guide rated New Zealand as the second most 'gay friendly' country in the world. Certainly we have some of the most advanced human rights legislation. Under the Human Rights Act 1993, discrimination on the basis of gender and sexuality was made illegal, and in 2013 the Marriage Act was extended to include same-sex couples. Research suggests, however, that New Zealand's relatively 'inclusive' social climate is not always reflected in our educational settings.

'Heteronormativity' is a term coined by Warner (1991) to describe the assumption that heterosexuality is the norm, to the detriment of alternatives. This book explores how such assumptions operate in education. We draw attention to the pervasiveness of heteronormativity within the everyday contexts of all sectors of education in New Zealand, and its discriminatory effects. We consider how this shapes thinking, policies and practices, and we ask what this means for teachers, students and parents in early childhood education, schools, tertiary and alternative settings. How can education settings become more socially just sites of inclusion for sexual and gender diversity?

Understanding more fully the way in which heteronormativity works in education will help empower every educator to work towards realising social change in educational facilities. Many are actively doing so already. We invite others to join us in resisting the many injustices perpetuated by the unchecked discriminatory discourses that have shaped New Zealand education historically, and continue to shape it today. Only once these have been critically appraised can we work towards a more equitable education system (and, by association, society). The chapters in this book are intended as a tool for raising awareness and a call to action.

The book includes research on, with and by queer students, queer and trans*[1] academics, community workers and heterosexual allies. We aim to demonstrate how the disruption of heteronormativity is achievable and in the interests of all.

In New Zealand education settings children and young people perform their gender in multiple ways and enact multiple sexualities, even though research demonstrates that heterosexuality is constituted as the 'normal' and supposedly most desirable form of sexual expression in these settings. In this book we document how children, young people and educators reproduce heteronormativity, and how it fosters homophobic and transphobic bullying, as well as the 'othering' of those who depart from the 'norm'. We also demonstrate how some children, young people, families and educators actively resist such discrimination.

Heteronormativity plays out in different ways in different contexts. In early childhood centres and primary schools, it is often assumed that families are headed by two opposite sex/gender parents. In some cases this has led to parents in same-sex relationships being denied information about their own and/or their partner's child. There is a failure to recognise the increasing diversity of family forms that exist in New Zealand, which include families headed by same-sex parents, two same-sex couples who share parenting responsibilities, or children produced with the aid of a sperm or egg donor who may or may not play a role in a child's life. In New Zealand, women in same-sex relationships are increasingly choosing to have children, something Bree (2003) terms the 'lesbian baby boom' (3).

In all education sectors there is a lack of queer material included in the curriculum – even in sexuality education, which is compulsory in New Zealand high schools. Furthermore, when same-sex desire *is* mentioned in the curriculum it can leave queer students feeling distressed. For instance, in Smith's (2006) research on six young lesbian/bisexual women's experiences of high school, one lesbian participant reported feeling a sense of unease when lesbianism was discussed in sexuality education in relation to oral sex and the use of dental dams.[2] The young woman, who was involved with another student at the time, was not open about her sexuality at school and stated that she felt exposed by the discussion.

---

1 As explained by Burford et al. in Chapter 10, trans* is a signifier for a number of distinct, yet connected non-normative gender identities. Using the * at the end of 'trans' reminds us that a number of words might follow it (such as feminine, masculine, gender, or sexual).
2 A dental dam is device for prevention of sexually transmitted diseases during oral sex.

In a more recent study, Painter (2009) conducted research with 105 students attending high schools in one region of New Zealand. Painter asked the participants (who were not asked to specify their sexuality) what were the 'challenges and supports queer students would find [at their] school'. Although the majority of participants could not remember queer desires being mentioned in class, an unspecified number reported watching *Heavenly Creatures*, *Billy Elliot* and *Brokeback Mountain* in film studies, all of which contain queer themes. Others said queer topics were discussed in social studies, religious instruction, English, classical studies and drama.

In many New Zealand high schools trans* and queer students or those assumed to be queer are subjected to bullying. Rossen, Luccassen, Denny and Robinson (2009) found that of 8002 students surveyed on their health and wellbeing, approximately 8 per cent reported being same- or both-sex attracted, or unsure of their sexual attractions. Although the majority of same/both-sex- (74 per cent) and opposite-sex-attracted students (85 per cent) reported that they felt safe at school, same/both-sex-attracted participants were more likely to report instances of bullying:

*Twice as many same/both-sex-attracted as opposite-sex-attracted students had been afraid that someone would hurt or bother them at school; nearly three times as many [had] stayed away from school the previous month because they were afraid that someone would hurt them or bother them; and about three times as many were bullied weekly at school (p. 26).*

Such statistics highlight how student peer groups can sometimes make schooling intolerable for queer youth.

Research on how heteronormativity is perpetuated and/or resisted in New Zealand's initial teacher education settings is scarce, yet that which has been done highlights how pre-service teachers, like their counterparts in high schools, find queer desire and sexuality seldom discussed in their classes. This is unfortunate because prospective teachers who are educated about sexual and gender diversity can incorporate this information into their teaching and work to affirm queer students, families and sexual diversity.

A number of chapters in this edited collection are embedded in queer theory, which draws on the work of Michel Foucault and especially *The History of Sexuality* (1978). According to Foucault, prior to the nineteenth century people's engagement in various sex acts, such as male-to-male sex, did not define them. Studies of sexuality in the nineteenth century, however, led to a 'new specification of individuals', according to Foucault. This identified those whose sexuality deviated from the so-called norm espoused by dominant biological, scientific and religious discourses of the time. Sexual normalcy was, of course, the ideal of the monogamous married heterosexual couple who had sex in the privacy of the family home for the primary purpose of procreation.

Among the raft of newly specified individuals came such categories as 'frigid' women, and what we currently understand by the term 'homosexual'. Foucault states that the homosexual became 'a personage, a past, a case history, and a childhood ... with an indiscrete anatomy and possibly a mysterious physiology' (43).

## Genealogy of childhood sexuality

Since this book centres on New Zealand education it is necessary to consider evolving understandings of childhood and sexuality in New Zealand. The scientific study of sexuality in the Victorian era produced understandings of 'normality' and 'perversity'. Children were seen as being both prone to and in danger from sexual activity (specifically masturbation); they were 'defined as "preliminary" sexual beings, on this side of sex, yet within it, astride a dangerous dividing line' (Foucault 1978, 104). It was up to adults to take control of children's sexual potential and to produce it in a safe manner.

Official attitudes to sexuality in early Victorian New Zealand society emulated those of Europe. Drawing upon notions of childhood innocence and ignorance, children were seen as needing protection from sex and sexuality. Close supervision of children, especially during bath and bedtimes, was deemed necessary if adults were to preserve the innocence of childhood. This pursuit of moral and physical hygiene was reinforced by new knowledge regarding the proper and scientific approach to child-rearing that swept the country in the early part of the twentieth century.

Truby King, a medical doctor, director of Seacliff mental asylum and founder of the Plunket Society, began instructing New Zealand mothers on how to raise healthy and moral children. King's work in psychiatry had convinced him that low mental health resulted from improper nutrition, hygiene and poor moral standards early in life. King designed a regimen for meeting the basic physical needs of infants and young children, which emphasised sanitation, self-control and routine.

Disseminated through the Plunket Society, King's regimen gained wide appeal and was effectively institutionalised through the appointment of King to the position of Director of Child Welfare in 1921. Through his appointment, government policy and Plunket doctrine on child health and child-rearing merged. By 1930, 65 per cent of all non-Māori infants in New Zealand were under Plunket care, and by 1947 the figure had risen to 85 per cent (Olssen 1981). Plunket, together with Truby King, promised all New Zealanders, especially mothers, that they would be able to produce healthier children.

The interest in child health and development gained momentum in the twentieth century as the scientific study of children increased. Norms for various domains of children's development were established, including an orthodoxy of the sexual child, in which Sigmund Freud's theses were hugely influential. Freud, who had studied sexuality and its development in the 1920s, published his findings in a series of essays that contributed to the development of a theory of sex (Freud 1925). In the second of these essays, a piece concerning infantile sexuality, Freud opposed the earlier Victorian suppression of associations of childhood and sexuality. He believed that the healthy and well-adjusted child would inevitably grow up heterosexual, and considered homosexuality a form of arrested development.

Freud's work paved the way for child developmentalists to develop a multidisciplinary theory about childhood and the development of sexuality, in which childhood sexual behaviour was normalised and explained according to age and stage theory. These ideas were to be entrenched in New Zealand society after a 1937 visit from British child psychologist Susan Isaacs, whose 'ability to translate complex psychological theories into meaningful rationales and suggestions for teachers and parents ... made her writing popular' (May 1997, 168). Like Freud, Isaacs posited that 'normal' sexuality development followed a heterosexual trajectory. She advocated sensitive management of sexual activity in children. If a boy child was found fondling his genitals, for instance, Isaacs' advice to parents was to ignore the behaviour, because if attention were drawn to it, he may develop intense feelings of distress and shame. Isaacs described children's interest in their bodies as an 'expression of the intense inner conflict of the child's feelings towards his parents' (Isaacs 1929, 111). For a boy, it was an outward expression of his struggle to 'overcome his desire for absolute passion for his mother ...[and] a common thing in the ordinary course of development' (Isaacs 1929, 11–12). The associations between childhood and sexuality were again cast as dangerous.

As the twentieth century advanced, more moderate views eventually prevailed, and by the late 1960s associations between concepts of 'children' and 'sexuality' were rendered ordinary and generally non-problematic. In education settings, teachers' practices became imbued with the notion of a normalised sequence of child development, and teachers educated parents on what to expect of their children with respect to normal sexual play and behaviour. In the latter decades of the twentieth century, however, the connotation of danger in relation to children and sexuality came back into the public consciousness.

In November 1991 five early childhood teachers from Christchurch's Civic Crèche, four female and one male, were charged with committing sexual indecencies against children in their centre. After depositions, charges were dropped against the women, but Peter Ellis was tried on 25 charges, found guilty on 16 of these and sentenced to 10 years in prison. The case reverberated throughout the country and education officials moved quickly to establish children's safety, as well as to allay parental fears. A heightened state of anxiety about children and sex erupted.

At the beginning of the 21st century the sensitivity continues, with growing fears about the hypersexualisation of young people, as well as the dangers of sexual predation made ever more possible by technological advancements and social media. It is within this discursive context that this book is situated.

## Terminology

A number of specific terms are used in the chapters of the book and we define some of them here. Some have been criticised by queer theorists and academics and we briefly discuss these views. We acknowledge that different authors may use these terms differently and therefore these definitions are meant as a guide to their use is this book only.

### Queer

The term queer is used regularly as both a noun and a verb and in relation to the social and political theory 'queer theory'. Reclaimed by non-heterosexual activists and subjects, queer is an umbrella term that refers to subjects who perform their gender and/or sexuality in non-normative ways, including asexuals, lesbians, gay men, bisexuals, pansexuals, genderqueers, cross-dressers, intersexed, trans* persons, fa`afafine and takatāpui. Queer is a term usually favoured by younger people, while some older same-sex-attracted people wonder if such a term can ever be totally reclaimed from its past usage as a homophobic epithet.

Queer as an adjective is used as a challenge to all forms of normalcy, including sexual identity categories and traditional educational practices.

### *Homophobia/Heteronormativity*

The term homophobia is also used in the collection, but is a term that has been critiqued by numerous queer academics. Hinson (1996) explains that the 'phobia' part of the word suggests that when someone meets a queer subject they may experience a pathological response, similar to how someone who is arachnophobic would react when they encounter a spider. The homosexual fear or panic response has historically been used as a legal defence in trials of people accused of enacting violence against queer people.

Although we will at times refer to homophobia, this book privileges the use of the term heteronormativity because this term places heterosexuality rather than same-sex-attraction under investigation. We acknowledge that the term homophobia is more widely used in society and is likely better understood in education settings. The New Zealand Post Primary Teachers' Association's resources to schools, aimed at affirming sexuality and gender diversity, use the term homophobia.

### *Cisgender and cisnormativity*

In educational research it is common for the term heteronormativity to be used to address the concerns of lesbian, gay, bisexual and trans* people. Queer is also used to highlight the experiences of lesbian, gay, bisexual and trans* students in New Zealand schools, but trans* students are seldom included in research on queer populations. In relation to the similar but different form of prejudice experienced by trans* people, researchers sometimes use the label cisnormativity, to describe the privileging of people who identify their gender as consistent with the sex they were assigned at birth.

## The book's chapters

This book's authors are multiply positioned by our age, ethnicity, gender, sexuality performance and so forth, so we use a range of terms and theories. Some chapters adopt a queer theoretical framework, others Bourdieuian theory, and some can be considered to take up a liberal feminist approach.

We hope that by using a variety of theoretical perspectives and terms, we may attract a larger and more diverse audience than had we written with queer theory alone. All authors, however, are invested in disrupting the (hetero)normative status quo. As a collection, this book's chapters provide a contemporary account of how heteronormativity operates in New Zealand educational settings, with the goal of change.

In Chapter 2 Alexandra Gunn draws upon several recent studies to discuss how heteronormativity shapes experiences for children, families and teachers of the very young. She argues that a close reading of the early childhood curriculum framework *Te Whāriki* establishes heteronormativity as intolerable in early childhood education. The chapter claims that changes must be made if the radical inclusive potential of the curriculum framework is to be realised. Gunn concludes by arguing that small acts of resistance, through queer questionings, can lead to significant gains in disrupting the status quo.

In Chapter 3 Ann Hardie reflects on the fact that few school libraries contain children's picture books depicting same-sex parented families. She argues that exclusion of such resources restricts learning conversations that have the potential to develop, among children, understandings of diversity and different identities. While non-normative sexualities are increasingly in the public eye, they remain largely invisible within school settings, where heterosexuality is promoted. To interrupt this, Hardie introduces several picture books depicting same-sex-parented families and clusters them according to theme. She shows how some of these books simply reflect the sexual status quo while others can be used as classroom resources to challenge heteronormativity.

Primary school children are immersed in popular cultural texts, argues Susan Sandretto in Chapter 4. Drawing from New Zealand research into critical literacy and providing a framework for critical analysis that will support students to question discourses of heteronormativity, Sandretto shows how teachers can help students question discourses that are frequently taken for granted in such texts. She supports the reader to engage in a critical analysis of an episode of *The Simpsons*, an advertisement for a Calvin Klein fragrance, and a cartoon from the *School Journal* series. Such exemplars are designed to help educators to work alongside students as they investigate ways to explore the hegemony of the heterosexual matrix.

In Chapter 5 Steven Sexton explores how male secondary school students regulate and negotiate their masculinities in friendship groupings.

Using a framework developed by McCormack (2012), Sexton explores how language is constantly evolving. He shows how the term 'that's so gay' is not purely a homophobic epithet, but is an example of 'gay discourse' that in some contexts is not intended to offend same-sex-attracted subjects. Sexton's analysis recognises how a school's culture and student friendship groups expand and constrain understandings of acceptable masculinity.

In New Zealand popular culture and media, the school formal is constructed as a relentlessly heterosexual social sphere. Some schools openly ban or discourage queer students from attending the formal with their same-sex partners. In Chapter 6 Lee Smith investigates the policies of three New Zealand secondary schools – a co-ed, a girls' and a boys' school – in regard to queer students attending the school formal. She also looks at student attitudes in those schools. Her research shows the extent to which the school formal, as a heteronormative site, is influenced by the gender make-up of the student body, policy, and perceptions of risk and safety.

In Chapter 7 Louisa Allen examines the way heteronormativity is produced in typically unexplored dimensions of schooling. Consistent with an identified 'spatial turn' in the social sciences (Kalervo, Gulson & Symes 2007), and renewed concerns with materialisation (Bennett, 2010), the chapter asks us to consider the multiple intersections of people, bodies, places and things. Allen draws on photographs from a study of sexual cultures of schooling (Allen 2009) to illuminate how heteronormativity is both (re)produced and disrupted at school.

In Chapter 8 Katie Fitzpatrick documents experiences of Māori and Pasifika students in a South Auckland secondary school, exploring how the students' views of gender and sexuality play out in their school environments. Fitzpatrick shows how dominant narratives of gender and sexuality that are reproduced in schools serve to reinscribe a narrow range of social norms. She then documents the potential for teachers to disrupt such norms through their engagements with students.

In Chapter 9 Kathleen Quinlivan reflects on the im/possibilities and conundrums of researching sexuality education queerly. She draws on Derrida's notion of 'aporia' or the double bind, to explore what it might mean to research queerly in schools – in ways that are open to knowing the unexpected more fully. Writing from a study of student Queer–Straight Alliances in New Zealand secondary schools, she explores double binds of the sort that queer researchers confront as they attempt to work queerly in schools where normalcy is a dominant discourse and an often desired state of being.

In recent years a proliferation of studies have identified and examined the effects of heteronormativity across education cultures. These studies have largely failed to address the concerns of trans* students, and the ways in which cisnormativity also shapes education cultures. In Chapter 10 James Burford, Joey MacDonald, Samuel Orchard and Phillip Wills, who identify as and/or have investments in the well-being of trans* communities, begin a conversation in New Zealand education studies about the place of cisnormativity in education.

Teenage mothers are often marginalised and excluded from 'mainstream' educational contexts. Becoming a mother is a significant turning point in a young woman's life and often encourages young women to reconsider the importance of education to their own and their child's future opportunities. In Chapter 11 Jenny Hindin-Miller and Rebeccah Hibbert report on a group of young mothers' perspectives of their re-engagement in education at a Teen Parent Unit. Attending the unit provides the young women with affirmation and support of their non-normative sexuality and gender identities.

In Chapter 12 Vicki Carpenter and Debora Lee explore the climate of a pre-service teacher education faculty. They present findings of two research studies conducted in 2002 and 2009, which explored staff and student attitudes, beliefs and practices in relation to sexual orientation and their professional work. They found that while some small and positive changes were evident after seven years, the teacher education climate in 2009 appeared to remain essentially heteronormative. There has been considerable progress since 2009, however, and the faculty in 2014 is far more inclusive of queer lives and perspectives.

As pre-service teacher educators, lisahunter, Debi Futter-Puati and Janette Kelly work to have students recognise and affirm sexual diversity, but their attempts have often been met with resistance. Using a Bourdieuian framework and drawing on their own teaching experiences, in Chapter 13 they create a fictional narrative in which they provide examples of how heteronormativity is typically reproduced and/or resisted in encounters between pre-service teachers. The authors include a number of questions for use by teacher educators and pre-service teachers in challenging heteronormativity in their pedagogy and practice.

The concluding discussion in Chapter 14 weaves together threads of activism and action from this collective work. We comment on this

What might happen if we were to take Michel Foucault, Pierre Bourdieu and Judith Butler with us into New Zealand's education settings? *Sam Orchard*

collection's limitations and areas of possible future research, and we reassert the challenge our authors and their research participants bring to the field of education in Aotearoa/New Zealand: to find ways of teaching that are more socially just, inclusive and respectful of social diversity, and which support many and varied gender and sexual cultures.

# References

Allen, L. (2009), '"Caught in the act": Ethics committee review and researching the sexual culture of schools', *Qualitative Research*, 9(4), 395–410.

Bennett, J. (2010), *Vibrant Matter: A political ecology of things*, Durham: Duke University Press.

Bree, C. (2003), 'Lesbian Mothers: Queer Families. The experience of planned pregnancy', (Master's thesis), Auckland University of Technology, Auckland.

Foucault, M. (1978), *The History of Sexuality: An introduction* (R. Hurley, trans.), New York: Random House.

Freud, S. (1925), 'The sexual aberrations', (A.A. Brill, trans.), in *Three Contributions to the Theory of Sex* (1–36), New York and Washington: Nervous and Mental Disease Publishing.

Hinson, S. (1996), 'A practice focus approach to addressing heterosexist violence in Australian schools', in L. Laskey & C. Beavis (eds), *Schooling and Sexualities: A practice focus approach to addressing violence in Australian schools* (241–58), Deakin: Deakin Centre for Education and Change.

Isaacs, S. (1929), *The Nursery Years. The mind of the child from birth to six years*, London: Routledge & Kegan Paul.

Kalervo, N., Gulson, S. & Colin, S. (2007), 'Knowing one's place: Educational theory, policy, and the spatial turn', in N. Kalervo, S. Gulson & S. Colin (eds), *Spatial Theories of Education: Policy and geography matters* (1–16), New York: Routledge.

May, H. (1997), *The Discovery of Early Childhood*, Auckland: Bridget Williams Books & New Zealand Council for Educational Research.

McCormack, Mark (2012), 'Queer masculinities, gender conformity and the secondary school', in J.C. Landreau & N.M. Rodriguez (eds), *Queer Masculinities: A critical reader in education* (Vol. 21, 35–46), Dordrecht: Springer.

Painter, H. (2009), 'How safe?: How safe and inclusive are Otago secondary schools? Ae ranei he haumaru, he wahi whāi kit e katoa ngā kura tuarua o Otago?' A report on the implementations from the 'Safety in our schools – Ko te harumaru i o tatou kura' action kit: He purongo ūruhi i ngā tuanaki a te kete mahi 'Safety in our schools – Ko te harumaru i o tatu kura', Dunedin, NZ: OUSA Queer Support.

Rossen, F.V, Lucassen, M.F.G., Denny, S. & Robinson, E. (2009), *Youth '07 the health and wellbeing of secondary students in New Zealand: Results for young people attracted to the same or both sexes*, Auckland: University of Auckland.

Smith, L. (2006), 'Un/silencing Lesbian and Bisexual Students: Some women's experiences of how their high schools met their needs', (Master's thesis), University of Otago, Dunedin.

Warner, M. (1991), 'Introduction: Fear of a queer planet', *Social Text*, 29, 3–17.

# 2.
# The potential of queer theorising in early childhood education

Disrupting heteronormativity and practising for inclusion

Alexandra C. Gunn

In the early childhood setting heteronormativity plays out along related trajectories of the family, genders and sexualities (Gunn 2011). It inheres in children's play, adults' expectations about gender and sexualities development, and related policies and practices. Yet New Zealand's early childhood curriculum framework *Te Whāriki* (Ministry of Education 1996, hereafter MOE) establishes that heteronormativity in early childhood education is intolerable.

Heteronormativity is the effect of construing particular forms of gender, sexuality and the family as normal. In doing so, we simultaneously establish the grounds upon which different things are known as *other*-than-normal (or abnormal). Such forms of binary thought are fundamental to creating and maintaining meaning (Davies 1994) and also reflect and uphold asymmetrical power relationships in society. In a binary formation, the first term represents a standard against which the second or sub-ordinate term is measured or understood (Burr 1995); the second term is conceptualised as troubling because it represents a deviation from the norm (MacNaughton 2005).

In this chapter I draw upon several New Zealand-based studies related to sexualities and early childhood education, to discuss how heteronormativity shapes experiences in this domain. I argue that small acts of resistance, through queer questioning, can lead to significant gains in disrupting the heteronormative status quo, and explore ways in which early childhood teachers might work with and against particular forms of binary thinking. My purpose is to help teachers imagine and realise early childhood education that resists heteronormative discourses – or what I refer to as practising beyond the (hetero)norm.[1] To illustrate my arguments, I draw on data from the study 'We're a Family', which explored how lesbians and gay men in Aotearoa/New Zealand were creating and maintaining families within the context of then recent legislative change (Gunn & Surtees 2009; 2010).[2] The study involved interviews with parents from 19 families, and found continued issues of homophobia and heteronormativity in families' encounters with New Zealand education settings. It called for recognition of parents' work in supporting their children to navigate others' negative responses to their family structures; it also illustrated how parents may represent themselves and their families so that others might come to understand and value their diversity. The study, while not solely focused on education or early childhood, sits alongside several others conducted in early childhood education within a New Zealand context (Gunn 2008; Jarvis 2010; Lee 2010; Surtees 2006).

Together, this body of research indicates a growing awareness of, and interest in, social justice and diversity issues where sexualities are concerned. These authors seized upon affordances offered by progressive law changes[3] and inclusive education law and policy[4] to show how, despite the existence of support for socially just teaching, the practices of some teachers and institutions remained exclusionary and problematic. The research has also sought to exemplify how educators' teaching might change for the better. In this chapter I argue for early childhood education practices that more adequately address the challenges of practising beyond the (hetero)norm.

## Supporting family competence, parental identity and social inclusion

Often the first formal institution that parents and children encounter is the early childhood setting. Professionals within these settings play an important role in supporting family competence, parental identity and social inclusion (Casper & Schultz 1999; Lee & Duncan 2008; Oates 2010).

---

1   The bracketed (hetero) in this term denotes the fact that the so-called norm in sexualities terms is heterosexual sexuality. The bracketed (hetero) is a queer strategy that both calls to attention and questions this cultural framing.
2   The study referred to here was funded by the New Zealand Families Commission as part of the Blue Skies Research Fund. Data included in this paper are reported in the study's official report (Gunn & Surtees 2009) and from a presentation about the research, not published elsewhere (Gunn & Surtees 2010).
3   For example, the New Zealand Human Rights Act (1993), the Civil Union Act (2004), the Care of Children Act (2004).
4   Such as the Education Act 1989, and the Ministry of Education's (2008) licencing criteria for centre-based early childhood education and care services.

One of the ways that teachers may support families is through recognition of the uniqueness of relationships within any given family constellation. In a context where heteronormativity prevails, however, the 'heterosexual presumption' (Epstein & Johnson 1994, 198) can mean some relationships are missed. This was the case for lesbian parents in Gunn and Surtees' (2009) study, who reported that they were asked 'Who are you?' or were referred to as 'grandmother', 'aunt', 'friend', and so on. When faced with incorrect assumptions, parents are forced to decide whether or not to correct these. As may be appreciated, at the very beginning of a relationship with a new early childhood setting or school this can be difficult for parents to manage. Challenging another person's heterosexual presumptions may involve having to cope with any ensuing embarrassment or homophobia; to do this in front of children and perhaps other parents is doubly confronting. It is up to teachers, therefore, to be aware of their assumptions so that families may find recognition and feel welcomed, whatever their legal or biological connection to the child may be.

Children in households with parents of the same gender are often considered to be 'motherless' or 'fatherless'. This is because the normalising effects of heteronormativity lead us to assume that there will only be two parents in any child's life. But if a gay couple has a child with the support of a surrogate, that surrogate may still have an ongoing relationship with the family. Similarly, an anonymous donor parent with no continuing practical or material relationship with a child may be openly acknowledged in a child's family. This is illustrated in the response of Penny, a three-year-old child of participants in Gunn and Surtees' (2009) study, who reportedly gave an account of her (anonymous donor) father to a 'man at the library' one day, saying, 'Oh my dad's a very kind man. I don't even know him. My mum doesn't even know what he looks like. He gave us some sperm' (Gunn & Surtees 2009, 34).

It is up to educators and institutions to be open to the diversity they will encounter and to create an inclusive environment for learning. When policies and practices respond to family diversity and families are welcomed on their own terms, it can lead to empowerment, enhanced family security, and security over future events (Kelly & Surtees 2013; Surtees 2011; Terreni, Gunn, Kelly & Surtees 2010).

## Heternormativity shapes early childhood contexts

There are many ways to perpetuate heteronormativity: it may be overt, unintentional, sustained or fleeting. Even with the best policies in place, heteronormative practices – historically established in early childhood education (Gunn 2009) – can still have a negative impact on families' experiences (Cloughessy & Waniganayake 2013a; Jarvis 2010; Lee 2010; Terreni et al. 2010). Heteronormativity inheres in children's everyday play, and in adults' expectations about gender and sexuality. Mothers parenting alone may be told their children are 'missing out' on important male role models; parents of boys whose performances of gender do not conform to hegemonic forms of masculinity may be asked if they are 'worried' about their son being gay; and strict adherence to narrow interpretations of privacy laws may lead teachers to deny non-biological parents access to information about their children (Gunn 2008). Moana's reflection about her daughter's early childhood teachers' practices is illustrative: '[L]ast year she made a fathers' day card and they just gave it to me and I thought, hmmm, now should I give this to Sue or should I keep it myself?!' (Gunn & Surtees 2010).

As a pervasive discourse in early childhood education, heteronormativity relies upon dominant and traditional ideas about gender, sexuality and the family that are mutually reinforcing (Gunn 2011). The concept of the traditional nuclear family, for instance, relies upon understandings of 'normal' heterosexuality and opposite-gender attraction for its coherence. The idea that there are only two 'proper' genders – male and female – plays to understandings of so-called 'normal' sexuality development, which invariably assume that 'normally' developing young children will grow up to be heterosexual (Gunn 2008). These enduring and traditional constructions of sexuality, family and gender persist in everyday language and actions. In order to expand understandings of diverse realities, early childhood educators must be attuned to their own entanglements in binary forms of thought – and catch themselves in the act of perpetuating these. It is equally important to encourage children to transcend these by supporting them in their play, for example by acknowledging that it is possible for girl best-friends to grow up, love and marry each other in New Zealand; or by accepting a boy's desire to wear high heels and a dress to kindergarten.

Teachers can play a big role in opening up understandings of family, sexuality and gender diversity. Several families in Gunn and Surtees' (2009; 2010) research talked about how teachers advocated this for them. Lesbian mother Sacha said: '[Reggie's peers] just couldn't understand it [the family], they couldn't quite get their heads around it ... the children were, "I just can't understand how it works", they do tend to regard Kari as the nanny looking after my baby who pops down to visit quite often' (Gunn & Surtees 2010). In this case Reggie's teacher intervened, saying that Reggie did have two mums and there were 'lots of ways to have families' – a factual and neutral response that both Kari and Sacha appreciated (Gunn & Surtees 2010).

Despite recent progressive law changes in New Zealand and generational shifts in recognising and living more openly with sexual, gender and family diversity (Gunn & Surtees 2009; Kelly & Surtees 2013; Power et al. 2012), moving beyond heteronormativity remains challenging. Many teachers still feel ill equipped to resist heteronormative discourses (Cloughessy & Waniganayake 2013b; Gunn 2008; Jarvis & Sandretto 2010; Souto-Manning & Hermann-Wilmarth 2008), and some people still consider non-heterosexual sexualities, diverse family structures and post-structural understandings of gender immoral, improper and abnormal. How then might the teacher who desires to disrupt heteronormativity proceed?

## Using *Te Whāriki* as a tool for advocating practice beyond the (hetero)norm

The curriculum framework *Te Whāriki* (MOE 1996) provides statements about the kinds of learning environments teachers in early childhood education are expected to build. Using the framework, teachers should work in collaboration with children and families to enact curriculum that is empowering, holistic, inclusive of family/whānau and community aspirations for children, and relationships based. These expectations are encapsulated in the four principles of the curriculum. *Te Whāriki* acts not as a syllabus for practice but as a guide for thinking. It is founded on the key aspiration: for children to 'grow up as competent and confident learners and communicators, healthy in mind, body, and spirit, secure in their sense of belonging and in the knowledge that they make a valued contribution to society' (9). Some aspects of the curriculum framework, including the aforementioned principles, have been prescribed since 2008 (New Zealand Government 2008).

The framework's text includes provocative questions for reflection, such as 'What aspects of the environment help children feel that this is a place where they belong?' (58), and 'In what ways and how well is the curriculum genuinely connected to the children's families and cultures?' (66). A teacher with a desire to work beyond the constraints of heteronormativity could arguably use the curriculum framework to support her or his work. Two of the principles are key: that of whānau tangata/family and community, and that of relationships/ngā hononga (MOE 1996). The first of these holds that the wider worlds of family and community have an integral part to play in the early childhood curriculum; the second, that children learn through responsive and reciprocal relationships with people, places and things.

Te Whāriki raises questions about how teachers can know that all family members who are important in children's lives are included in the early childhood community and supported within curriculum. It asks teachers to think about what is done to ensure that everyone who wishes to participate in curriculum is supported to do so. If heteronormativity prevails in the early childhood learning environment, however, some goals may be unattainable. For instance, the first curriculum strand, mana atua/wellbeing, contains goals for children to experience environments where 'their health is promoted [and] their emotional well-being is nurtured' (MOE 1996, 46). The strand of mana whenua/belonging stipulates that children and their families 'feel a sense of belonging' (54); and the mana tangata/contribution strand describes children developing 'confidence that their family background is viewed positively within the early childhood education setting' (66). If teachers are to realise these goals in practice, they must resist and disrupt heteronormativity.

I have long argued that the curriculum framework offers licence for teachers to work against heteronormative discourses (Gunn 2008), yet the extent to which it might provide impetus for such work has been questioned (Surtees 2003). Having engaged in a content analysis of Te Whāriki, Surtees investigated how sexuality was reflected in the framework and considered the resultant implications for children's learning about and development of sexuality. Initially her analysis challenged Te Whāriki and suggested that heteronormativity may have been central to its construction because of the way sexuality is rendered absent in the framework's texts.

Drawing on the work of Tobin (1997) it is possible to understand how the invisibility of sexuality is linked to the theoretical bases of Western early childhood practices. From the Western perspective, understandings of children's development regularly privilege cognition over other developmental domains; as a result, adults may question the relevance of sexuality to young children's lives. Complicating this further, dominant discourses of childhood innocence – which separate out notions of (adult) sexuality from (childhood) asexuality and ignorance – make it easy for matters of sexualities to remain unspoken and disconnected from children (Robinson 2012b; Surtees 2005). Surtees (2003, 136) wrote:

> [C]onsider the principle of 'Empowerment'. In reading about 'Empowerment', as it is described in Te Whāriki, I see the intent is to 'enable' children to develop their 'identity', 'personal dignity', 'self-worth' and 'confidence' (to list but a few of the relevant qualities described in the document). Placing this particular conception of empowerment under scrutiny, I query the potential for all children to experience empowerment and to be enabled without access to information about the full spectrum of sexual orientation.

If narrow readings of the curriculum framework are possible, albeit in my view indefensible, how else then might activist-oriented teachers work to resist heteronormativity?

## Using queer theory to practise beyond the (hetero)norm

Queer theory forms one of a number of late twentieth-century post-structural theories, which brought to light the means by which people use, and are entangled within, discourses of modernity that imbue the body with power, and demarcate boundaries between society's so-called 'normal' and 'abnormal' persons. Brought to prominence in works by feminist scholars Judith Butler (1990) and Eve Kosofsky Sedgwick (1990), queer theory was quickly taken up by others with an interest in genders, sexualities and the like. It became a conceptual tool with which people could disrupt heteronormativity, the concept of which is central to queer theory. The displacement of heterosexual sexuality as the dominant and so-called 'normal' (moral and healthy) form of sexuality is viewed as *the* key project of queer scholars and queer research (Cameron & Kulick 2003; Jackson 2003; Sumara & Davis 1999; Warner 1991).

The term 'queer' itself, however, brings with it a history of multiple emergent and contemporary meanings. It represents an historically derogatory nomenclature for gay men, which has subsequently been reclaimed and used positively as an identity category to name those who claim non-heterosexual sexualities (Alexander 1999; Halberstam 1996; Phelan 1997; Pinar 1998; Slagle 1995). 'Queer' refers to an approach to research that questions normativity (Britzman 1995, 1998; Morris 1998;

Spargo 1999; Taylor & Richardson 2005; Valocchi 2005). It can become an analytic strategy that helps to determine relationships between sexuality, gender, power and notions of normal and deviant (Blaise & Taylor 2012; Cooper 2002; Dilley 1999; Jarvis & Sandretto 2010; Robinson 2012a; Valocchi 2005). Because heteronormativity binds us all to particular social patterns where inequitable power relations reside, I believe teachers do not have to name themselves 'queer' to engage with queer theory.

Surtees (2003) used queer theory to read *Te Whāriki* for ways in which it could support teachers to work against heteronormativity. She found options for 'queering the whāriki' (148)[5] as she reports:

> *I see that while the principles and strands used to weave the metaphor are not overtly queer this invisibility does not necessarily equate with either the presence of heteronormativity or the absence of queerness ... perhaps queer possibilities (and indeed a multitude of other meanings) can be read into the text. The whāriki may provide a space for alternative threads to be woven (Surtees 2003, 150).*

In the following and final section of the chapter, I take up Surtees' argument and, using queer theory, describe two strategies for how teachers may proceed. I also share examples of practices parents have found useful for disrupting the heteronormative status quo.

## Realising the full potential of *Te Whāriki* and practising beyond the (hetero)norm

At the start of the chapter I described how heteronormativity draws upon binary forms of thought for its power and coherence: in particular, the heterosexual/homosexual binary. Comprehending binary thinking as cultural means we must accept that assumptions and understandings associated with binaries might change. Armed with this concept we can work to disrupt binary thinking; doing so would be considered a classic queer theory-inspired move (Cooper 2002). Working queerly, a teacher

---

5   In this instance Surtees uses the word 'whāriki' on its own and not as part of the title of the early childhood curriculum framework. Whāriki means 'woven mat' in te reo Māori (the Māori language). The whāriki metaphor in the early childhood curriculum refers to the act of a collective weaving of a mat upon which all members of an early childhood community can stand. Each early childhood service's whāriki will be unique to that service's social-historical-cultural context and relevant to that community and its aspirations for itself and its children.

might consider what the world would look, sound and feel like if concepts in a given binary were positioned in reverse. For example, if we imagined that it was normal to raise children in same-gender rather than opposite-gender parented families, how might we reflect those opposite-gender parented families' experiences and realities in the learning environment? In considering *Te Whāriki*'s question 'In what ways and how well is the curriculum genuinely connected to the children's families and cultures?' (MOE 1996, 66), how might we respond if we were to view it from the perspective of a woman who had given birth to a child and was raising that child together with a gay couple?

The possibilities for thinking queerly are vast, especially if one takes seriously queer theory's call to question normativity (Britzman 1995, 1998; Morris 1998; Spargo 1999; Taylor & Richardson 2005; Valocchi 2005). Early childhood education is replete with normative thinking: teachers work with particular notions of normal childhood, normal development, of play as the normal site of learning – to name a few instances. Blaise and Taylor (2012) use the strategy of questioning normativity in their consideration of gender development and early childhood education. Through queer theory they ask: Are there any normal expressions of gender? And furthermore, how are understandings of so-called 'natural' and 'normal' gender connected to those of so-called 'normal' sexuality? I asked similar questions in my doctoral study when mapping trajectories of knowledge about young children's gender and sexuality in early childhood (Gunn 2008), and showed how these played out in early childhood policy and practice in New Zealand (Gunn 2009). Jarvis and Sandretto (2010) also engaged this strategy when they wrote concerning how teachers might query children's working theories about sexual subjectivities: for instance, a teacher in that study asked a two-year-old why he or she chooses the mummy and daddy finger-puppets. Jarvis and Sandretto argue that teachers who engage with such queer strategies are actively working towards social justice and a positive response to social diversity.

In another example of querying normativity, Hernamm-Wilmarth and Souto-Manning (2007) queried children's stereotypical thinking about good, evil and notions of desire. By deliberately reading stories to children that provided counter-narratives to well-known tales such as *The Three Little Pigs*, they helped children identify and resist their normative thinking; in doing so, they queried and queered the enacted curriculum through their work. I believe that teachers who become attuned to their normative thinking and trouble their investments in normative discourses will find ways to challenge normative discourses and work towards early childhood education beyond the (hetero)norm.

Beyond these two queer theory-inspired strategies, Gunn and Surtees' (2009) study revealed a number of teaching practices that participants considered important for disrupting heteronormativity. First, parents talked about teachers who created a welcoming climate, what we might call practising with an 'overt philosophy of whānau'. Since the term 'whānau' enables a broader view of who might 'belong' in any family constellation and care for children, this approach has the potential to broaden teachers' conceptualisations of family beyond the (hetero)norm. Metge (1995, 134) states: 'When a whānau functions as a unit, adult members describe each other's children as "ā mātou tamariki" (the children of us many), as distinct from "ā māua tamariki" (the children of us two).' When teachers recognise that all children may be the children of many, growing up 'in the midst of a "surrounding world of kinsfolk"' (Metge 1995, 138) they are more likely to recognise and respond to diverse family forms.

This overt philosophy of whānau is evident in the language teachers use, in the policies and forms they develop, and in the curriculum they enact. For example:

- Terms such as 'partner', rather than 'wife' or 'husband' are used, and questions such as 'Who is part of your family group?' and 'Who is important in the lives of your children?' are asked.
- Documents provide space to accurately record those in a parenting role and those with caregiving responsibilities for a child. They are inclusive of same-gender parented families and families where the care of children occurs across more than a single household.
- The curriculum positively reflects the diversity of family formations, including same-gender parented families.

A second practice for working beyond the (hetero)norm focuses on the development of a pedagogy of relationships for early childhood education. The study demonstrated that teachers who made it a priority to get to know children and their families well supported family wellbeing and participation in early childhood education. This does not mean, however, that the onus should remain on same-gender parented families to have to 'out' themselves and their family. Teachers must consider how best they might create conditions to support a family's openness. Celia, a parent, reflected: 'The kids were in settings [where] we had really strong relationships with the teachers, so that was all very affirming and ... affirming of who we were as a family' (Gunn & Surtees 2010).

Those teachers who made children's families visible in ways that contributed positively to parents' and children's sense of belonging were also considered to practise inclusively. This is because their practices recognised and reflected a diversity of family forms and celebrated these in a positive light. This made Heather and Penny, a lesbian couple with children, feel more willing to be involved in the curriculum, extra-curricular activities and the management of their child's early childhood services (Gunn & Surtees 2009). They recalled, 'It was coming up to Mother's Day ... and she came home with two big Mothers' Day cards. And Hana [the teacher] had obviously asked her what she calls her parents because one of them has "Mummy" and one of them has "Mum"' (Gunn & Surtees 2010). This was quite a different experience to that of Moana, reported earlier in the chapter, whose receipt of a Fathers' Day card brought a mixture of amusement and despair.

Early childhood policies and practices that name homophobia, heterosexism and heteronormativity as intolerable are likely to support teachers to work beyond the (hetero)norm. As mentioned earlier, it is easy in early childhood education to ignore matters of sexualities and gloss over instances where, whether by design or by ignorance, someone has been injured by the effects of heteronormative discourses and practices. To lessen the likelihood of such prejudice, teachers can work systematically with centre managers and owners to bring issues of heteronormativity to the fore. Inclusive education, employment and anti-discrimination policies should name sexuality as one of the grounds upon which discrimination will not be tolerated. By taking a stand, the early childhood setting can meet its current and future communities from a position of strength and inclusion.

## Conclusion

Early childhood teachers must practise beyond the prejudices of heteronormativity in order to realise inclusive and socially just early childhood education. Several New Zealand-based studies concerning sexualities in the early twenty-first century have responded to progressive law and policy and illustrate how early childhood teachers can both perpetuate and resist the (hetero)norm. Building on this work, this chapter brings a queer theory perspective to the debate, urging teachers to think and practise 'at odds' with heteronormativity. By using the tools of queer theory it is possible to recognise and respond differently to cultural forms of thinking that bind us to power relations in which normative thinking resides. The New Zealand studies of sexualities and early childhood education have provided evidence of effective teaching strategies for social justice and inclusion. Concepts of whānau, a pedagogy of relationships, and practices designed to increase belonging have all been important markers of inclusive practice. The curriculum policy provides impetus for change. Teachers must now combine forms of thinking and forms of practice if they are to rise to the challenge of practising beyond the (hetero)norm.

## References

Alexander, J. (1999), 'Beyond identity: Queer values and community', *Journal of Gay, Lesbian and Bisexual Identity*, 4(4), 293–314.

Blaise, M. & Taylor, A. (2012), 'Using queer theory to rethink gender equity in early childhood education', *Young Children*, 67(1), 88–98.

Britzman, D. (1995), 'Is there a queer pedagogy? Or, stop reading straight', *Educational Theory*, 45(2), 151–65.

Britzman, D. (1998), *Lost Subjects, Contested Objects. Toward a psychoanalytic inquiry of learning*, New York: State University of New York Press.

Burr, V. (1995), *An Introduction to Social Constructionism*, London: Routledge.

Butler, J. (1990), *Gender Trouble: Feminism and the subversion of identity*, New York: Routledge.

Cameron, D. & Kulick, D. (2003), *Language and Sexuality*, Cambridge: Cambridge University Press.

Care of Children Act (NZ), (2004).

Casper, V. & Schultz, S.B. (1999), *Gay Parents/Straight Schools: Building communication and trust*, New York: Teachers College Press.

Civil Union Act (NZ), (2004).

Cloughessy, K. & Waniganayake, M. (2013a), 'Early childhood educators working with children who have lesbian, gay, bisexual and transgender parents: What does the literature tell us?', *Early Childhood Development and Care*. DOI: 10.1080/03004430.2013.862529

Cloughessy, K. & Waniganayake, M. (2013b), '"Raised eyebrows": Working with lesbian-parented families. Experiences of childcare centre directors in Australia', *Children and Society*. DOI: 10.1111/chso.12065

Cooper, B. (2002). 'Boys don't cry and female masculinity: Reclaiming a life and dismantling the politics of normative heterosexuality', *Critical Studies in Media Communication*, 19(1), 44–63.

Davies, B. (1994), *Poststructuralist Theory and Classroom Practice*, Geelong, Australia: Deakin University Press.

Dilley, P. (1999), 'Queer theory: Under construction', *Qualitative Studies in Education*, 12(5), 457–72.

Epstein, D. & Johnson, R. (1994), 'On the straight and narrow: The heterosexual presumption, homophobias and schools', in D. Epstein (ed.), *Challenging Lesbian*

and *Gay Inequalities in Education*, (197–230). Buckingham and Philadelphia: Open University Press.
Gunn, A.C. (2008), 'Heteronormativity and early childhood education: Social justice and some puzzling queries', Doctoral thesis, University of Waikato, New Zealand.
Gunn, A.C. (2009), '"But who are the parents?": Examining heteronormative discourse in New Zealand government early childhood reports and policy', *Early Childhood Folio: A collection of recent research, 13*, 27–31.
Gunn, A.C. (2011), 'Even if you say it three ways, it still doesn't mean its true: The pervasiveness of heteronormativity in early childhood education', *Journal of Early Childhood Research, 9*, 280–90.
Gunn A.C. & Surtees, N. (2009), '"We're a family": How lesbians and gay men are creating and maintaining family in New Zealand', Wellington: New Zealand Families Commission Te Komihana ā Whānau.
Gunn, A.C. & Surtees, N. (2010), 'Lesbian and gay parents talk about teaching: What can we learn?' Keynote presentation to The Gathering – 2010, 21 August 2010, University of Canterbury, Christchurch.
Halberstam, J. (1996), 'Queering lesbian studies', in B. Zimmerman & T.A.H. McNaron (eds), *The New Lesbian Studies: Into the twenty-first century*, (256–68), New York: The Feminist Press, City University of New York.
Hermann-Wilmarth, J. & Souto-Manning, M. (2007), 'Queering early childhood practices: Opening up possibilities with common children's literature', *International Journal of Equity and Innovation in Early Childhood, 5*(2), 5–16.
Human Rights Act (NZ), (1993).
Jackson, S. (2003), 'Heterosexuality, heteronormativity, and gender hierarchy: Some reflections on recent debates', in J. Weeks, H. Holland & M. Waites (eds), *Sexualities and Society* (69–83), Cambridge: Polity.
Jarvis, K. (2010), 'Exploring heteronormativity: Small acts towards queer(y)ing early childhood education', Master's thesis, University of Otago, Dunedin.
Jarvis, K. & Sandretto, S. (2010), 'The power of discursive practices: Queering or heteronormalising?', *New Zealand Research in Early Childhood Education, 13*, 43–56.
Kelly, J. & Surtees, N. (2013), 'We are a family: Legal issues for lesbian and gay parented families in New Zealand', *Plymouth Law and Criminal Justice Review, 1*, 39–49.
Lee, D. (2010), 'Gay mothers and early childhood education: Standing tall', *Australasian Journal of Early Childhood, 35*(1), 16–23.
Lee, D. & Duncan, J. (2008), 'On our best behaviour: Lesbian parented families in early childhood education', *Early Childhood Folio: A collection of recent research 12*, 22–26.
MacNaughton, G. (2005), *Doing Foucault in Early Childhood Studies: Applying poststructural ideas*, London and New York: Routledge.
Marriage (Definition of Marriage) Amendment Act (NZ), (2013).
Metge, J. (1995), *New Growth from Old: The whānau in the modern world*, Wellington: Victoria University Press.
Ministry of Education (1996), *Te Whāriki. He whāriki mātauranga mō ngā mokopuna o Aotearoa: Early childhood curriculum*, Wellington: Learning Media.
Ministry of Education (2008), *Licensing Criteria for Early Childhood Education and Care Centres 2008 and Early Childhood Education Curriculum Framework*, Wellington: New Zealand Government.
Morris, M. (1998), 'Unresting the curriculum: Queer projects, queer imaginings', in W.F. Pinar (ed.), *Queer Theory in Education*, (275–86), London: Lawrence Erlbaum.
New Zealand Government (2008), 'Education (Early childhood education curriculum framework) Notice 2008', *New Zealand Gazette*, Notice no. 6504, 4 September 2008.
Oates, J. (2010), *Supporting Parenting: Early childhood in focus 5*, Milton Keynes, UK: The Open University, Child and Youth Studies Group.
Phelan, S. (1997), *Playing with Fire: Queer politics, queer theories*, New York: Routledge.

Pinar, W.F. (1998), *Queer Theory in Education*, London: Lawrence Erlbaum.
Power, J., Perlesz, A., McNair, R., Schofield, M., Pitts, M., Brown, R. & Bickerdike, A. (2012), 'Gay and bisexual dads and diversity: Fathers in the work, love, play study', *Journal of Family Studies, 18*(2–3), 143–54.
Robinson, K. (2012a), 'Childhood as a "queer time and space": Alternative imaginings of normative markers of gendered lives', in, K.H. Robinson, C. Davies & B. Davies (eds), *Rethinking Research and Professional Practices in terms of Relationality, Subjectivity and Power: Queer and subjugated knowledges: Generating subversive imaginaries*, (110–39), United Arab Emirates: Bentham Science.
Robinson, K. (2012b), '"Difficult citizenship": The precarious relationship between childhood, sexuality and access to knowledge', *Sexualities, 15*(3–4), 257–76.
Sedgwick, E. (1990), *Epistemology of the Closet*, Los Angeles: University of California Press.
Slagle, R.A. (1995), 'In defense of Queer Nation: From identity politics to a politics of difference', *Western Journal of Communication, 59*(2), 85–103.
Souto-Manning, M. & Hermann-Wilmarth, J. (2008), 'Teacher inquiries into gay and lesbian families in early childhood classrooms', *Journal of Early Childhood Research, 32*(1), 10–18.
Spargo, T. (1999), *Foucault and Queer Theory*, Cambridge: Icon Books.
Sumara, D. & Davis, B. (1999), 'Interrupting heteronormativity: Toward a queer curriculum theory', *Curriculum Inquiry, 29*(2), 191–208.
Surtees, N. (2003), 'Unravelling the woven mat: Queering the whāriki', *Waikato Journal of Education, 9*, 143–53.
Surtees, N. (2005), 'Teacher talk about and around sexuality in early childhood education: Deciphering an unwritten code', *Contemporary Issues in Early Childhood, 6*(1), 19–29.
Surtees, N. (2006), 'Sexualities matters in early childhood education: The management of children/bodies and their unsettling desires', Master's thesis, University of Canterbury.
Surtees, N. (2011), 'Family law in New Zealand: The benefits and costs for gay men, lesbians and their children', *Journal of GLBT Family Studies, 7*, 245–63.
Taylor, A. & Richardson, C. (2005), 'Queering home corner', *Contemporary Issues in Early Childhood, 6*(2), 163–73.
Terreni, L., Gunn, A.C., Kelly, J. & Surtees, N. (2010), 'In and out of the closet: Successes and challenges experienced by gay- and lesbian-headed families in their interactions with the education system in New Zealand', in V.A. Green & S. Cherrington (eds), *Delving into Diversity: An international exploration of issues of diversity in education*, (151–61), New York: Nova.
Tobin, J. (1997), *Making a Place for Pleasure in Early Childhood Education*, Ann Arbor, Michigan: Edwards Brothers.
Valocchi, S. (2005), 'Not yet queer enough: The lessons of queer theory for the sociology of gender and sexuality', *Gender and Society, 19*, 750–70.
Warner, M. (1991), 'Introduction: Fear of a queer planet', *Social Text, 29*, 3–17.

# 3.
# Conversations with potential

Teaching for inclusion

## Ann Hardie

I comb city bookshops for children's picture books that include a gay or lesbian parent or same-gender parents in storylines.[1] Although accustomed to the scarcity and hardened to disappointment, that sense of frustration and despair rises again. I put energy into justifying and explaining the rationale for stocking this sort of book, expressing disbelief to bookshop managers that they have none available. This is emotional work. As Evans (2002, 33) describes it: 'the promulgation of heteronormativity creates more potential emotionally laden situations for those in the sexual minority'.

The purpose of this chapter is to raise teachers' awareness of picture books that encompass sexuality and family diversities, to provide a critique of this style of picture book, and to suggest how teachers might include such stories in their literacy programmes. I come to this work from several positions: as a teacher-educator who works with pre-service teachers; as a lesbian grandmother who reads with her grandchildren; and as an advocate for social justice. These positions motivate me to work with student teachers, colleagues, librarians, booksellers and teachers because I want to initiate change in practice. I am encouraged by fresh, socially aware teachers who bring with them an enthusiastic sense of social justice, and a metaphorical bundle of diversity books under their arms. This chapter encourages educators' capacities to teach for diversity and inclusion where matters of sexuality and family diversities are concerned.

---

1  I use the terms 'gay men', 'lesbians' and 'same-gender parents' to reflect that some children live in households with one parent who may be gay or lesbian, while others live in households where same-gender parent couples raise them, or even across multiple households where many parents are involved. My principle interest in the chapter is, however, in recognising and reflecting children's families where gay men, lesbians or same-gender couples parent.

## Background

My interest in picture books that tell stories of lesbian or gay parented families stemmed from The No Outsiders Project Team (2008) research conducted in England, in which school communities, teacher-researchers and academics collaborated to use picture books as tools to combat homophobia in schools. On learning of this project, I researched library catalogues in Wellington schools and found a distinct lack of picture books inclusive of diverse family structures (Hardie 2011). This finding has motivated my continued work in this domain.

I believe inclusive education is about recognising and upholding the rights of all people in a school community, including children, their families, and adults who work in the school. Working inclusively involves showing respect for diversity. Inclusion is not a reality in many educational settings; for many children and their families, 'inclusion remains at the level of rhetoric' (Gordon-Burns, Gunn, Purdue & Surtees 2012, 7).

In my work in initial teacher education (ITE) I use picture books to open dialogue about sexualities, difference and advocacy, as well as inclusive, fair, and equitable teaching practices. I pursue a social justice agenda through this work. My intention is to develop awareness of how the exclusionary status quo is constructed and maintained with respect to sexuality and family diversity. I want to puncture the complacency that characterises teaching practice and move beyond the rhetoric. It is imperative that ITE improves awareness of such issues so that beginning teachers are opened to difference and more willing to practise inclusively.

Deliberately bringing the topic of sexualities into ITE or primary classrooms remains difficult, however, especially if family diversity is not reflected in that environment. Sexuality already exists in classrooms as 'heterosexual sexuality' (Surtees & Gunn 2010, 42); by introducing inclusive picture books, I believe teachers can inspire classroom conversations about family diversity.

## Inclusive curriculum

ITE students examine *The New Zealand Curriculum* (Ministry of Education, 2007), its vision, values and principles. The principles promote a non-discriminatory inclusive curriculum that recognises and affirms students' identities and supports a sense of belonging. It encourages the provision of learning experiences that facilitate explorations of, and learning about, different kinds of values and worldviews. The early childhood curriculum

*Te Whāriki* (Ministry of Education 1996) also seeks to affirm individuals and ensure a sense of belonging. *Te Whāriki* encourages an environment in which children 'experience the stories and symbols of their own and other cultures' with 'an expectation that words and books can amuse, delight, comfort, illuminate, inform, and excite' (78).

These official curriculum documents advocate inclusive education because they expect teachers to practice culturally inclusive pedagogy. However, awareness of inclusion for children from same-gender parented families has not been promoted as part of this. Some teachers may consider that they teach inclusively even though they never include sexual and family diversity in their work. I argue that in such instances the curriculum is not fully realised. As sexual diversity is not always outwardly displayed, teachers may not be aware that some children in their classrooms live in households where gay men, lesbians or same-gender parents are raising the children, particularly if family members choose not to reveal their personal details. An Australian study of lesbian-parented families (Lindsay et al. 2006) recognised a continuum of disclosure practices families engage in when dealing with schools: proud (open), private (concealed) or selective (depending on the school circumstances). New Zealand same-gender parented families report similar practices (Terreni, Gunn, Kelly & Surtees 2010). Inclusive teachers who have knowledge of the issues that emerge for families with sexually diverse parents can consciously counter the discrimination and exclusion they face. Many schools and teachers remain unaware or indifferent, however, and this prevents the voicing of alternative perspectives. In such environments heteronormativity abounds.

## Evaluating children's books that counter heteronormativity

One way to practise inclusively with respect to sexualities is through children's literature. In this next section I consider a range of children's picture books that contain narratives inclusive of gay, lesbian and same-gender parents and their families. My aim is to provoke curiosity in their storylines and to promote interest in and access to them by teachers. Awareness of and access to books of this nature may be limited, however, as they are scarce (Hardie 2011; Rowell 2007; Spence 2000; Sunderland & McGlashan 2012).

Charmaz (2006) provides guiding questions that assist in my text analysis and which use a grounded theory approach. These questions focus on understanding a text's purposes and embedded meanings, and the realities represented by the text. In picture books it is necessary to evaluate words and pictures because both are relied upon to convey meaning to a reader. Day (2011) poses further questions with particular relevance to my interest in children's picture books with gay and lesbian content. These ask a reader to consider the potential impact of the book on children's self-esteem, and the portrayal of relationships between characters. Day's purpose is to recognise how texts can provide positive influences for gay and lesbian people.

Inquiries like mine are not new. Others have engaged in similar reviews of picture books with gay and lesbian content (Day 2011; Rowell 2007; Sapp 2010; Spence 2000; Sunderland & McGlashan 2012). While some researchers are interested in a specific aspect of a picture book's representation (Epstein 2012), Sunderland and McGlashan's (2012) study is illustrative. They worked quantitatively to examine the representation of gay- and lesbian-parented families in children's picture books, and asked, specifically: whether a two-mother couple differed from a two-father couple; what the nature of the visual representation of physical contact was like; and what textual strategies the authors used to convey positive attitudes. Their analysis concluded that all the books in the sample promoted 'acceptance, understanding and/or celebration' (146), and emphasised commonalities between same-gender and opposite-gender parented families. In the study, more books portrayed families with two mothers – a fact the authors suggest may either indicate that women are seen as 'natural carers' (150), or may simply make the books more marketable. Texts were found to focus on family issues; sexuality was relegated to the background. The authors argue that 'all these stories could feasibly and in principle be told using heterosexual parents with no real impact on the narrative [but importantly, here they are not]' (169).

## Method

For the purposes of my inquiry I read 47 children's picture books with gay and lesbian family themes and 'clustered' them according to their storylines. I eliminated books that made non-specific reference to difference, selecting only those that denoted same-gender parents or strongly suggested this possibility, and which were published from 2000 onwards. Of the original 47 books, 21 were chosen for analysis. I will discuss the books in four clusters: same-gender parents; same-gender weddings; issue stories; and family forming. Following Charmaz (2006), I comment on their purpose, embedded meanings and realities.

## The books

### *Same-gender parents*

For children of gay and lesbian parents, the depiction of same-gender parented families in picture books gives visibility to their kind of family, affirming their reality while simultaneously educating other adults and children about such family lives. In Lesléa Newman's (2009) books *Mommy, Mama and Me* and *Daddy, Papa and Me*, the storylines express the pleasure same-gender parents experience while interacting and playing with their children. Accompanied by language rhythms and rhymes, the pictures motivate shared reading. In *Mommy, Mama and Me* the child is portrayed with each mother in turn, ending with, 'Now I'm tucked in nice and tight. Mommy and Mama kiss me goodnight.' *Daddy, Papa, and Me* concludes with the fathers collapsing under a tree to rest after a hectic day of activity with their child. The books depict love and care within the family and affection between the adults.

Another pair of books is *The Tale of Two Daddies* and *The Tale of Two Mommies* (Oelschlager 2010; 2011). The first shows two children in a friendly conversation that develops from a boy's comment: 'My friend Lincoln says you have two dads.' The second begins with a question from two children to a boy with two mothers: 'If you have a momma and a mommy, who fixes things when they break?' The author is deliberate with words: in the second book the word 'if' opens up possibilities for discussion between the reader and the listener around stereotypical gender roles. Does a father usually fix things in families? The reply is eloquent: 'Mommy has the tools. There's nothing she can't fix or make.'

Both Oelschlager's (2010; 2011) narratives are told from children's perspectives. Parents are silent: only their hands and legs are depicted in the illustrations. The texts follow a rhythmic two questions followed by two responses. The characters' questions, such as which father helps with homework and which mother coaches T-ball, refer to familiar activities for school-age children – the books' intended audience. Concluding questions foreground the characters' relationships with their parents and ask which parent is available when the children need love and someone to talk to. In these stories, the characters reply that both parents are there (of course), and the books end with an image of the child holding the parents' hands. There are gender differences in the author's depictions of girls and boys in these books: the girl is portrayed as needing love, whereas the boy needs someone to talk to. This prompts me to wonder: are the books promoting gender-stereotyped behaviour, or does this difference simply provide variety to the storylines?

*And Tango Makes Three* (Richardson & Parnell 2005) tells of two male penguins in a New York zoo, and an observant zookeeper who provides the penguins with the opportunity to satisfy their parenting instincts. The zookeeper notices the penguins' relationship and nesting behaviours and provides them with an egg, which eventually hatches into the chick Tango. Based on real events, this story is significant as it demonstrates that same-gender parenting occurs in the animal world. Tango's family is described as 'just like all the other penguin families. And all the children who came to the zoo could see Tango and her two fathers playing in the penguin house with all the other penguins.' I recommend this book as a resource for school libraries. It could be useful at all levels of the school and in various learning areas such as science, literacy, health and social sciences.

Family stories may include same-gender parents as incidental rather than central characters. This deliberate strategy suggests that the family 'just is', and in this way implies that family diversity is 'normal'. *The Different Dragon* (Bryan 2006) is about a boy and one of his mothers making up a bedtime story. In my view, the representation of a child and parent imagining a story together has strong appeal. *Spacegirl Pukes* (Watson 2005) tells of a girl with two mothers who becomes ill while playing out her space adventure. The theme of the story is family kindness; the same-gender parenting is not the central focus of the story. *City Life* (Ferreira 2010) is about a girl with two mothers who visualises what it will be like the next day when she goes out and about in the city.

Two New Zealand publications are *My Favourite Places* (Bailey 2008) and *Milly, Molly and Different Dads* (Pittar 2002). The first features a boy who, after imaginary adventures, eventually returns home for his dinner. Two women prepare the meal. Although sexuality is not explicit, the possibility exists for readers to interpret this family as they choose to. An early childhood setting is the context for *Milly, Molly and Different Dads*, a story that depicts a teacher and children having a mat-time discussion about their fathers. One child says she has two, and the accompanying illustration shows her family playing dress-ups. The teacher listens as each child shares something unique about their fathers, and concludes by saying, 'So there we are ... all dads and families are different. That's just the way it is.' This story portrays a range of differences in a straightforward and simple way.

Parr (2001; 2003) has authored two brightly illustrated books for preschoolers that depict non-specified difference. *It's Okay to be Different* states, 'It's okay to have different moms … different dads.' All sorts of families are mentioned in *The Family Book*, including those that 'have two moms or two dads'. That these books are open to interpretation and uncertainty increases the possibility for children's explanations and life experiences to emerge during discussions about the content.

## Same-gender weddings

In New Zealand the legalisation of same-sex marriage and civil unions has resulted in an increase in ceremonies of commitment. Picture books are useful tools for reflecting social customs and change, and as such can be used as vehicles to explain the complexities of real events in ways that children can understand. Importantly, the stories I introduce next portray same-gender commitment ceremonies and marriages as authentic family celebrations.

The family event in *Donovan's Big Day* (Newman 2011) builds anticipation about a particularly special occasion. The central character, Donovan, has been taking care of his parents' wedding rings. He has an important role to play in the ceremony; after he hands one ring to Mommy and one to Mama, they hold hands and are pronounced 'wife and wife'. Illustrations and text combine in this picture book to convey absolute pleasure in this family celebration. Epstein (2012) argues that foregrounding the child's perspective in stories such as *Donovan's Big Day* enables a child reader 'to better imagine him/herself in that situation' (146). The book depicts elements of familiar traditional weddings; as children often attend family weddings, many readers are likely to relate to the excitement of *Donovan's Big Day* and bring their experiences of same- or opposite-gender ceremonies to a classroom discussion.

In contrast, *Uncle Bobby's Wedding* (Brannen 2008) takes an anthropomorphic approach to same-gender commitment ceremonies. This story features guinea pigs which convey human emotions such as joy and jealousy. Sunderland and McGlashan (2012, 154) classify stories like *Uncle Bobby's Wedding* as 'animal-real world' because they tell of a realistic situation and substitute animals for human characters. In this story, Chloe's Uncle Bobby is marrying Jamie; Chloe is jealous and afraid that she is being displaced. Her uncle declares, however, 'when we get married you'll have an Uncle Jamie too', which brings a happy ending. Once again the families are delighted with the wedding.

The traditional fairy tale genre usually involves castles with kings and queens, and princes and princesses involved in a quest. De Haan and Nijland (2000) disrupt traditional fairy tale norms to present a postmodern take on love and marriage in their story *King and King*. O'Neil (2010) discusses how postmodern picture books 'present an alternative point of view or outcome, often in a way that questions the validity of conventional mores and leaves much of the meaning up to the reader' (43). In this story the queen wishes to retire and expects her son, the prince, to find a suitable princess to marry – despite the fact that the prince 'has never much cared for princesses'. The prince watches with little interest as princesses from all over the world are paraded before him. Eventually Princess Madeleine arrives with her brother Prince Lee: 'At last, the prince felt a stir in his heart. It was love at first sight.' He has fallen in love with Prince Lee.

Teachers frequently use fairy tales and traditional stories as resources for literacy programmes. Such stories are valuable for prompting children's thinking and for motivating writing that allows children to create alternative endings for traditional stories. The non-normative ending of *King and King* (De Haan & Nijland 2000) provides a strong model for writing from an alternative perspective. It supports imagining that is not limited by, or to, traditional common beliefs.

## *Issue stories*

As heteronormativity is pervasive, same-gender parented families occupy a minority position that is exacerbated by issues of discrimination and invisibility. Some children's picture books confront these issues through storytelling, creating a tension for authors between portraying realistic or idealistic situations. Others portray harmonious gay, lesbian or same-gender parented families who look and behave much like conventional families (Sunderland & McGlashan 2012). In the latter, characters participate in caring relationships and go about their daily lives with no overt mention or recognition of the same-gender status of their parents. Epstein (2012) introduces the term 'nuclear gay family' (142) to indicate the family arrangement of two same-gender parents and a child or children.

Esposito (2009) argues for a realistic depiction of lesbian-parented families in picture books that fairly represents the complexities of relationships, families, power and privilege. She questions why children's books 'pretend that the world is a perfect place' (77). Three books address Esposito's (2009) argument, portraying issues of prejudice and misunderstanding in their storylines: *In Our Mothers' House* (Polacco 2009), *Molly's Family* (Garden, 2004) and *What Can You Do with Two Mommies?* (Hill 2012). These stories depict parents providing explanations to children to enable them to resolve confrontations or problems. In two of the books the onus is put on children to teach others about their same-gender parented families. Faced with climates characterised by heteronormativity, the characters explain and justify their alternative family constellations to peers and friends.

Ford (2011) states that 'a child narrator can only offer what she sees, knows, thinks and is told' (206). In *In Our Mothers' House* (Polacco 2009) the child narrator describes various situations experienced by members of her extended family. She discusses her family's multiculturalism and reminisces over neighbourhood occasions. She lingers over a particular neighbour's negative attitude toward her family. The neighbour is homophobic and her prejudice is strongly conveyed when she glares at the children and their mothers, stops her children sleeping over, and confronts the mothers with the comment, 'I don't appreciate what you two are!' The narrator and other child characters ask their mothers what the matter is and one explains, 'She is full of fear, sweetie. She's afraid of what she cannot understand: she doesn't understand us.' This story also conveys family love and joy as the characters are visited by grandparents and have family celebrations.

The issue of what constitutes family is raised in *Molly's Family* (Garden 2004) when Molly draws a picture at kindergarten of her two mothers. Tommy comments, 'That's not a family … where's your daddy?' Although another boy points out that he does not have a daddy either, Tommy claims that Molly 'can't have a mommy and a mama'. Tommy's assertion and apparent certainty illustrates how heteronormative understandings are forcefully acted out and reinforced through peer interactions. In her analysis of lesbian-themed books for children, Esposito (2009) concludes that the angst Molly experiences from having to describe and justify her family is not explicit. Molly is distressed and uncertain about her family but Esposito explains, 'We are not privy to the real and sometimes painful conversations that occur when people come up against tradition and difference' (74). Tales with overzealous or didactic explanations can, however, result is less appealing stories, whereas Molly's distress will maintain interest and prompt further discussion. A teacher could deliberately use this story to explore difference and prejudice.

The home environments of *Molly's Family* (Garden 2004) and *In Our Mothers' House* (Polacco 2009) reflect the contrasting ways the authors have presented the respective issues. *Molly's Family* exemplifies a tidy, orderly environment in which issues are resolved. *In Our Mothers' House* (Polacco 2009) depicts spontaneity and disarray, and issues are open for readers and listeners to discuss. Both these books deserve to be read and shared in classrooms, but will appeal to different age groups: *Molly's Family* is better suited to junior school (Years 0–4), whereas *In Our Mothers' House* could stimulate class discussion up to Year 6.

An instructive approach is used in *What Can You Do with Two Mommies?* (Hill 2012). This story is about the emotions Annie experiences when her friend asks her why she has two mothers, and where her father is. One of her mothers explains that her father left and his whereabouts are unknown. Although Annie queries why she does not have 'real parents', she loves her family. This book would suit children in Years 2–4, as the child characters appear to be about seven years of age. Issues of difference and the child's emotional responses are explicit.

## Family forming

Some books offer explanations of how same-gender parented families form. In *Molly's Family* (Garden 2004), Molly's mothers explain to her how her family came about: '"When mama Lu and I were first living together … we decided we had so much love that we wanted to share it with a baby." Mamma Lu added, "So your mommy had you … she's your birth mommy … I'm your adopted Mommy."' Mama Lu tells Molly, 'There are lots of different kinds of families.'

Three ethnically different children and their mothers constitute the family in *In Our Mothers' House* (Polacco 2009). Whether any of the children is adopted or fostered is unknown. The narrator, one of the children, says, 'When my mothers told me about how they brought me home to live with them shortly after I was born, their eyes would shine and glisten and they'd grin from ear to ear.' The circumstances of each child's arrival in the family is left open to interpretation, making this a versatile book for classroom discussion about family formation.

*King and King and Family* (De Haan & Nijland 2004) is the sequel to *King and King* (De Haan & Nijland 2000), mentioned earlier. The kings Bertie and Lee, now happily married, go on a jungle holiday and notice all the animal families, which in turn prompts their wish for 'a little one of our own'. When they return home, they seem to have a bulky, heavy suitcase that, surprisingly, contains a child from the jungle. The kings proclaim her as the child they have 'always wanted' and Princess Daisy is adopted, a process entailing a lot of 'documents and stamps'. This improbable child arrival is in stark contrast to the planned parenthood represented in *Felicia's Favorite Story* (Newman 2002). This book gives a serious account of baby Felicia's arrival into her family after her birth in Guatemala where, because her birth mother was unable to care for her, she was adopted by her two mothers. The retelling of this tale is Felicia's much-loved bedtime story and conveys how her mothers came to love and adopt her. The stories *Molly's Family* (Garden 2004), *Felicia's Favorite Story* and *In Our Mothers' House* (Polacco 2009) are likely to resonate with many children's life experiences, as they portray realistic methods of family formation, and may encourage children to share their own personal stories of family.

## Discussion and implications

Temple, Martinez and Yokoto (2006) argue that a good children's book has particular qualities, including the potential to 'expand awareness' (8) of perspectives without teaching or moralising to excess. This chapter has described several books teachers might share with children in their efforts to support thinking about family beyond normative assumptions. Books that tell non-normative stories can open minds to alternative perspectives and experiences which, O'Neil (2010) maintains, 'can work to expand a child's sense of justice and equity [and develop a] sense of agency' (p. 44). These particular books give visibility to diverse families; they open discussion and promote understanding of difference; and they will enrich literacy programmes.

Children's picture books that include narratives and promote discussion of sexual and family diversity can provide useful tools for teachers and families to correct misinformation and assumptions. Sharing stories is an initial step towards awareness; however, subsequent discussion, activated by teachers who have developed their own sense of social justice, is necessary if children are to ask questions and develop thinking and understanding beyond their own experiences and worldviews. Surtees and Gunn (2010) argue that silence around sexuality and family diversity in early childhood teaching 'masks possibilities for understanding the world beyond the constraints of the (hetero)norm' (45). Kelly (2012) describes the 'hesitancy to ask probing questions or fully engage with children's thinking ... as missed opportunities' (296). In reading such books teachers must engage with children over book content, otherwise they continue to perpetuate silence and restrict learning about diverse families. Robinson (2005) argues for anti-homophobia and anti-heterosexist education in early education since prejudice is already present. Similarly, Sapp (2010) suggests that acknowledgment of diverse family structures needs to begin in the early years, otherwise the task becomes 'unlearning prejudice instead of preventing it' (33).

Day (2011) questions whether the portrayal of lesbian and gay relationships in books would bolster or diminish a readers' self-esteem. Without exception, I argue that the books discussed in this chapter portray positive, loving family relationships in which parents are engaged with their children. Some stories showed that children's self-esteem may be troubled when they experience heteronormativity, disbelief and homophobia; however, they also showed how children may be supported through issues. Fiction is an effective way to challenge heteronormativity and promote understandings of prejudice, but not all books provide resolution to the issues. *In Our Mothers' House* (Polacco 2009) is an example of this. Resources such as these create opportunities for teachers to introduce social justice-oriented discussions to the curriculum.

Books in which same-gender parenting appears incidental to the plot may be more broadly acceptable, as they do not necessarily confront traditional beliefs. Conversely, a risk brought about by obscuring sexuality and family diversity is that issues may not be discussed because subtle messages could be missed, avoided, or deliberately left unexplored. Children from gay- or lesbian-parented families have a right to see their realities, lives and family experiences included in classrooms and programmes.

New Zealand teachers are expected to encourage full participation of all children in education. A first step for teachers who want to pursue inclusive teaching is to examine their personal worldviews for any prejudice (by omission or design). Astute children do notice casual remarks that portray discriminatory attitudes. Second, teachers must select and use classroom resources that provide a balance of worldviews and promote inclusion. In this chapter I have identified picture books that can be easily integrated into literacy programmes or studies of topics about health and wellbeing, families, recreation, celebrations and caring for others.

Teaching through a curriculum that recognises and respects the social and cultural contexts of learners is recognised as effective pedagogy in New Zealand education settings (Ministry of Education 2007). Even though official curriculum documents advocate non-discriminatory and inclusive programmes, the onus is on teachers, schools and early childhood centres to acquire and use book resources representative of diverse social and cultural contexts. Doing so will allow teachers to address the breadth of curriculum and to practise in ways that open up conversations of potential.

## References

Charmaz, K. (2006), *Constructing Grounded Theory: A practical guide through qualitative analysis*, Los Angeles: Sage.

Day, F.A. (2011), *Lesbian and Gay Voices: An annotated bibliography and guide to literature for children and young adults*, Westport, Connecticut: Greenwood Press.

Epstein, D. (2012), 'The nuclear gay family: Same-sex marriage in children's books', *Gay and Lesbian Issues and Psychology Review*, 8(3), 142–52.

Esposito, J. (2009), 'We're here, we're queer, but just like heterosexuals: A cultural studies analysis of lesbian themed children's books', *Journal of Educational Foundations*, 23(3), 61–78.

Evans, K. (2002), *Negotiating the Self: Identity, sexuality, and emotion in learning to teach*, New York: RoutledgeFalmer.

Ford, E.A. (2011), 'Why Lesléa Newman makes Heather into Zoe', in M.A. Abate & K. Kidd (eds), *Over the Rainbow: Queer children's and young adult literature* (201–14), Ann Arbor, Michigan: University of Michigan Press.

Gordon-Burns, D., Gunn, A., Purdue, K. & Surtees, N. (eds) (2012), 'Introduction: Thinking differently about early childhood inclusive education in Aotearoa New Zealand', in *Te Aotūroa Tātaki Inclusive Early Childhood: Perspectives on inclusion, social justice and equity from Aotearoa New Zealand* (1–20), Wellington: New Zealand Council for Education Research Press.

Hardie, A. (2011), 'Inclusive primary school libraries: Stories of diverse families', *New Zealand Journal of Educational Studies*, 46(2), 95–102.

Kelly, J. (2012), 'Two daddy tigers and a baby tiger: Promoting understandings about the same gender parented families using picture books', *Early Years: An International Journal of Research and Development*, 32(3), 288–300.

Lindsay, J., Perlesz, A., Brown, R., McNair, R., de Vaus, D. & Pitts, M. (2006), 'Stigma or respect: Lesbian-parented families negotiating school settings', *Sociology*, 40, 1059–77.

Ministry of Education (2007), *The New Zealand Curriculum*, Wellington: Learning Media.

Ministry of Education (1996), *Te Whāriki: He whāriki mātauranga mō ngā mokopuna o Aotearoa: Early childhood curriculum*, Wellington: Learning Media.

O'Neil, K. (2010), 'Once upon today: Teaching for social justice with postmodern picturebooks', *Children's Literature in Education*, 41, 40–51.

Robinson, K. (2005), 'Doing anti-homophobia and anti-heterosexism in early childhood education: Moving beyond the immobilising impacts of "risks", "fears" and "silences". Can we afford not to?', *Contemporary Issues in Early Childhood*, 6(2), 175–88.

Rowell, E.H. (2007), 'Missing! Picture books reflecting gay and lesbian families', *Young Children*, 62(3), 24–30.

Sapp, J. (2010), 'A review of gay and lesbian themed early childhood children's literature', *Australasian Journal of Early Childhood*, 35(1), 32–40.

Spence, A. (2000), 'Controversial books in the public library: A comparative survey of holdings of gay-related children's picture books', *The Library Quarterly*, 70(3), 335–79.

Sunderland, J. & McGlashan, M. (2012), 'Stories featuring two-mum and two-dad families', in J. Sunderland (ed.), *Language, Gender and Children's Fiction* (142–72), London: Continuum Logo.

Surtees, N. & Gunn, A.C. (2010), '(Re)marking heteronormativity: Resisting practices in early childhood education contexts', *Australasian Journal of Early Childhood*, 35(1), 42–47.
Temple, C., Martinez, M. & Yokota, J. (2006), *Children's Books in Children's Hands* (3rd edn), Boston: Pearson Education.
Terreni, L., Gunn, A., Kelly, J. & Surtees, N. (2010), 'In and out of the closet: Successes and challenges experienced by gay- and lesbian-headed families in their interactions with the education system in New Zealand', in V. Green & S. Cherrington (eds). *Delving into Diversity: An international exploration of issues of diversity in education*, (151–61), New York: Nova Science.
The No Outsiders Project Team (2008), 'Using children's literature to challenge homophobia in primary schools', in R. De Palma & E. Atkinson (eds), *Invisible Boundaries* (139–44), Stoke on Trent: Trentham.

## Picture Books

Brannen, S. (2008), *Uncle Bobby's Wedding*, New York: Putnam's Sons.
Bryan, J. (2006), *The Different Dragon*, Ridley Park: Two Lives.
Bailey, M. (2008), *My Favourite Places*, Wellington: Mallinson Rendel.
de Hann, L. & Nijland, S. (2000), *King and King*, Berkeley, CA: First Tricycle.
de Hann, L. & Nijland, S. (2004), *King and King and Family*, Berkeley, CA: First Tricycle.
Ferreira, J. (2010), *City Life*, Lavergne, TN: Books for all Families.
Garden, N. (2004), *Molly's Family*, New York: Farrar, Straus and Giroux.
Hill, T. (2012), *What Can You Do with Two Mommies?*, Lavergne, TN: Hills Quills.
Newman, L. (2011), *Donovan's Big Day*, Berkeley, CA: Tricycle.
Newman, L. (2009), *Daddy, Papa and Me*, Berkeley, CA: Tricycle.
Newman, L. (2009), *Mommy, Mama and Me*, Berkeley, CA: Tricycle.
Newman, L. (2002), *Felicia's Favorite Story*, Ridley Park: Two Lives.
Oelschlager, V. (2010), *The Tale of Two Daddies*, Akron, Ohio: Vanita.
Oelschlager, V. (2011), *The Tale of Two Mommies*, Akron, Ohio: Vanita.
Parr, T. (2001), *It's Okay to be Different*, Boston: Little, Brown.
Parr, T. (2003), *The Family Book*, New York: Little, Brown.
Pittar, G. (2002) *Milly, Molly and Different Dads*, Gisborne, NZ: MM House.
Polacco, P. (2009), *In Our Mothers' House*, New York: Philomel.
Richardson, J. & Parnell, P. (2005), *And Tango Makes Three*, New York: Simon and Schuster.
Watson, K. (2005), *Spacegirl Pukes*, London: Onlywomen.

## 4.
# 'I like my beer cold, my TV loud and my homosexuals f-laming'

Using critical literacy to draw attention to heteronormative hegemony in texts of popular culture

### Susan Sandretto

Discourses of heteronormative hegemony – discourses that normalise heterosexuality (Warner 1991) – are pervasive in many popular culture texts, such as *The Simpsons*. In the quote in the title of this chapter, Homer Simpson would like 'Other' sexualities to be explicit, or 'flaming' in his words. As I will explain, Homer's stance serves to reinscribe the binary of normal/other or heterosexual/homosexual. In this chapter, I will examine the use of critical literacy as a tool to support students to deconstruct the heterosexual/homosexual binary and the workings of heteronormativity in texts of popular culture.

The term 'text' can refer to any combination of the audio, gestural, linguistic, spatial or visual semiotic systems that have been constructed to communicate something to someone (Bull & Anstey 2010). Texts of popular culture include such things as advertisements, movies, books or music, that represent 'a terrain of exchange' (Morrell 2002, 73) between different social groups. What constitutes this terrain of exchange is itself a contested concept. I draw upon the concept of popular culture as everyday culture (Hagood 2008), a stance that positions readers as agentic subjects rather than either mindless, uncritical consumers, or solely resistant producers of alternative interpretations (Hagood 2008). Viewing popular culture as everyday culture encourages us to consider the diversity of engagement with popular culture texts: we cannot predict what readings students will make of the texts of popular culture they encounter daily.

Teachers in New Zealand can draw upon popular culture texts to inform the development of relevant and engaging curriculum, when they follow the eight principles of curriculum decision-making as explained in *The New Zealand Curriculum* (Ministry of Education 2007). Inclusion forms one of these principles. While a number of descriptions of inclusion circulate, I subscribe to the view that 'inclusive education is concerned with reducing all exclusionary pressures, and all devaluations of students whether on the basis of disability, attainment, "race", gender, class, family structure, life-style or sexuality' (Booth, Ainscow & Dyson 1997, 338). This chapter provides one strategy to support teachers to develop inclusive curriculum and pedagogies.

In the sections that follow I consider heteronormative hegemony as a theoretical tool to support the critical analysis of popular texts. I then recommend critical literacy (Sandretto with Klenner 2011) as a means to support students to develop the practice of text analysis. Next, I consider three texts from popular culture: an episode of *The Simpsons*; an advertisement for fragrance; and a cartoon from the *School Journal* series. I conclude by urging teachers to work with the texts of popular culture as a means to deconstruct the discourses of heteronormativity that exclude many students.

## Heteronormative hegemony as a theoretical tool

Theories are useful tools to prompt 'thinking otherwise' (Ball 1995). Here I use heteronormative hegemony (Ludwig 2011) to draw attention to the ways in which the texts of popular culture frequently (re)inscribe discourses that position heterosexuality as the norm – and thus the 'desirable' – sexuality. Attention to the construction of heterosexuality cannot proceed without considering the construction of gender, and how the concepts of gender and sexuality are related.

Judith Butler theorised that we are made into intelligible, gendered subjects through the heterosexual matrix (Butler 1999). The matrix describes the ways in which

> *bodies, genders, and desires are naturalized ... [This] model of gender intelligibility ... assumes that for bodies to cohere and make sense there must be a stable sex expressed through a stable gender (masculine expresses male, feminine expresses female) that is oppositionally and hierarchically defined through the compulsory practice of heterosexuality (194).*

The gendering of a subject via the matrix results in only two options: male or female. Following the logic of the matrix, it is possible to see the biology of a male body is suggestive of a male gender that desires a female subject. Thus gender is constituted through 'compulsory heterosexuality' (Rich

1980), in which male and female subjects only make sense when placed in binary opposition to each other within the frame of heterosexuality. Queer theory draws our attention to the construction of binary pairs, or 'unfair pairs' (MacLure 2003, 10; see also Sedgwick 1990) – 'unfair' because the ascendant member of the pair (in this case heterosexuality) maintains its dominance at the expense of the non-dominant member (homosexuality). A focus on deconstructing the binary of heterosexual/homosexual allows us to catch heteronormativity at work.

Heteronormativity has been described as taken for granted, like 'the air we breathe' (Quinlivan & Town 1999, 510). It takes ongoing work to maintain the normative status of heterosexuality (Atkinson & DePalma 2009). We maintain it as the privileged sexuality through the disavowal or rejection of any subjects positioned outside of the matrix (Butler 1993). For heterosexual male and female subjects to be constituted as recognisable and normal, we need gay, lesbian, transgendered and 'Others' to provide the 'threatening spectre' (Butler 1993, 3) and to shore up the normal/abnormal binary. It is possible to capture momentary glimpses of the maintenance work of heteronormativity in many popular culture texts.

The heterosexual matrix has proven a useful theoretical tool for 'exposing the ways in which boys' and girls' normative gender identities are inextricably embedded and produced within hegemonic representations of heterosexuality' (Renold & Ringrose 2008, 314). Atkinson and DePalma (2009), however, warn us of its limitations: 'through naming and believing the heterosexual matrix and identifying evidence of its operation, we reify, reinforce and reinscribe it, even as we attempt to subvert, unsettle or deconstruct it' (17). In addition, the abstract nature of the matrix and the lack of clarity in terms of how subjects take up power within it, suggest the concept needs revising to better account for the complexities of gender and sexuality.

Gundula Ludwig (2011) argues convincingly for a redesign of Butler's matrix as heteronormative hegemony. Antonio Gramsci's (Simon 1991) theory of hegemony offers promise in terms of (re)thinking the ways in which heteronormativity works. Like hegemony, heteronormative hegemony is a power formation that functions not through top-down repression or coercion, but through consent (Ludwig 2011). It is both a site of social struggles and a product of them. That is to say, it absorbs the contestations and compromises of social actors as it continually reinvents itself. Like Butler's matrix, heteronormative hegemony is co-constitutive of gendered subjects. Unlike the matrix, however, it provides us with opportunities to catch ourselves in the act of becoming gendered, sexual subjects both within and against everyday practices that normalise heterosexuality.

To suggest that teachers should address heteronormative hegemony invites careful consideration of sexuality – an area usually targeted as off-limits outside the sexuality education classroom (DePalma & Atkinson 2010). Researchers have identified that teachers across the early childhood, primary and secondary sectors are hesitant to address heteronormativity because sexuality is deemed to be located in the realm of the personal and private, not to be discussed in public (Epstein & Johnson 1998). Constructions of children as innocent (Robinson, 2002) or teachers as heterosexual (Evans 2002) do nothing to address persistent discourses of heteronormativity within the spaces of schooling.

Despite the challenges involved, a number of educators and researchers have argued persuasively that teachers have a responsibility to develop inclusive practices (e.g. Ferfolja 2007; Robinson, Irwin & Ferfolja 2002). Teachers can learn to analyse the ways in which they may inadvertently privilege discourses of heteronormativity (Jarvis & Sandretto 2010; Robinson & Ferfolja 2001); students can be introduced to the notion that sexuality and gender are constructed and contested concepts (e.g. Letts & Sears 1999). Teachers who support students to develop the skills of text analysis (Sandretto with Klenner 2011) can develop inclusive spaces in which students may begin to expose heteronormative hegemony. Promoting critical analysis of texts of everyday or popular culture encourages teachers to position students as agentic readers who can 'both critique and redesign texts in contextually significant ways' (Hagood 2008, 542). In the next section I look to critical literacy as a tool to support deconstruction of the heterosexual/homosexual binary, and the critique of heteronormative hegemony.

## Critical literacy as a tool to deconstruct heteronormative hegemony

Using critical literacy to analyse texts enables readers to contemplate matters of inclusion, exclusion and representation; they are able to relate texts to their own lives, and ultimately to consider how texts influence their thoughts and actions (Sandretto with Klenner 2011). Critical analysis encourages readers to question the construction and effects of texts. In terms of classroom practice, it involves supporting students to become aware that:

- Texts are social constructions
- Texts are not neutral
- Authors draw upon particular discourses (often majority discourses) and assume that readers will be able to draw upon them as well
- Authors make certain conscious and unconscious choices when constructing texts
- All texts have gaps, or silences, and particular representations within them
- Texts have consequences for how we make sense of ourselves, others and the world.

(Sandretto & Critical Literacy Research Team 2006, 24)

In short, critical literacy involves 'the analysis of how texts and discourses work, where, with what consequences, and in whose interests' (Luke 2012, 5). We can apply the process to popular culture texts to consider how to disrupt the heterosexual/homosexual binary and to see how discourses of heteronormativity work to include some groups and exclude others.

Few studies have used critical literacy to deconstruct discourses of heteronormativity in texts. In one project, designed to support adolescent girls to interrogate texts about the body and the effects of them, Lalik and Oliver (2007) found some resistance when the participating girls were presented with opportunities to resist heteronormativity. During the process of co-constructing a survey, the girls challenged one of the researcher's attempts to include questions that might be interpreted by other students as 'gay'. Given the complexities and sanctions of pursuing what might be interpreted as a queer 'agenda', the researcher did not persist with her desire to include questions that encompassed multiple sexualities.

In addition to critical literacy, other strategies used to draw attention to heteronormative hegemony involve using texts that have lesbian, gay, bisexual, transgender or queer (LGBTQ) characters or themes (Blackburn & Smith 2010), or drawing upon pedagogies 'that call into question the conceptual geography of normalization' (Britzman 1995, 152). Researchers such as Martino (2009) and MacIntosh (2007) have found that school programmes that merely encourage tolerance, or superficially add LGBTQ content, do not address the ways in which heteronormative hegemony works to position sexualities other than heterosexuality as deviant or abnormal.

Queer theorists remind us that for many, the workings of heteronormativity remain invisible, tacit and taken-for-granted (Warner 1991).

This awareness brings us back to the affordances of critical literacy. Teachers and students who develop their skills of text analysis can explicitly address the relationships between language and power as they make visible the ways that heterosexuality is frequently normalised in the texts of popular culture.

## Analysing texts of popular culture: What it might look like?

In this section I explore three popular culture texts: an episode of *The Simpsons*, a fragrance advertisement, and a cartoon from the *School Journal*. I provide a brief summary of each text and suggest the framework for a critical literacy analysis constructed to draw attention to heteronormative hegemony.

### *Homer's Phobia*

The 15th episode of the eighth season of the animated series *The Simpsons* aired in the United States in 1997. The episode centres on the Simpsons' new friend, John. Marge explains to Homer that John is gay:

*Marge: Homer, didn't John seem a little 'festive' to you?*
*Homer: Couldn't agree more, happy as a clam.*
*Marge: He prefers the company of men!*
*Homer: Who doesn't?*
*Marge: Homer, listen carefully. John is a ho – mo ...*
*Homer: Right.*
*Marge: ... sexual.*
*Homer: AAAAHHH! Oh my God! Oh my God! Oh my God! Oh my God! I danced with a gay!*
*Marge: I'm very sorry you feel that way, because John invited us out on a drive today, and we're going.*
*Homer: Whoa! Not me. And not because John's gay, but because he's a sneak. He should have the good taste to mince around and let everyone know that he's ... that way.*
*Marge: What on earth are you talking about?*
*Homer: You know me, Marge. I like my beer cold, my TV loud, and my homosexuals F-LAMING!*

For the remainder of the episode Homer embarks on a variety of stereotypical activities designed to address his own fear, expressed to his son Bart as 'He didn't give you gay, did he?' In this question Homer frames homosexuality as a disease that can be transmitted through association. The comment calls upon historical and pathological understandings of so-called deviant sexualities. Homer takes Bart to a steel mill, a setting he considers sufficiently masculine to inoculate Bart and steer him straight. According to Moe the bartender, however, 'the whole industry is gay', so Homer's intervention backfires. In the final attempt to consolidate Bart's masculine and therefore heterosexual status, Homer and his friends Moe and Barney take Bart hunting. Bart alludes to the potentially queer nature of the situation: 'Something 'bout a bunch of guys, alone, together in the woods. Seems kinda gay.' They are unable to find any deer to shoot and wind up at a reindeer farm where they are rescued by John, who addresses Homer's homophobia by concluding, 'Homer, I won your respect, and all I had to do was save your life. Now, if every gay man could just do the same, you'd be set.'

*Homer's Phobia* provides a rich popular-culture text for critical analysis. The episode won the Gay and Lesbian Alliance Against Defamation (GLAAD) Media Award for 'Outstanding TV – Individual Episode'. The award described the episode as: 'a shining example of how to bring intelligent, fair and funny representations of our community onto television' ('Homer's phobia' n.d.). I argue the intended reading of *Homer's Phobia* is that Homer's homophobic position is not the norm; no one other than Homer and Moe views John as abnormal. Without the support of critical literacy analysis, however, it is possible that children will side with Homer's heteronormative position, and the very stereotypes we seek to deconstruct will be reinforced.

So how might teachers use *Homer's Phobia* as a text for analysis in a critical literacy lesson? A starting place could be to discuss how Homer's repeated attempts at scaring Bart straight are focused on Bart's masculine and heterosexual subjectivities, and express Homer's desire for Bart to be seen as 'normal'. As noted by Ludwig (2011), subjects 'integrate hegemonic worldviews about female or male body care, sexuality and desires in their everyday practices by applying them in a way that makes sense and feels "normal" to them' (58). In other words, Homer wants Bart to be viewed as a normal, masculine and therefore heterosexual subject. Yet his strategies do not seem to have succeeded, because in this episode the joke is on Homer:

> Moe: Come on, don't take this so hard, Homer. You still got that other kid, uh ... Lisa. Let's, uh, take her out hunting tomorrow; make her into a man.
> Homer: Aw, she'd never go. She's a vegetarian.
> Moe: Oh, geez! Homer, geez! You and Marge ain't cousins, are you?

We cannot predict how students will read Homer's position. But as teachers, we can use texts such as this to open discussions with students around the ways in which heterosexuality is constructed as 'normal', and to discuss how such a construction excludes many people. Numerous students will have had experiences of friends or family members who are excluded by discourses of heteronormativity (Pallotta-Chiarolli 1999). Critical literacy analysis can support these, and indeed all students, to develop the resources to 'reflexively turn ... the gaze of language on itself' (Davies et al. 2004, 380) and consider the effects of heteronormative hegemony.

A teacher may wish to focus on a small excerpt of the show, or divide students into small groups to consider particular aspects. They may focus solely on the linguistic semiotic system, or the visual, or on how these systems work together. Questions to support critical analysis of the text might include:

- What do the words in *Homer's Phobia* suggest?
- What do the images in *Homer's Phobia* suggest?
- What makes the text fair or unfair?
- What knowledge does the viewer need to bring to the text in order to understand it?
- What makes *Homer's Phobia* funny?

## *Eternity advertisement*

Advertisements provide a means for teachers and students to explore heteronormative hegemony. Some readers may remember a popular advertising campaign for the Calvin Klein fragrance range *Eternity* from 1995, featuring the supermodels Christy Turlington and Mark Vanderloo, shot by photographer Peter Lindbergh. The series of print advertisements featured an idyllic heterosexual couple and family. The campaign was so popular, Calvin Klein has reissued it to celebrate the 25th anniversary of the fragrance. In one of the series of advertisements for the campaign we see what appears to be a loving family. The first frame shows the husband and wife cuddling. We suppose they are married because the woman's wedding ring is prominently displayed. The woman gazes upon the man lovingly and the words 'love sweet love' provide the bridge to the family picture below. The second photo seems to capture the happy family, complete with pet rabbit. The final line states: 'Calvin Klein, fragrances for men and women.'

The advertisement draws upon 'a heterosexual logic: sex is perceived as bringing about gender and desire' (Ludwig 2011, 45). The woman is pictured gazing upward in desire at her husband; her femininity and assumed heterosexual status is reinscribed by her focus on the object of her affection. In addition, we can argue that the advertisement portrays the common-sense purpose of heterosexual marriage: the production of offspring. Warner (1991) refers to this unspoken assumption of heterosexual logic as 'repro-narrativity: the notion that our lives are somehow made more meaningful by being embedded in a narrative of generational succession' (7). The unspoken purpose of marriage – reproduction – has clearly been fulfilled. The advertisement leaves little room for alternative constructions of family, gender or sexuality.

There are many ways to undertake a critical literacy analysis of a text (Sandretto with Klenner 2011). One option for analysing the *Eternity* advertisement could involve teachers and students considering who has been *excluded* from the text. The heteronormative hegemonic ideal of the nuclear family haunts children from their first drawings of their family, which they are asked to make at school or in early childhood centres. While not a malicious practice, it does frequently go unexamined. A critical literacy analysis encourages us to consider how a teacher might support students whose life worlds are not acknowledged at school (Pallotta-Chiarolli 1999). It can focus attention on the ways in which heterosexuality is privileged and normalised while all other sexualities are marginalised, Othered or, in the case of the *Eternity* advertisement, excluded. Questions such as those listed below can initiate conversations that may expose the privileged status of heterosexuality and the silencing of queer sexualities:

- Do you think the people in the advertisement are a family? Why or why not?
- Who is missing from the text?
- How else could the *Eternity* advertisement have been constructed?

In addition, critical literacy analysis can occur by questioning the representation of heteronormative hegemony via the taken-for-granted constructions of sexuality and gender portrayed in the advertisement

(Sandretto with Klenner 2011). Questions that draw students' attention to the heteronormative assumptions operating through the silences in the advertisement can illustrate how such hegemony works through popular culture texts. Teachers could use questions such as:

- What do the images in the advertisement imply?
- How is the woman/man/child represented in the text?
- What view of the world do the images present?
- What has been left out of the images?

As Janks (2005) suggests, not only should students be supported to deconstruct texts, they should be provided with opportunities to reconstruct texts. A question such as the earlier 'How else could the advertisement have been constructed?' could kick-start critical conversations and perhaps even lead the students into a multimodal (Bull & Anstey 2010) project in which they design their own inclusive advertisements.

## *School Journal*

Finally we consider the *School Journal*, a New Zealand-based literacy resource developed to support students in Years 4–8 (ages 7–13). All primary schools in New Zealand receive the publication free of charge; it forms a key element of guided reading programmes in many classrooms and is part of the everyday culture of New Zealand primary school students. The journal provides a rich opportunity to support students to 'understand ... that texts are not neutral, that particular points of view privilege some while silencing other voices' (Hagood 2008, 542).

To begin my analysis of aspects of the *School Journal*, I consider it as a text in itself. It is important that teachers not only support students to critically analyse texts, but also that teachers themselves critically analyse the texts that form their curriculum (see also Hickman 2012; Snyder & Broadway 2004). The *School Journal* online search tool and the key words 'wedding', 'love', 'girl' and 'boy' returned a variety of stories.[1] I have listed a brief representative selection of these in Table 4.1.

A number of authors have drawn our attention to the presence of heteronormative hegemony in the authorised texts in school. For instance, Sears (1999) stresses 'as cultural cops of the ancient regime, elementary

---

1   The search terms 'gay' and 'lesbian' returned no results. The terms 'two mums' and 'two dads' did not return any stories that challenged heteronormativity. The search tool may be found at http://journalsurf.learningmedia.co.nz/login.php

Table 4.1: *School Journal* search selected results

| KEY WORD | NO. OF ITEMS FOUND | TITLE & PUBLICATION DETAILS | BRIEF DESCRIPTION |
|---|---|---|---|
| **WEDDING** | 19 | *The Bendigo bride*<br>Part 3, No. 1, 1978 | A Dunedin serving girl, anxious to be married, agrees to travel to Cromwell to be wed. When the bridegroom does not appear she accepts a job as a barmaid at the Bendigo Gully saloon. She has many offers of marriage, but carefully chooses a steady young miner. She marries and lives happily ever after. |
| | | *I'm not wearing that!*<br>Part 3, No. 1, 2003 | Hannah's sister, Greta, is getting married. But Hannah doesn't want to be a bridesmaid and she definitely doesn't want to wear anything sparkly or fancy. |
| **LOVE** | 126 | *Love story*<br>Part 4, No. 1, 1996 | A New Zealand story from the World War II years. A girl falls in love with a classmate who's a recent immigrant from Germany. |
| | | *Write on*<br>Part 4, No. 1, 2000 | Solomon's got just 50 minutes to think up a message for Lara's Valentine's Day card. 'Your voice is like a guitar, ah! You're sweeter than a jar – a honey jar …' (Play with four characters). |
| **GIRL** | 145 | *Fred and his amazing night-time powers*<br>Part 3, No. 2, 1996 | On school camp, no one was keen to have Fred in their cabin. But his blindness proved an asset when it came to playing games in the dark and raiding the girls' cabin at midnight. |
| | | *The show-off*<br>Part 4, No. 1, 1984 | Much to Beverley's annoyance, Uncle Ted keeps showing off in front of his girlfriend when he brings her to stay at the farm. When Beverley tries to cure him, he has an accident, and his girlfriend is no longer impressed. |
| **BOY** | 195 | *Lovelorn schoolboy*<br>Part 4, No. 2, 1988 | A story from the 1920s when Denys was at secondary school, fell madly in love with Susan, and spent more money than he could afford on taking her out, all to no avail. |
| | | *The cuddly one*<br>Part 3, No. 2, 1979 | Jeannie's sister Susan teases her because she likes a Greek boy called Dimitri at school. But Jeannie insists that he is not her boyfriend, she just likes him. |

teachers unmindfully enforce "compulsory heterosexuality" through stories of nuclear ... families' (11). In the *School Journal* the silence of any sexuality other than heterosexuality is deafening. My search returned stories, poems and plays that were all underpinned by the heteronormative assumption that everyone is heterosexual, everyone desires the 'opposite' sex, and it is natural and 'normal' to marry someone of the 'opposite' gender. As a text the journal provides evidence of the regular maintenance involved in heteronormative hegemony (Atkinson & DePalma 2009).

Teachers and students may wish to conduct their own text sleuthing exercise to critically analyse a number of stories, poems and plays from the *School Journal* series to analyse the weight of representation. Such an exploration could consider:

- Which representations of sexuality can you find?
- Do these representations change over time?
- If you were to present your findings to the editors of the *School Journal*, what might you say?

By drawing attention to the weight of representation of heteronormative hegemony in the texts of the *School Journal* series, we can support students to consider ways to create spaces where more than one version of 'normal' could exist.

*She loves me, she loves me not ...*
From the *School Journal*, we now consider the cartoon *She loves me, she loves me not ...* (Esler 2003) (Figure 4.1) in which Claude agonises over whether a girl loves him. He engages in the traditional game of plucking the petals off a flower to determine whether the object of his affection returns his feelings. We can see the taken-for-granted workings of heteronormative hegemony when the assumption that the object of Claude's affection is a girl is reinforced through the pronoun 'she'. Furthermore, a critical literacy analysis draws attention to the (re)construction of this hegemony as it normalises the attraction Claude has to the unnamed girl. We can also see in this text how Claude 'applies heteronormative scripts in everyday performative practices' (Ludwig 2011, 49). The popular rhyme that Claude chants – 'she loves me, she loves me not' – is unquestioned. What would it be like if Claude used an alternative: 'he loves me, he loves me not'?

Heteronormative hegemony is maintained 'not only through what is said, but through silences, inferences and assumptions' (DePalma &

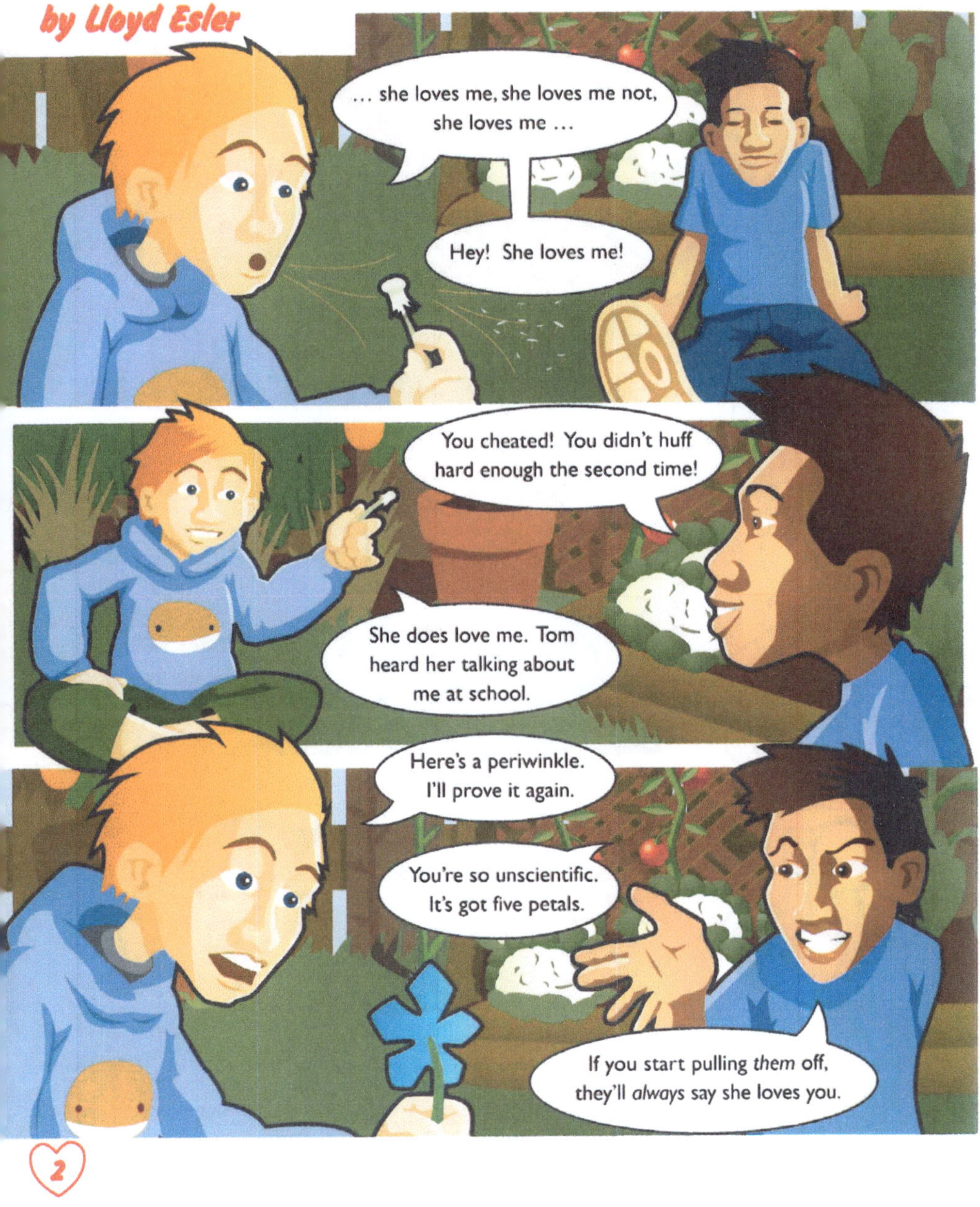

Figure 4.1. From *School Journal*, Part 4 (No. 3), 2–5, Ministry of Education, 2003. *Author Lloyd Esler; illustrator Courtenay Hopkinson.*

Atkinson 2010, 1671). Students could critically analyse the cartoon to identify instances of these silences. They could consider:

- What view of the world is the text presenting?
- When is it assumed or inferred that someone is heterosexual? Does it matter? Why or why not?
- What is missing (or silent) in the text?

And most importantly:
- How else could the text have been constructed?

## Why support students to analyse the discourses of heteronormative hegemony?

In this chapter I have argued that the discourses of heteronormative hegemony are pervasive in many popular culture texts. Ludwig's (2011) theoretical synthesis of Gramsci's hegemony and Butler's (1999) heterosexual matrix provides a means to understand how heteronormative hegemony operates as a power formation that is constantly undergoing transformation. The concept encourages us to interrogate the operation of heteronormativity in everyday practices, as well as our complicity in its reinscription (Ludwig 2011). Surveying the texts of everyday or popular culture (Hagood 2008) presents opportunities to deconstruct the heterosexual/homosexual binary and catch glimpses of heteronormative hegemony in action.

Critical literacy analysis of popular culture texts is an important step towards deconstructing such discourses and assists teachers to develop inclusive classrooms. If we accept the assertion of queer theorists such as Quinlivin and Town (1999) – that heterosexuality is as taken-for-granted as the 'air we breathe' – then we owe it to our students to support them to develop the critical literacy strategies to deconstruct those discourses. When used with the texts of popular culture, 'critical literacy opens up … the possibility of students and teachers becoming reflexively aware of the way speaking-as-usual constructs themselves and others' (Davies 1997, 25). The analysis of *Homer's Phobia*, *Eternity* and *She loves me, she loves me not* … reveals that critical literacy analysis focused on heteronormative hegemony may be conducted regardless of text type. Even in the award-winning episode of *The Simpsons*, arguably written to draw attention to the discourses of homophobia, we can create spaces to critically analyse and discuss how heteronormative hegemony works and what its potential effects may be.

I recognise that this is not easy terrain for teachers. Nonetheless it is very important work and we should not shy away from it. In fact, by engaging in critical analysis of texts in this way, teachers will be upholding the principle of inclusion as described in *The New Zealand Curriculum* (Ministry of Education 2007). There are sufficient studies documenting the harm of heteronormative hegemony (e.g. Robinson et al. 2002) to end the argument of whether or not we should make it a topic of critical analysis and discussion. A student in Quinlivan's (2004) study, which considered how to make schools more inclusive for lesbian and bisexual students, asked: 'Can you really change a problem that most people aren't aware of?' (96). The aim of using critical literacy analysis to highlight the workings of heteronormative hegemony in popular culture texts is to make more people aware of how it works, in turn creating spaces in which we may choose to withdraw our complicity in its (re)construction.

## Acknowledgements

The ideas presented here were developed from the results of Teaching and Learning Research Initiative (TLRI) grants with support from the University of Otago. Many thanks to the participating teachers and students.

## References

Atkinson, E. & DePalma, R. (2009), 'Un-believing the matrix: Queering consensual heteronormativity', *Gender & Education, 21*(1), 17–29. DOI: 10.1080/09540250802213149

Ball, S.J. (1995), 'Intellectuals or technicians? The urgent role of theory in educational studies', *British Journal of Educational Studies, 43*(3), 255–71.

Blackburn, M.V. & Smith, J.M. (2010), 'Moving beyond the inclusion of LGBT-themed literature in English language arts classrooms: Interrogating heteronormativity and exploring intersectionality', *Journal of Adolescent & Adult Literacy, 53*(8), 625+.

Booth, T., Ainscow, M. & Dyson, A. (1997), 'Understanding inclusion and exclusion in the English competitive education system', *International Journal of Inclusive Education, 1*(4), 337–55.

Britzman, D.P. (1995), 'Is there a queer pedagogy? Or, stop reading straight', *Educational Theory, 45*(2), 151–65. DOI: 10.1111/j.1741-5446.1995.00151.x

Bull, G. & Anstey, M. (2010), *Evolving Pedagogies: Reading and writing in a multimodal world*, Carlton, Australia: Curriculum.

Butler, J. (1993), *Bodies That Matter: On the discursive limits of 'sex'*, New York: Routledge.

Butler, J. (1999), *Gender Trouble: Feminism and the subversion of identity* (10th Anniversary edn), New York: Routledge.

Davies, B. (1997), 'Constructing and deconstructing masculinities through critical literacy', *Gender and Education, 9*(1), 9–30.

Davies, B., Browne, J., Gannon, S., Honan, E., Laws, C., Mueller-Rockstroh, B. & Petersen, E.B. (2004), 'The ambivalent practices of reflexivity', *Qualitative Inquiry*, 10(3), 360-89.

DePalma, R. & Atkinson, E. (2010), 'The nature of institutional heteronormativity in primary schools and practice-based responses', *Teaching and Teacher Education*, 26(8), 1669-76. DOI: 10.1016/j.tate.2010.06.018

Epstein, D. & Johnson, R. (1998), *Schooling Sexualities*, Buckingham, UK: Open University Press.

Esler, L. (2003), 'She loves me, she loves me not ...', *School Journal*, Part 4 (No. 3), 2-5.

Evans, K. (2002), *Negotiating the Self: Identity, sexuality, and emotion in learning to teach*, New York: RoutledgeFalmer.

Ferfolja, T. (2007), 'Schooling Cultures: Institutionalizing heteronormativity and heterosexism', *International Journal of Inclusive Education*, 11(2), 147-62. DOI: 10.1080/13603110500296596

Hagood, M.C. (2008), 'Intersections of popular culture, identities and new literacies research', in J. Coiro, M. Knobel, C. Lankshear & D.J. Leu (eds), *Handbook of Research on New Literacies* (531-51), New York: Lawrence Erlbaum.

Hickman, H. (2012), 'Handling heteronormativity in high school literature texts', in H. Hickman & B.J. Porfilio (eds), *The New Politics of the Textbook* (71-85), Rotterdam: Sense.

Homer's phobia (n.d.), Wikipedia: http://en.wikipedia.org/wiki/Homer%27s_Phobia - cite_note-16

Janks, H. (2005), 'Deconstruction and reconstruction: Diversity as a productive resource', *Discourse: Studies in the cultural politics of education*, 26(1), 31-43.

Jarvis, K. & Sandretto, S. (2010), 'The power of discursive practices: Queering or heteronormalising?', *New Zealand Research in Early Childhood Education*, 13, 43-56.

Letts, W.J. & Sears, J.T. (eds), (1999). *Queering Elementary Education: Advancing the dialogue about sexualities and schooling*, Lanham, MD: Rowman & Littlefield.

Ludwig, G. (2011), 'From the "heterosexual matrix" to a "heteronormative hegemony": Initiating a dialogue between Judith Butler and Antonio Gramsci about queer theory and politics', in M. Castro Varela, N. Dhawan & A. Engel (eds), *Hegemony and Heteronormativity: Revisiting 'The Political' in queer politics* (43-61), Surrey: Ashgate.

Luke, A. (2012), 'Critical literacy: Foundational notes', *Theory into Practice*, 51(1), 4-11, DOI: 10.1080/00405841.2012.636324

Macintosh, L. (2007), 'Does anyone have a band-aid? Anti-homophobia discourses and pedagogical impossibilities', *Educational Studies*, 41(1), 33-43. DOI: 10.1080/00131940701308874

MacLure, M. (2003), *Discourse in Educational and Social Research*, Maidenhead: Open University Press.

Martino, W. (2009), 'Literacy issues and GLBTQ youth', in L. Christenbury, R. Bomer & P. Smagorinsky (eds), *Handbook of Adolescent Literacy Research* (386-99), New York: Guilford.

Ministry of Education (2007), *The New Zealand Curriculum for English-Medium Teaching and Learning in Years 1-13*, Wellington: Learning Media.

Morrell, E. (2002), 'Towards a critical pedagogy of popular culture: Literacy development amongst urban youth', *Journal of Adolescent & Adult Literacy*, 46(1), 72-77.

Pallotta-Chiarolli, M. (1999), '"My moving days": A child's negotiation of multiple lifeworlds in relation to gender, ethnicity and sexuality', in W.J. Letts IV & J.T. Sears (eds), *Queering Elementary Education: Advancing the dialogue about sexualities and schooling* (71-81), Lanham: Rowman & Littlefield.

Quinlivan, K. (2004), 'So far so queer? Learning about intersections of gender and sexuality with young women in a single-sex girls' school', in L. Alice & L. Star (eds),

*Queer in Aotearoa New Zealand* (87–101), Palmerston North: Dunmore.

Quinlivan, K. & Town, S. (1999), 'Queer pedagogy, educational practice and lesbian and gay youth', *International Journal of Qualitative Studies in Education*, 12(5), 509–24.

Renold, E. & Ringrose, J. (2008), 'Regulation and rupture: Mapping tween and teenage girls' resistance to the heterosexual matrix', *Feminist Theory*, 9(3), 313–38. DOI: 10.1177/1464700108095854

Rich, A. (1980), 'Compulsory heterosexuality and lesbian existence', *Journal of Women in Culture and Society*, 5(4), 631–60.

Robinson, K. (2002), 'Making the invisible visible: Gay and lesbian issues in early childhood education', *Contemporary Issues in Early Childhood*, 3(3), 415–34.

Robinson, K. & Ferfolja, T. (2001), '"What are we doing this for?" Dealing with lesbian and gay issues in teacher education', *British Journal of Sociology of Education*, 22(1), 121–33.

Robinson, K., Irwin, J. & Ferfolja, T. (eds), (2002), *From Here to Diversity: The social impact of lesbian and gay issues in education in Australia and New Zealand*, New York: Harrington Park.

Sandretto, S. & Critical Literacy Research Team (2006), 'Extending guided reading with critical literacy', *SET: Research information for teachers* (3), 23–28.

Sandretto, S. with Klenner, S. (2011), *Planting Seeds: Embedding critical literacy into your classroom programme*, Wellington: New Zealand Council for Educational Research.

Sears, J.T. (1999), 'Teaching queerly: Some elementary propositions', in W.J. Letts IV & J.T. Sears (eds), *Queering Elementary Education: Advancing the dialogue about sexualities and schooling* (3–14), Lanham, MD: Rowman & Littlefield.

Sedgwick, E.K. (1990), *Epistemology of the Closet*, Berkeley, CA: University of California Press.

Simon, R. (1991), *Gramsci's Political Thought: An introduction* (revised edn), London: Lawrence & Wishart.

Snyder, V.L. & Broadway, F.S. (2004), 'Queering high school biology textbooks', *Journal of Research in Science Teaching*, 41(6), 617–36. DOI: 10.1002/tea.20014

Warner, M. (1991), 'Introduction: Fear of a queer planet', *Social Text* (29), 3–17.

# 5.
# How are teenage male students redefining masculinity and heterosexuality?

Steven S. Sexton

In 1985 I was in my final year of high school. I would rather have died than let anyone know I was gay.[1] I was never a member of the inner circle of high school, but worked very hard at being a regular guest. I was friends with a couple of the most popular girls. I had spent the previous five years working my way up the social ladder and would have done almost anything to keep this position. My entire self-worth was based on what others thought of me. I cultivated an image of myself that I hoped allowed me to blend into the assumed heterosexuality (Cooper 2013). I was always worrying about whether I had said the right thing or laughed long enough at the sexual innuendoes of my friends; and if I bought this designer shirt, these pants, this jacket, would I make it up the next rung of the ladder. I knew this would all end the minute anyone found out I liked boys.

I suppressed who I was and refused to accept I was gay. Growing up in the Bible Belt of the United States had not helped my self-esteem; nor had growing up with a bi-polar alcoholic parent. I decided in the 9th grade (equivalent to Year 10 in New Zealand) that university was my ticket out – and I was getting out. I drew a 2000-kilometre circle around my house and refused to look at any university within this circle. It took another 10 years, however, before I was able to come to terms with who I really was, before I felt confident and comfortable enough in my identity to tell my family and friends I was gay. I will never forget the fear I felt walking back and forth in front of the first gay bar I ever stepped into. Nor will I forget how I cried the first time a man said he loved me and I knew he meant me, the real me, the me that only a handful of people knew.

Now, as a university academic and teacher educator, I wonder has anything changed since my time in high school? To explore this in 2013

---

1 'Gay' is my preferred descriptor of who I am and my use of this term results from my own personal experiences.

I conducted a study in which I inquired into the regulation of each others' masculinities by queer and heterosexual male secondary school-aged students within friendship circles. I was keen to find out whether teenage boys are any more confident and comfortable in their identities. Mark McCormack's (2012b) work *The Declining Significance of Homophobia* would seem to indicate that some are, at least in the three schools in the UK where he conducted his research. His book details how the intersection of masculinity, sexuality, homophobia and education has shifted dramatically over time in the three schools. He explains how, a few years before his work was published, much of the behaviour he observed would have likely been coded as 'gay' and resulted in bullying. According to McCormack, all three schools are now 'gay-friendly'. The change in culture is significant.

International (Phoenix, Frosh & Pattman 2003; Ratele et al. 2007) and national (Rout 1992; Town 1999) research has highlighted how discourses of hegemonic masculinity, which are reinforced in official school practices and student cultures, have a strong impact on young men's behaviour in high schools – an impact that varies, however, between schools and among young men themselves.

## Teenage boys, sexuality and schooling

Many students experience bullying in secondary schools, especially those who belong to marginalised groups (Goodenow, Szalacha & Westheimer 2006; Poteat, Mereish, DiGiovanni & Scheer 2013; Rossen, Lucassen, Denny & Robinson 2009; Swearer, Turner, Givens & Pollack 2008). In 2007 Rossen et al. (2009) conducted a study into the health and wellbeing of 9107 New Zealand students. When asked about their sexual attractions, a total of 343 (4.2 per cent) reported they were attracted to the same or both sexes, or were not attracted to anyone. Same- or both-sex-attracted students reported five times as many instances of bullying (33 per cent) as their opposite-sex-attracted counterparts (6 per cent). Rossen et al. (2009) also found that 'three times as many same/both-sex-attracted students were bullied weekly at school compared to opposite-sex-attracted students' (26).

Using social cognitive domain theory, Horn (2006) explored the age-related differences in boys' attitudes towards homosexuality and their treatment of gay and lesbian peers. She noted that as young men passed through adolescence their acceptance and/or tolerance of 'Others' changed. She argues that in early adolescence (12–14 years) boys start to develop an understanding of societal conventions and their own identity; between 14 and 16, boys tend to become 'invested in rigid adherence to the conventions of their particular normative reference group' (423). Horn (2006) states that it is not until 19–26 years of age that young men become more secure in their own sexuality and identity and therefore more tolerant of others. Although Horn's (2006) age-and-stage theory can be considered deterministic, other research has also found that homophobic language peaks in young men aged around 15 years and is directed at anything that signifies a lack of allegiance to the expectations of peer groups (Plummer 2001).

Poteat (2007) examined the influence of peer groups on individual group members' attitudes and behaviours in a co-educational school in the United States, and found that measureable similarities in attitude could be identified within friendship circles, while distinct variations existed across friendship groupings. Poteat (2007) maintains that members of a peer group not only influence each other but also develop similar views, attitudes and behaviours.

Of particular relevance to this present chapter, Nairn and Smith (2003) and Painter (2009) conducted research on how queer students in New Zealand secondary schools experienced their school culture. Nairn and Smith (2003) surveyed 821 secondary students and 438 school staff, and reported that only 5 per cent of students and 8 per cent of school staff believed that their school would be a safe space for queer students. They also found that 31 per cent of students and 33 per cent of school staff were aware of the use of homophobic language in their schools. While one in 12 students in New Zealand self-identifies as queer (Le Brun, Robinson, Warren & Watson 2004), participants in Nairn and Smith's (2003) study reported that they were unaware of any queer students in their school. Nairn and Smith suggest that this might be because queer students felt too unsafe to be open about their sexuality.

Painter (2009) conducted research on how safe, supportive and inclusive high schools are for queer students. The study involved youth and teachers from one geographical region of New Zealand. Survey and interview methods were used. Painter asked 150 high-school students (103 female and 38 male, none of whom were asked to specify their sexuality) about what challenges queer students would face at their schools. Two-thirds identified homophobic language and bullying. Painter interviewed queer youth as part of the study (n=12); six of them (three male and three female) also identified homophobic language as the commonest form of bullying they experienced.

Some went on to explain that there was no point reporting these incidences because staff 'ignored' them. For instance, one student said, 'If there is other bullying going on, they'll deal with it to a huge extent ... whereas when it comes down to this sort of subject [homophobic bullying], [they are] a little bit more, "oh, it's alright"' (Painter 2009, 12).

Male student peer groups are a site where many of the codes of acceptable masculine behaviour are taught, learned and policed (Connell 1995: Mac An Ghaill 1994). A teacher in Painter's (2009) study said that in New Zealand secondary schools many young men are attempting to sort out their identities while wanting to fit in at the same time. As the dominant group usually regulates 'acceptable' forms of masculinity, young men are likely to 'play along' for fear of retribution if they do not live up to a perceived ideal.

In Western societies, 'hegemonic masculinity' refers to the most dominant and socially rewarded form of masculinity that exists (Connell & Messerschmidt 2005). It is characterised by heterosexuality, boasting about heterosexual conquests, homophobia and, in specific relation to the New Zealand context, playing rugby and drinking beer (Campbell, Law & Honeyfield 1999; Connell & Messerschmidt 2005; Town 1999). A hegemonic masculinity is also forged in relation to 'sub-ordinate' masculinities, such as gay masculinities, as well as the masculinities of young men who engage in non-traditional gender displays, such as those who prefer chess or art to rugby (Carrigan, Connell & Lee 1985; Sexton 2012; Town 1999).

## Gay discourse

McCormack's (2012b) report of significant change in school environments that had shifted from homophobic to gay-friendly, referred to earlier, was in part based on his observation of boys' use of what he terms 'gay discourse'. Building on Pascoe's (2005) notion of 'fag discourse' (language used within homophobic settings for a range of intentions, including to marginalise a person's sexuality and to regulate other young men's behaviour) and Anderson's (2009) 'homohysteria' (the fear of being thought homosexual because of one's atypical gender performance), McCormack (2012b) developed a model of homosexually themed language (Figure 5.1). The model ranges from homophobic language used for negative social effect, to pro-gay language used for positive social effect.

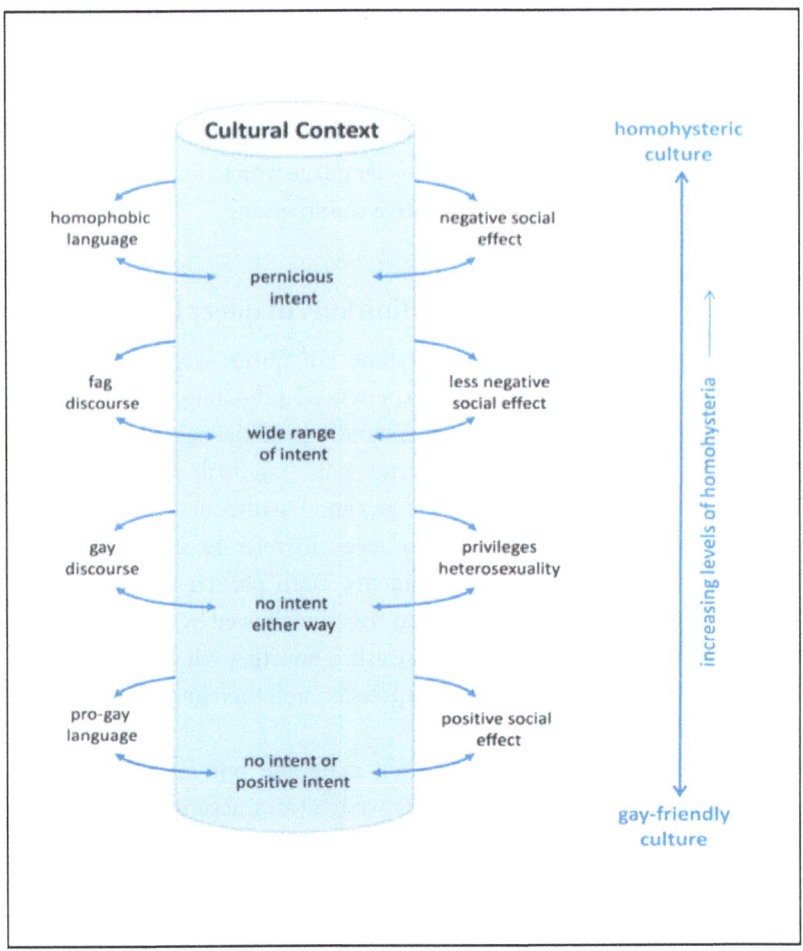

Figure 5.1: Model of homosexually themed language (reproduced with permission). *McCormack 2012b.*

McCormack's model draws attention to the multiple meanings of language. For example, the expression 'that's so gay' may be used with or without negative intent (McCormack 2012b). In gay discourse, the expression is often used as a verbal statement of 'dissatisfaction or frustration' (McCormack 2012b, 119); while the language is not pro-gay, in this context the use of the word 'gay' has no relationship to same-sex attraction, and no marginalisation is intended. McCormack acknowledges, however, that some would argue the phrase 'that's so gay' is, and always will be, homophobic language, because of the historical deployment of the term 'gay'.

The concept of 'cultural lag' is a useful tool in understanding the development of gay discourse. Cultural lag occurs when 'two social variables become dissociated because their meanings change at different rates' (McCormack 2012b, 114). Gay discourse recognises that, as a result of cultural lag, some people today employ language which, for them, may have no association with its previous negative connotation.

## New Zealand's shifting definitions of queer language

In 2011 I conducted research into how ten queer[2] secondary students from one region of New Zealand experienced schooling, and how those experiences impacted on their understandings of the role of the teacher and teaching (Sexton 2012). Two participants (one male and one female) appeared to agree with the notions of gay and fag discourse. They reported hearing the expression 'that's so gay' used to refer to anything causing concern or frustration for other students. Both participants went on to explain that the term 'that's so gay' was usually followed by 'you know what I mean' or 'no offence'. When they were asked how they felt when they heard the phrase, both said it was just an expression and therefore not meant as a personal attack.

The other eight participants (seven male and one female), however, reported that homophobic comments were always negative and intended to wound the subject. Consequently, they appeared to view homophobic epithets in accordance with McCormack's description of homophobic language. The seven male participants made comments explaining how homophobia was a mechanism for policing young men's behaviour (McCormack 2012b). The female participant attended a school in which a negative view of homosexuality reflected its religious foundation. Because of the school's special character she felt compelled to suppress her sexuality but considered this worthwhile given the opportunities the school provided.

### *Methodology*

This chapter reports on a study that explored how queer and heterosexual male secondary school-aged students regulate their own and each other's masculinities in their friendship circles. As focus groups facilitate a 'friendly research method that is respectful and not condescending' (Morgan &

---

2  In the 2011 study and this chapter, 'queer' is used to denote those who self-identify as gay, lesbian, bisexual, transgendered, takatāpui, fa`afafine or intersex.

Krueger 1993, 18), these were chosen as the data-collection method for the study. Research has shown how focus groups have helped enable participants to share personal experiences (Carey 1994; Kitzinger 1995; Zeller 1993). Carey (1994) highlights the importance of the leader establishing trust, fostering an accepting atmosphere and encouraging members to interact with and respond to each other. As a result, 'group members can describe the rich details of complex experiences and the reasoning behind their actions, beliefs, perceptions, and attitudes' (Carey 1994, 226).

In order to gather participants I contacted teachers from schools throughout one province of New Zealand, in the hope of procuring introductions to groups of young men who were known to have strong friendship circles, and who might be willing to participate in this study. Through a third party I was also put in touch with a group for self-identifying queer students. I informed all potential participants that the focus of this research was to investigate their friendship circles and, specifically, to investigate how they initiated, maintained and regulated the behaviour of their peers in their friendship groupings.

Of my six focus groups, one comprised queer students only; the remainder included heterosexual students. While the queer focus group involved students from a range of schools, each of the the other five groups consisted of participants who attended the same school (see Table 5.1). In all, eight schools were involved. Due to the nature of this study, self-identified queer and heterosexual students were not included in the same focus group. In an endeavour to help them feel safe enough to share personal information, I informed the queer participants that I self-identified as gay (Carey 1994; McCormack 2012a).

Thirty-eight young men aged 13–18 participated in the study. I use pseudonyms to protect the identity of the participants. Due to the limited number of secondary schools in the region where the research was carried out, I do not provide descriptions of the schools the participants attended, in order to protect the identity of the schools concerned.

The focus-group sessions averaged 48 minutes in duration. Students in Year 7–8 groups had the longest, lasting over an hour. These groups also elicited the most responses, with peers often talking over each other to provide further details, explanations or examples. The Year 11–12 sessions were the shortest, lasting approximately 30 minutes; these participants were more reticent in their responses.

Table 5.1: Participant demographics

| FOCUS GROUP SIZE | YEAR GROUP | AGE | SCHOOL TYPE | QUEER/ HETEROSEXUAL |
|---|---|---|---|---|
| 7 | 13 | 18 | single-sex | heterosexual |
| 6 | 11 to 12 | 16–17 | co-educational secondary | heterosexual |
| 6 | 9 to 10 | 14–15 | co-educational secondary | heterosexual |
| 7 | 7 to 8 | 12–13 | co-educational full primary | heterosexual |
| 6 | 7 to 8 | 12–13 | co-educational intermediate | heterosexual |
| 4 | 11 to 12 | 16–17 | both co-educational and single-sex secondary | queer |
| 2 | 13 | 18 | | |

## *Homosexually themed language in New Zealand*

In his model of homosexually themed language (Figure 5.1), McCormack (2012b) makes several distinctions between types of language. For example, gay discourse privileges heterosexuality, occurs in a social setting of little or no homophobia, and lacks any negative social effects. It is not intended to marginalise anyone or cause offence. Fag discourse, on the other hand, occurs mostly in a homophobic setting and is used for a wide range of purposes, which may or may not have negative social effects. Fag discourse is more often employed to regulate other young men's behaviour than to marginalise a person's sexuality. In this study, the difference between whether the participants classified a comment as an example of gay or fag discourse was based on the social position of who was talking, who they were talking to, and who they were talking about.

## *'That's so gay' vs 'gay'*

Participants in each focus group were asked about their thoughts regarding the expression, 'that's so gay', which is frequently used in New Zealand high schools (Painter 2009). They were also asked to comment on a media story about John Key, New Zealand's prime minister, who referred to a man's shirt as 'that gay red shirt'.[3] All participants were able to make comments on the

---

3   See www.youtube.com/watch?v=8ppB9Mf4OhM

expression 'that's so gay'; however, only the focus group consisting of Year 13 students had knowledge of the 'gay red shirt' episode.

For the Year 13 group, the phrase 'that's so gay' had the same intended meaning whether applied to an object or a person. Even those who self-identified as queer stated 'that's so gay' was a common expression and not intended to hurt. The word 'gay', however, has come to mean something that is not very good. After showing and explaining the 'gay red shirt' reference to all focus groups, the consensus among participants was summed up by Adam (Year 13 focus group, heterosexual), who commented, 'I would take the comment as downgrading the shirt.' All participants believed that when an object is referred to as 'gay' it does not imply any negative social intent; they agreed the comment was about the shirt and not about the person wearing the shirt.

When talking about a person, all the participants saw the term 'gay' as having the same meaning: something about the person it was directed at was 'bad' or 'not right'. However, there were differences in the way the heterosexual and queer participants viewed the intent of the term. The heterosexual participants reported that calling a person 'gay' suggests that something about them is wrong. For example, Charlie (Year 9–10 focus group, heterosexual) commented that it is a way of 'trying to make them feel down about themselves'. The heterosexual participants stated that the degree to which they wanted to make a person feel 'down' determined whether they employed the term in order 'to wind someone up' (an example of fag discourse, described as 'playing around, giving them a hard time but not making fun of them … or put[ting] them down in any way' (David, Year 11–12 focus group, heterosexual)) or to 'rip on them' (an example of homophobic language, 'more like making fun of people, more like an insult' (David, Year 11–12 focus group, heterosexual)). Participants in each heterosexual focus group also stated that the term 'gay' 'would be offensive to direct at a person' because it 'offends gays' (Edward, Year 7–8 focus group, heterosexual). These discussions would seem to imply that while 'that's so gay' may be an acceptable and inoffensive expression among school students, most still view the term 'gay' as having a degree of negative social intent when applied to people, i.e. it becomes homophobic language.

## *Language within friendship circles*

Regardless of sexuality, all participants stated that what could be said within their friendship circle was different to what could be said to people beyond the circle. For example, Frank (Year 13 focus group, heterosexual) commented, 'The things we say to each other would never be okay to say to someone else.' George (Year 13 focus group, heterosexual) also commented, 'we tease each other all the time; they [people outside our friendship group] wouldn't understand it as well, they wouldn't know us'. The participants' comments highlighted that there was a greater acceptance of joking or teasing within their friendship circles. All agreed that among their circle there was no negative intent implied by the term 'gay', and joking and teasing were done in a non-threatening and humorous manner.

However, the participants said that if gay-themed comments were directed at them by people outside their friendship circle, then they 'might take it different[ly]' (Jack, Year 9–10 focus group, heterosexual). While the heterosexual participants stated that they would feel awkward or uncomfortable in this situation, the queer students reported that they would be scared or worried.

### Performing masculinity in an educational setting

Performing one's masculinity in an educational setting is context-dependent and situational (Frank, Kehler, Lovell & Davison 2003). Frank et al. (2003) highlight that socially acceptable codes of masculinity change in different locations, although they do note common threads in what are seen as 'appropriate' male behaviours in schools. The school environment appeared to have less impact on how the Year 7–8 participants enacted their masculinity. These young men, who were just embarking on their secondary schooling years, willingly talked about crying in front of their peers and also explained that they expected physical comforting from their friends. They appeared more relaxed around each other and far more willing to defend each other from those outside their friendship circle than participants from any other year-group. It should be noted that there were no self-identified queer participants in this age range.

For the young men in Years 9 and 10, the acceptance of physical contact between male friends had changed. These participants reported they were aware that physical contact between males was considered unacceptable, except within the context of sports or physical fighting. When asked to explain why they thought this, the participants attributed it to older male students and teachers policing the behaviour of younger males.

Participants from all other year-levels reported that young men in Years 9–10 were the most aggressive. This would suggest that male students in this age range are attempting to enact their masculinity in accordance with societal discourses of hegemonic masculinity (Carrigan, Connell & Lee 1985; Connell & Messerschmidt 2005), in which physicality and aggression are considered acceptable and desirable qualities in men (Frosh, Phoenix & Pattman 2002; Martino 1999; Sadowski 2013).

No participants in the Year 9-10 age group self-identified as queer; however, the six participants in Years 11-13 who did identify as queer reflected on this time. They reported that in Years 9-10 they had experienced confusion and awkwardness as they began to acknowledge their queer attractions while at the same being aware that contact amongst males was seen as taboo. It was during this time that five of these students sought, and the sixth was introduced to, a queer group. When asked why they had made contact with a queer group, the five participants reported that they wanted to be around people who knew what they were going through. The sixth said he had not felt confident enough to seek out a queer group but was thankful a teacher at his school had introduced him to this group.

The importance of queer youth groups in establishing a positive queer self-identify has been well documented in literature reporting on queer students' experiences in high schools (Doty, Willoughby, Lindahl & Malik 2010; Ratele et al. 2007; Sadowski 2013). In these groups, queer youth can meet one another and discuss any issues they may be experiencing. The six queer participants agreed that being a member of a queer group provided a safe environment where they could be themselves without fear of censure. For instance, Michael (Year 11-12 focus group, queer) explained that attending a queer group 'lets me be me for a few hours without worrying what anyone else thinks'.

*Stability of friendship circles*

Participants at all year-levels reported that they experienced the greatest change of membership in their friendship circle during Years 9-10, and suggested this was because young men begin to develop and pursue different interests at this age. When asked to reflect back on this time, participants in Years 11-13 commented that this was when the newest members had joined their current friendship circle.

When comparing themselves to students in the 'junior' school (Years 7-10), participants in Years 11-12 reported that they felt they were starting to mature. The Year 11 and 12 heterosexual students explained that although several of their friends were no longer in their classes, or had moved to different schools, membership of their friendship circle was no longer dependent on these factors.

Four of the six queer participants were in the Year 11–12 group. Of these, only one – Nicholas, who attended a gay-friendly school – reported that he had not had dramatic changes to his friendship circle during this period; most of his current friends had been his friends since Year 7. The other three noted their friendship circles at school had undergone dramatic change and were now smaller and less familiar. These three said they had no friends at school to whom they could disclose their sexuality. For emotional support they turned to their queer groups because, as Oliver (Year 11–12 focus group, queer) stated, 'they understand what it's like'.

The Year 13 heterosexual participants considered themselves the most mature students in school and therefore viewed themselves as role models. They had the most positive view of their schooling and stated that bullying was unacceptable at their age. For example, Paul (Year 13 focus group, heterosexual) said, 'these days [bullying] is seen as not really the okay thing to do'. The heterosexual Year 13 participants considered that although they might attend different universities or enrol in different courses at the end of the school year, they would be able to maintain their friendship circle.

The two queer participants in Year 13, however, reported that this year was the worst of their schooling. These young men explained how they were attempting to be a part of their school culture while at the same time trying to ensure that no one found out about their sexuality. As his peers were increasingly 'bragging' about their supposed heterosexual exploits, Quentin (Year 13 focus group, queer) explained that his final year of school was like walking through a minefield and he was finding it increasing difficult to feign interest in their conversations. Quentin and Roger (Year 13 focus group, queer) stated that they just wanted to get through their final year of schooling, go to university and start living without the constraints of high school. When asked how and why they thought university was going to be different, both young men said university would likely be more like Nicholas' high school, where no one would care about who is or is not gay.

## Conclusion

Research has highlighted the influence of school culture on a student's self-image, referring to this as the intersection of schooling and self (Rasmussen 2006). Participants in this study appeared to modify their relationship between school and their self-image as they progressed through their secondary schooling. Students in Years 7 and 8, who were new to the culture of secondary school, were only just beginning to understand their school's social conventions. By Years 9 and 10, participants were aware of their school's expectations of male behaviour (Horn 2006; Martino 1999), which were based on heteronormative assumptions (Cooper 2013; Plummer 2001). Year 11–13 students provided evidence of what McCormack refers to as 'cultural lag'. While the use of language such as the phrase 'that's so gay' privileges heterosexuality, for these students the phrase was uttered in friendship circles where there was little or no homophobia, and was not intended to marginalise; despite this, students' recognised that 'gay' equated with something 'bad' and could be used with homophobic intent or to tease friends.

A school's culture has significant influence on how young men shape their understandings of acceptable displays of masculinity (Frosh et al. 2002; Sadowski 2013). Young men have to negotiate competing forms of masculinity; however, some talk openly about the close, emotionally supportive or personal nature of their relationships with other young men in their friendship circles at school. This study provides insight into how young men in New Zealand high schools negotiate their masculine subjectivities, and the ways in which friends influence their self-concept. It also provides an understanding of how language and meanings shift over time and contexts, and how terms once seen as derogatory and demeaning may no longer be considered exclusively as such.

## References

Anderson, E. (2009), *Inclusive Masculinity: The changing nature of masculinities*, New York: Routledge.
Carrigan, T., Connell, B. & Lee, J. (1985), 'Toward a new sociology of masculinity', *Theory and Society, 14*(5), 551–604.
Connell, R. (1995), *Masculinities*, Berkeley: University of California Press.
Carey, M.A. (1994), 'The group effect in focus groups: Planning, implementing and interpreting focus group research', in J.M. Morse (ed.), *Critical Issues in Qualitative Research Methods* (225–41), Thousand Oaks, CA: Sage.
Cooper, A.J. (2013), *Changing Gay Male Identities*, London: Routledge.
Connell, R.W. & Messerschmidt, J.W. (2005), 'Hegemonic masculinity', *Gender & Society, 19*(6), 829–59. DOI: 10.1177/0891243205278639
Doty, N.D., Willoughby, B.L.B., Lindahl, K.M. & Malik, N.M. (2010), 'Sexuality related social support among lesbian, gay, and bisexual youth', *Journal of Youth and Adolescence, 39*, 1134–47. DOI: 10.1007/s10964-010-9566-x

Frank, B., Kehler, M., Lovell, T. & Davidson, K. (2013), 'A tangle of trouble: Boys, masculinity and schooling – future directions', *Educational Review, 55*(2), 119–33.

Frosh, S., Phoenix, A. & Pattman, R. (2002), *Young Masculinities: Understanding boys in contemporary society*, Houndmills, England: Palgrave.

Goodenow, C., Szalacha, L. & Westheimer, K. (2006), 'School support groups, other school factors, and the safety of sexual minority adolescents', *Psychology in the Schools, 43*(5), 573–89. DOI: 10.1002/pits.20173

Horn, S.S. (2006), 'Heterosexual adolescents' and young adults' beliefs and attitudes about homosexuality and gay and lesbian peers', *Cognitive Development, 21*, 420–40. DOI: 10.1016/j.cogdev.2006.06.007

Kitzinger, J. (1995), 'Qualitative research: Introducing focus groups', *British Medical Journal, 311*, 299–302.

Le Brun, C., Robinson, E., Warren, H. & Watson, P.D. (2004), 'Non-heterosexual youth. A profile of their health and wellbeing: Data from Youth 2000, Auckland: University of Auckland.

Mac An Ghaill, M. (1994), *The Making of Men: Masculinities, sexualities and schooling*, Buckingham, England: Open University Press.

Martino, W. (1999), '"Cool boys", "party animals", "squids", and "poofters": Interrogating the dynamics and politics of adolescent masculinities in school', *British Journal of Sociology of Education, 20*(2), 239–63.

McCormack, M. (2012a), 'Queer masculinities, gender conformity and the secondary school', in J.C. Landreau & N.M. Rodriguez (eds), *Queer Masculinities: A critical reader in education* (Vol. 21, 35–46), Dordrecht: Springer.

McCormack, M. (2012b), *The Declining Significance of Homophobia: How teenage boys are redefining masculinity and heterosexuality*, New York: Oxford University Press.

Morgan, D.L. & Krueger, R. (1993), 'When to use focus groups and why', in D.L. Morgan (ed.), *Successful Focus Groups: Advancing the state of the art* (3–19), Newbury Park, CA: Sage.

Nairn, K. & Smith, A.B. (2003), 'Taking students seriously: Their rights to be safe at school', *Gender and Education, 15*(2), 133–49. DOI: 10.1080/09540250303853

Painter, H. (2009), 'How safe?: How safe and inclusive are Otago secondary schools? Ae ranei he haumaru, he wahi whāi kit e katoa ngā kura tuarua o Otago?' A report on the implementations from the 'Safety in our schools – Ko te harumaru i o tatou kura' action kit: He purongo ūruhi i ngā tuanaki a te kete mahi 'Safety in our schools – Ko te harumaru i o tatu kura', Dunedin, NZ: OUSA Queer Support.

Pascoe, C.J. (2005), '"Dude, you're a fag": Adolescent masculinity and the fag discourse', *Sexualities, 8*(3), 329–46. DOI: 10.1177/1363460705053337

Phoenix, A., Frosh, S. & Pattman, R. (2003), 'Producing contradictory masculine subject positions: Narratives of threat, homophobia and bullying in 11–14 year old boys', *Journal of Social Issues, 59*(1), 179–95.

Plummer, D.C. (2001), 'The quest for modern manhood: Masculine stereotypes, peer culture and the social significance of homophobia', *Journal of Adolescence, 24*, 15–23. DOI: 10.1006/jado.2000.0370

Poteat, V.P. (2007), 'Peer group socialization of homophobic attitudes and behavior during adolescence', *Child Development, 78*(6), 1830–42.

Poteat, V.P., Mereish, E.H., DiGiovanni, C.D. & Scheer, J.R. (2013), 'Homophobic bullying', in I. Rivers & N. Duncan (eds), *Bullying: Experiences and discourses of sexuality and gender* (75–90), Hoboken, NJ: Taylor and Francis.

Rasmussen, M.L. (2006), *Becoming Subjects: Sexualities and secondary schooling*, New York: Routledge.

Ratele, K., Fouten, E., Shefar, T., Strebel, A., Shabalala, N. & Buikema, R. (2007), '"Moffies, jock and cool guys": Boys' accounts of masculinity and their resistance in context', in T. Shefar, K. Ratele, A. Strebel, N. Shabalala & R. Buikema (eds), *From Boys to Men:*

*Social constructions of masculinity in contemporary society* (112–27), Lansdowne, South Africa: UCT Press.

Rossen, F.V., Lucassen, M.F.G., Denny, S. & Robinson, E. (2009), *Youth '07. The health and wellbeing of secondary school students in New Zealand: Results for young people attracted to the same sex or both sexes*, Auckland: University of Auckland.

Rout, B. (1992), 'Being staunch: Boys hassling girls', in S. Middleton & A. Jones (eds), *Women and Education in Aotearoa* (2nd edn, 169–80), Wellington: Bridget Williams.

Sadowski, M. (2013), *In a Queer Voice*, Philadelphia, PA: Temple University Press.

Sexton, S.S. (2012), 'Queer Otago secondary students' views of their schooling environment', *New Zealand Journal of Educational Studies, 47*(1), 93–105.

Swearer, S.M., Turner, R.K., Givens, J.E. & Pollack, W.S. (2008), '"You're so gay!": Do different forms of bullying matter for adolescent males?', *School Psychology Review, 37*(2), 160–73.

Town, S. (1999), 'Queer(y)ing masculinities in schools: Faggots, fairies and the first XV', in R. Law, H. Campbell & J. Dolan (eds), *Masculinities in Aotearoa/New Zealand* (135–52), Palmerston North: Dunmore.

Walker, J. (1988), *Louts and Legends: Male youth culture in an inner city school*, Sydney: Allen and Unwin.

Zeller, R.A. (1993), 'Focus group research on sensitive topics: Setting the agenda without setting the agenda', in D.L. Morgan (ed.), *Successful Focus Groups: Advancing the state of the art* (167–83), Newbury Park, CA: Sage.

# 6.
# Queer students and same-sex partners at the school formal

## Lee A. Smith

The New Zealand media constructs the school formal as 'a right of passage' (Tay 2007, C6) for New Zealand youth and the highlight of the school year for senior students. Given these depictions, it is surprising that there is a paucity of research on the school formal in a New Zealand context. Participants in research studies focusing on queer students' experiences in New Zealand secondary schools report, however, that their schools have implemented policies that impede the ability of queer students to attend the formal with same-sex partners (Painter 2009; Smith 2006). Such practices highlight how the school formal in New Zealand, like the prom in North America, upholds 'heterosexuality as the desired and assumed expression of sexuality' (Grace & Wells 2005, 248–49).

Under the 1993 Human Rights Act (HRA) it is illegal to discriminate on the basis of sexuality or gender in New Zealand (Smith 2006). Consequently, the Human Rights Commission[1] (HRC) has received numerous complaints from queer students (or their parents), who have been denied permission by their schools to attend the formal with their same-sex partners (McCullough 2009). In these cases the HRC has encouraged negotiation between schools, parents and students, and reports that the issues have been satisfactorily resolved for all involved (although they do not explain how).[2] Nevertheless, the complaints brought to the HRC highlight how the issue of schools banning queer students attending the school formal with same-sex partners is a current social justice concern.

In 1993 the New Zealand government ratified the United Nations Convention on the Rights of the Child (UNCROC) (United Nations 1989), which spells out children's rights of participation, protection and participation. Under UNCROC children and young people under 18

---

[1] The HRC is a government department that mediates in cases where human rights have been breached (www.hrc.co.nz).
[2] See www.hrc.co.nz/enquiries-and-complaints-guide/faqs/the-school-ball

are legally entitled to 'the right to protection from discrimination on any grounds', and the right to safety. In New Zealand secondary schools, however, queer students are more likely to experience bullying than their heterosexual counterparts, which can have a negative effect on the wellbeing of some same-sex-attracted students (Le Brun, Robinson, Warren & Watson 2004; Rossen, Luccassen, Denny & Robinson 2009).

In order to explore how schools are meeting their responsibilities under legislation such as UNCROC and the HRA, in this chapter I report on the policies of three New Zealand secondary schools – one boys', one girls' and one co-educational – regarding queer students attending the formal with same-sex partners. Since student cultures are more likely than official school policies to be hostile to same-sex attraction, in each participating school the student attitudes toward queer students attending the formal with same-sex partners are also documented (Epstein & Johnson 1994). I also examine how staff and students at each participating school reproduce and/or challenge New Zealand media constructions of the school formal as a heteronormative social event (Hewson 2009; Tay 2007). Key tenets of post-structural theory are employed in the chapter and are used to make sense of school policies and students' subject positioning.

## Post-structural theory, gender and sexuality

The term 'discourse' refers to communication between two or more people, whether verbal or written. In post-structural theory, however, the term refers to groups of statements that give meaning to everything in the social world – a definition developed by Foucault, who described discourse as the language or speech acts that we draw upon to describe things, which in turn 'form the objects of which they speak' (Foucault 1972, 54). For example, different discourses surrounding the school formal are promoted in the New Zealand media, some of which constitute the event as a 'night to remember' (Smith 2008, 10) and a feminine space (Hewson 2009). Others construct the formal and associated after-parties as problematic events, since students may consume excess alcohol on the night of the event (see Beech 2009; Lewis 2008). These and other discourses influence people's understandings of the formal and constitute its meaning.

According to post-structural and queer theorist Judith Butler (1990), our sense of being intrinsically gendered is not genetic, but is created through bodily performances that define us as masculine/feminine subjects. That is, men and women move and shape their bodies in conjunction with normative gender codes, so that others will view them as legitimate masculine/feminine subjects. Many young women, for instance, in their desire to appear feminine, are likely to spend considerable time and energy on their appearance for the formal (Best 2000). This is because make-up (Dellinger & Williams 1997) and highly styled hair (Weitz 2001) are considered markers of femininity in Western societies.

Normative gender codes and discourses are forged by heteronormativity – the entrenched societal belief that heterosexuality is the 'normal' sexuality (Blaise & Taylor 2012; Warner 1993). In accordance with the heteronormative framework, a person can only be considered a legitimate human being if their gender ties to their sex (men must perform masculinity and women femininity), and they are attracted to members of the 'opposite' sex or gender (Butler 1990). Same-sex attracted subjects and those who perform their gender in non-normative ways are invalidated within this 'heterosexual matrix' (Butler 1990, 151). As a result, queer people often experience considerable harassment and abuse in society, including in high schools (New Zealand Post Primary Teacher's Association 2012).

Furthermore, some gender displays are more highly valued than others. Hegemonic masculinity is the most desired form of masculinity that exists in society (Connell 1987). In order for boys/men to perform hegemonic masculinity they must be heterosexual and skilled in particular sports (rugby, in the New Zealand context) (Rout 1992), and be considered heterosexually experienced by other boys/men (Kehily 2002). In high schools, male students who perform hegemonic masculinity are frequently held in high regard, while boys who perform alternative versions of masculinity, such as those who prefer drama, music or chess, are considered to enact inferior masculinities (Martino 2000).

Paired with hegemonic masculinity is the concept of 'emphasised femininity', a type of femininity that focuses on pleasing men (Connell 1987). Discourses of emphasised femininity promote attractiveness, sexual availability and submissiveness as desirable qualities in girls/women. However, because there is slightly less pressure placed on girls/women to conform to normative gender codes than boys/men (Wyss 2004), more acceptable variations in young women's performances of femininity exist than in young men's enactments of masculinity (Connell 1987). In this chapter, I document how young women have more 'leeway' when it comes to performing their gender than their male counterparts. For instance, participants of both genders reported that young women are more likely to be accepted by their peers if they attend the formal with a same-sex partner than are their male counterparts.

## Methodology

I employed multiple methods of data collection in my study, however only data collected in semi-structured individual interviews, conducted with students at the participating schools, is reported here. The schools were located within the same New Zealand urban centre and had mid-decile ratings.[3] All participants chose their own pseudonyms to be used in the project.

All the participants were going to their school formal but would be likely to attach different understandings to the event. Since I wanted to capture a detailed picture of young people's understandings of gender/sexuality, individual interviews were selected as a means of data collection (Bryman 2004). I was hopeful that the space of the one-on-one interview would result in young people feeling safe enough to give open and honest responses when I asked questions that challenged common-sense understandings, such as what would happen if a young man wore a dress to the formal (Bennett 2004).

In 2008 I conducted 30 interviews (19 before and 11 after the formal), with 19 Year 13 students (17–19 years of age). Five peer researchers in the participating boys' school took part in a photo-elicitation[4] interview after the formal instead of a second individual interview. Three participants also withdrew from the study during the course of the research. The focus of the first interview was gathering information about the participant's

---

3   Decile ratings are allocated to all New Zealand schools by the Ministry of Education, based on the number of students from low socio-economic backgrounds that the school attracts. 'Decile 1 schools are the 10 per cent of schools with the highest proportion of students from low socio-economic communities, whereas decile 10 schools are the 10 per cent of schools with the lowest proportion of these students': www.minedu.govt.nz/Parents/AllAges/EducationInNZ/SchoolsInNewZealand/SchoolDecileRatings.aspx, para. 3

4   Five participants in the boys' school were employed as peer researchers to take photographs of what they considered to be 'typically gendered behaviour' at the formal and then discussed the images in a photo-elicitation interview (see Allen, 2009 for an explanation of photo-elicitation interviews). Photography was abandoned as a data collection method in the other participating schools due to issues with gaining consent for photographs to be taken at the formal.

understandings of and expectations for the formal, while the second focused on the young people's experiences of their school formal. The interviews were 25–50 minutes in duration.

New Zealand schools are self-governing and can establish their own policies when it comes to the school formal. In order to gather information on each participating school's policy on queer students attending the formal with same-sex partners, senior staff members (SSM) responsible for organising the formal at each school were also interviewed. The SSMs were all women and these interviews lasted from 50 to 150 minutes. Participants were reimbursed for their time with vouchers or formal tickets. Interview transcripts were returned to the participants so they could delete any passages they did not want included in the analysis, which none did.

As I transcribed the interviews I noted a number of initial themes that were common across the participants' responses (Maykut & Morehouse 1994). The transcripts were then entered into the qualitative data analysis computer programme TAMS (Text Analysis Mark up System) where codes were attached to initial themes that had been identified. TAMS was employed because it made working with the large number of transcripts easier (Neumann 2006). While this coding was taking place, I conducted a thematic analysis in conjunction with a discourse analysis. For example, I identified when the participants made heteronormative statements, and when discourses that perpetuate the authority of specific groups over others were being reproduced, such as the dominant positioning of heterosexual masculinity in the masculine/feminine and heterosexual/homosexual binaries (Cameron 2001; Gee 1996).

When the coding was completed, 82 themes had been identified; these were then grouped into nine overarching categories. Two of these categories – heteronormativity/homophobia and 'acceptance' of queer students – are the focus of this chapter. The co-educational and girls' schools had similar policies regarding queer students attending the formal with same-sex partners, and student participants in both schools reported similar accounts of how they thought students in their schools would react if queer students attended the formal with same-sex partners. Consequently, the school policy and student attitudes of both schools are jointly discussed.

## The official policies of the co-educational and girls' schools

When I initially met with the SSM of the co-educational school to discuss my research, she said there was a 'zero tolerance for homophobia' in the school (Journal Entry 28 March 2008). She also said the school had a climate of celebration of diversity:

> There's a lot of acceptance of girls taking girls [to the formal] if they want to, or girls going by themselves, or boys going by themselves, or boys going with boys and I think that's terrific and I will never discourage it ...

By permitting students to take same-sex partners to the formal, the SSM is acknowledging that sexualities of all types exist in the school and is not constructing the school formal as a heteronormative sphere (Epstein et al. 2001). Her comments highlight how the school is not only meeting its legal responsibilities to create a safe and inclusive learning environment for all its students, but is also affirming the diversity of sexualities that exist in the school.

The SSM at the girls' school said the school had no policy regarding students taking same-sex partners to the formal:

> No ... in taking a same-sex partner I don't make any assumption about their sexual orientation ... a number of our students just bring their friends, you know. In fact one girl said to me, 'Now I want you to know ... that I'm taking so and so but it doesn't mean that I'm actually gay.'

One reading of this SSM's comments is that the school recognises sexual diversity and therefore queer students are welcome to attend the formal with same-sex partners. Although the girls' school permits students to attend the formal with a same-sex partner, at no time does the SSM mention that lesbian/bisexual students exist in the school. Instead she explains that students who take same-sex partners to the formal are usually 'friends'; she goes on to refer to one young woman who stated that although she would be attending the formal with a female partner, this was not an indication of her sexual preferences. I argue that the SSM is attempting to distance the school from any notion of queerness, perhaps because she is aware that girls' schools are often constituted as lesbian enclaves (Griffin 2000; Watson 1996) – and she does not want to jeopardise the school's reputation in the educational marketplace.

There is a second way to interpret these comments. During their teenage years, young women experience considerable societal pressure to have a boyfriend and demonstrate their heterosexuality (Griffin 2000). In many cases this results in young women abandoning their same-sex friendships in favour of romantic relationships. By permitting young women to attend the formal with their female friends, the girls' school is not forcing young women to prioritise romantic relationships over their friendships, and is simultaneously implementing a socially just policy that is inclusive of queer students.

The female student who states that bringing a same-sex partner does not mean she is gay illustrates how a young woman may distance herself from any notion of lesbianism and reinscribe her own 'hetero-normal' femininity (Griffin 2000). Such a comment highlights how heterosexual femininity is forged in relation to 'the "spectre" of lesbianism' (Griffin 2000, 238).

## 'Acceptance' of queer students attending the formal with same-sex partners

All participants from the co-educational and girls' schools reported that students in their schools would be accepting of queer students bringing same-sex partners to the formal. For instance:

*Hungus: I don't think people would really care in this day and age, they'd just think, oh yeah, cool.*[5]
*Jen: There's a couple of girls in our form that I know are taking people of the same sex and, like, we don't care, we don't judge them on it.*

In New Zealand schools queer students are often bullied because of their non-normative sexuality/gender displays. The above comments suggest that not all students are homophobic, however, and some openly accept their queer classmates (Nairn & Smith 2003; Smith 2006). This counters much of the research on queer students' experiences in New Zealand high schools, which depicts queer youth as lonely and unhappy at school (Nairn & Smith 2003, Smith 2006; also see Britzman 1997).

Perhaps because of the increasing visibility of queerness in New Zealand society, queer sexualities are becoming more accepted. In New Zealand, there are numerous 'out' queer entertainers (such as the Topp Twins and

---

5  Hungus is female.

Urzila Carlson) and celebrities (such as Alison Mau and Tamati Coffey), and queer characters regularly feature on New Zealand television (for example on *Shortland Street, Nothing Trivial* and *Winners and Losers*) (Vincent & Ballard 1997). The 2004 Civil Union Act gave same-sex relationships recognition in law, while the 2013 Marriage Amendment Act has extended marriage to same-sex couples. The growing cultural recognition of queerness may explain why Hungus comments that no one cares if queer students bring same-sex partners to the formal, and may also explain why Jen knows some of her peers are taking same-sex partners to the formal.

The New Zealand Post Primary Teacher's Association (2012) maintains that if senior school staff counter bullying in all its forms (including homophobia) and affirm diversity, this can foster a school climate that is safe and welcoming for all students and staff. Perhaps because the co-educational and girls' school had school-wide policies that were inclusive of sexual diversity, this filtered down to student cultures in both schools and created a more positive environment for queer youth. However, when I asked Ziggy (co-educational school), the only 'out' queer participant in the study, if he thought it would be safe for queer students to bring same-sex partners to the formal, he said:

*Ziggy: I think it would definitely be safe enough for them to do it but most of the time they generally don't, just because while it would be safe there would always be some comments here and there ... It's just that sort of position where people ... don't really want to put themselves ...*
*Lee: Do you think it's fair if ... a queer student would, that there would be comments made that ...*
*Ziggy: Would make them feel uncomfortable ... Not necessarily, but I think it's just the way it is, there's no really escaping it [laughs] ... I was thinking about doing it and then I thought to myself well actually, I just want to have a great night ... so I'm just taking [names female friend], which is nice and easy.*

Ziggy's comments highlight how discourses of acceptance reported by the co-educational student participants were inconsistent with his own experience as a queer student. Perhaps because of their normative positioning as heterosexual (or non-disclosing 'passing' queers), the co-educational student participants perceive that all students have the freedom to attend the formal with a partner of the gender of their choice. Ziggy's comments reveal that this is not the case, however, and highlight how some queer students feel unable to attend the formal as queer young people (Best 2000). The excerpt also shows that heteronormativity is so pervasive that Ziggy simply takes it for granted and cannot see any alternatives to the socially unjust sexual order (Quinlivan & Town 1999).

## Utilising the terms gay/lesbian to police gender norms

The participants in the co-educational school were asked if students would have the same reaction to two males attending the formal as partners, as they would to two females. All of the participants said it would be harder for a young man to bring a male partner. These comments are typified by the following:

*Natasha: I mean there are lots of girls taking other girl friends from other schools and everyone knows it's, you know, taking a friend. If a guy took another guy, if he took his friend then it wouldn't really be a big deal either, it might be kind of funny, but not really, but if everyone knew that was like, they were in a relationship ... people might talk about it ... especially if it was someone who went to your school and ... they took someone, you'd just be interested ... I think it would definitely be harder for guys ...*
*Lee: How come, do you think it's okay for girls to take their girl friends but if a guy takes a guy then it would be ... funny?*
*Natasha: I don't know, I guess they'd just make jokes about them being gay.*

In order to perform hegemonic masculinity a man/boy must be considered heterosexual (Connell 1987). Having a girlfriend and being considered 'good looking' by young women may, in part, also constitute a young man as a hegemonic masculine subject (Connell 2000; Kehily 2002; Martino 1999). If young men take male partners to the formal, they are challenging hegemonic masculinity and therefore are more susceptible to jokes about being gay. Natasha's comments – that if two young men attended together people would joke about their sexuality – attests to how the term 'gay' and homophobic humour work in conjunction to reinscribe hegemonic masculinity (Kehily & Nayak 1997).

Despite the co-educational school participants stating it would be acceptable for two females to attend the formal together, Ellen (girls' school) went to the formal with a female partner and had heteronormative jokes made about her sexuality. I argue therefore that young women are just as likely to be subjected to homophobic humour as young men (Charlton 2004). Ellen initially reported that she was going to the formal with a male partner, but in the second interview she said:

> Ellen: *I didn't like who I was taking so I decided I'd rather go out and have a good time, but I took a girl [laughs] ... and it was the best move I ever made, it was so much better.*
> Lee: *How come?*
> Ellen: *'Cause, well, we were just really good friends and, and ... it's just like going out for dinner with your friend and ... having a good night with your friend, which is awesome.*

In order to be considered legitimate feminine subjects girls/women must centre their gender performances on masculinity (Renew 1996). By taking a same-sex partner to the formal Ellen transgressed normative codes of femininity, as she was not making masculinity the focus of her formal experience (Renew 1996; Smith 2006). Since Ellen was performing her gender in a non-normative way, some male formal-goers made jokes about her sexuality:

> *All the boys they go, like, obviously joking but yeah, they're all the whole 'I didn't know you were that way inclined' type thing ... but I just played along with it quite well [laughs].*

In taking a female partner to the formal Ellen resists the authoritative positioning of masculinity in the gendered order because she shows how girls/women do not need male partners to have a good time. Women's challenges to the authoritative positioning of masculinity in the binary construction of gender are often policed by heteronormativity, however (Holland, Ramazanoglu, Sharpe & Thompson 1998). This is because heteronormativity reproduces male domination and desires which in turn reproduce normative gender codes. Since Ellen's decision to take a female partner threatens authoritative masculinity, the male formal-goers make heteronormative jokes about her sexuality in order to police Ellen's gender performance. The jokes are heteronormative because Ellen would not be the subject of humour if she attended the formal with a male partner.

I also propose a second reading of this excerpt. Ellen did not challenge the heteronormative jokes made by the male formal-goers. Instead she pretended that she was in a relationship with her female friend. By playing along with the male formal-goers' heteronormative jokes, Ellen is helping to reinscribe the authority of masculinity to regulate normative displays of heterosexual femininity and construct the girls' school formal as a heteronormative site (Holland et al. 1998). It should be acknowledged, however, that by pretending to be lesbian and 'playing along' with the young men's jokes, Ellen's behaviour is also transgressive (albeit in a limited way). This is because she is blurring the boundaries between heterosexuality and queerness when she plays the role of lesbian, which challenges the rigid heterosexual/homosexual binary. Ellen's performance of lesbianism shows that anyone can perform sexuality categories regardless of their sexual attractions, which highlights the 'fluidity and changeability' (Quinlivan & Town 1999, 522) of sexual identity categories.

Although Ellen was the target of jokes as a result of her action, the policing of students attending the formal with same-sex partners was more pronounced in the boys' school.

## The official policy of the boys' school

When I asked the SSM of the boys' school if her school had any policy regarding students attending the formal with same-sex partners, she said:

SSM: *Yeah, we would discourage that. They've never actually, I don't think they've ever actually asked to do that.*
Lee: *How come you would discourage it?*
SSM: *We, we would rather than that, we would just say … look, buy two single tickets … but they're certainly not allowed to bring a male partner from another school.*
Lee: *Even if they're in a relationship?*
SSM: *Yeah even if they were in a relationship … we haven't moved with the times that much yet I think.*
Lee: *Can I ask how come?*
SSM: *I actually think it would be to protect them from comments that other students might make through ignorance more than anything else, umm, and there's a lot that young people put up with that they don't need to put themselves in those sort of situations. It might be a situation that they would come to regret … and … I do honestly think it's for their own protection in days, weeks and perhaps months to come.*

This SSM's comments illustrate how perceived homophobia within a school can dictate a school's official course of action (Epstein & Johnson 1994; Smith 2006). It also highlights how student peer groups may be more effective in reinscribing heteronormativity than official school discourse (Epstein & Johnson 1994). Furthermore, the SSM states that same-sex attracted students do not 'need to put themselves in those sort of situations'. This comment implies that if a young man encountered harassment, it would be his fault for taking a same-sex partner in the first place rather than a failure on the part of the school to address its heteronormative learning environment (Hinson 1996). Such comments imply that the boys' school is a hostile space for queer students, and highlight how school management is in breach of its legal responsibilities under UNCROC.

## Student culture and gender and sexuality at the boys' school

When I asked the student participants in the boys' school what would happen if a student attended the formal with a male partner, they all said he would be harassed. For instance:

*Bob: Umm, they'd be like, 'Oh shit he's gay' [laughs] they'd be like gobsmacked, 'Oh my god, a gay guy came to the formal, Jesus', but they'd get over it pretty quick apart from the whole ripping the crap out of them, which they would get to this day, but I guess after a while, but as long as they didn't stand there and slow dance and hook up in the middle of the thing, if they did that then that's almost like social suicide [laughs] when it comes to a male school's formal.*

Hegemonic masculinity is partly formed by boys/men divorcing themselves from homosexuality and femininity as well as bullying others who perform their gender/sexuality in non-normative ways (Mac An Ghaill 2000; Martino 1999; 2000). Bob's comments attest to his perception that young men in the boys' school reproduce their status as 'real' men through harassment (Martino 1999). If this is the case, the boys doing the harassing remove themselves from homosexuality, while simultaneously constructing queer male students as 'Other' to their own 'hetero-normal' masculinity (Kehily & Nayak 1997; Mac An Ghaill 2000).

Simon, however, reports that in some cases it would be acceptable for two young men to attend the formal together:

*Simon: If it was, I dunno, names out of a hat [names two popular boys] everyone would just crack up ... but if it was ... you know, [a] suspiciously feminine-looking guy, then I don't know what people would say.*

Simon mentions two boys in the school who could bring male partners because other students would find it humorous. Since the two young men mentioned by Simon are popular, they have the necessary social status to attend the formal with a male partner and have it seen as a joke rather than an indication of their sexuality.

Simon's comment – that he does not know how students would react if a 'suspiciously feminine-looking' student bought a male partner to the formal – highlights how he equates being gay with being feminine. Simon cannot comprehend that a boy/man can be sexually attracted to another boy/man and still be masculine (Sedgwick 1993). This is consistent with normative societal gender codes, in which anyone 'who desires a man must by definition be feminine, whether that person is a man or woman' (Sedgwick 1993, 72).

Not all the participants in the boys' school reported that they would have negative responses to students attending the formal with male partners. I asked John how he thought students in the boys' school would react if two young men attended the formal together:

*If, if they're out and proud at our age then they'll be loved by their peers I reckon, because I mean, if you have that confidence to drop a bombshell like that at an all boys' school then you've got to be ... someone that's, they can take anything and still keep on running.*

Although homophobia is associated with male behaviour in most secondary schools, in boys' schools it is more pronounced (Brutsaert 2006; Epstein & Johnson 1994). This is why John states a boy who 'comes out' at a boys' school needs to be able to 'take anything and still keep on running'. Nevertheless, John's comments indicate that even in boys' schools, which are more likely to be homophobic, some students would 'accept', befriend and indeed love gay students.

## Conclusion

On an official level, the participating co-educational and girls' schools were more accepting of sexual diversity than the boys' school, where heteronormativity remained unchallenged. The SSMs of the girls' and co-educational schools reported there were no policies in place that would hinder students taking same-sex partners to the formal. In contrast, the SSM at the boys' school said her school would discourage students from attending the formal with male partners because of the potential harassment they could receive. This indicated that the boys' school would likely be an unsafe environment for queer students. This finding replicates findings of other research conducted in New Zealand schools, which also reports that boys' schools are more likely to be hostile towards queer attractions than girls' and co-educational schools (Nairn & Smith 2003).

All the participants in the boys' school reported that if young men brought male partners to the formal, they would be harassed. Such comments highlight how students in the boys' school construct their own heterosexual masculinity through harassing others who perform non-normative sexualities or genders (Dalley-Trim 2007; Martino 1999).

Even a school that strives to affirm diversity cannot guarantee that queer students will meet with acceptance. The co-educational school student and staff participants reported that queer students bringing a same-sex partner to the formal would be accepted; however, Ziggy, an 'out' queer student in the co-educational school, chose to bring a female friend in order to avoid the comments that would be made if he brought a male partner. The discourses of acceptance were therefore inconsistent with the experiences of a queer student. Perhaps this is because heteronormativity is so entrenched in society that students learn from other sites, such as families or the media, that it is acceptable to make disparaging remarks about gay men/lesbians, and queer students like Ziggy come to expect homophobic comments (Quinlivan & Town 1999; Warner 1993).

The New Zealand Post Primary Teacher's Association (2012) reports that the majority of New Zealand secondary schools affirm diversity among their students in regard to gender, dis/ability, ethnicity and socioeconomic background, but that many schools fail to even recognise sexual diversity and homophobic harassment often goes unchecked. That this situation still remains in the middle of the second decade of the twenty-first century is intolerable. Heteronormativity and homophobic harassment can have damaging effects on the health and wellbeing of queer youth (see Le Brun et al. 2004; Rossen et al. 2009). School management not only has a legal duty to address homophobia within the school, it also has a moral responsibility to do so (New Zealand Post Primary Teacher's Association 2012). One way schools can do this is by encouraging queer students to attend the formal with their same-sex partners and thereby affirm sexual diversity.

## References

Allen, L. (2009), '"Snapped": Researching the sexual cultures of schools using visual methods', *International Journal of Qualitative Studies in Education* 22(5), 549–61.

Beech, J. (28 March 2009), 'School denies "booze culture"', *Otago Daily Times*, 17.

Bennett, P. (2004), 'Putting the 'L' in counselling: Promoting visibility in New Zealand', Master's thesis, University of Otago, Dunedin.

Best, A. (2000), *Prom night*, New York: Routledge.

Blaise, M. & Taylor, A. (2012), 'Using queer theory to rethink gender equity in early childhood education', *Young Children, 67* (1), 88–97.

Britzman, D. (1997), 'What is this thing called love?: New discourses for understanding lesbian and gay youth', in S. deCastell & M. Bryson (eds), *Radical Interventions: Identity politics and difference/s in educational praxis* (183–206), New York: State University of New York Press.

Brutsaert, H. (2006), 'Gender-role identity and perceived acceptance among early adolescents in Belgian mixed and single-sex schools', *Gender & Education, 18*(6), 635–49.

Bryman, A. (2004), *Social Research Methods*, Oxford: Oxford University Press.

Butler, J. (1990), *Gender Trouble: Feminism and the subversion of identity*, New York: Routledge.

Cameron, D. (2001), *Working with spoken discourse*, London: Sage Publications.

Charlton, E. (2004), 'Disrupting heteronormativity: What about the girls?', Paper presented at the Australian Association for Research in Education, Melbourne, Australia.

Civil Union Act (2004): www.legislation.govt.nz/

Connell, R.W. (1987), *Gender and Power: Society, the person and sexual politics*, Cambridge: Polity.

Connell, R.W. (2000), *The Men and the Boys*, St Leonards: Allen & Unwin.

Dalley-Trim, L. (2007), 'The boys' present ... hegemonic masculinity: A performance of multiple acts', *Gender and Education, 19*(2), 199–217.

Dellinger, K. & Williams, C.L. (1997), 'Makeup at work: Negotiating appearance rules in the workplace', *Gender & Society, 11*(2), 151–77.

Epstein, D. & Johnson, R. (1994), 'On the straight and narrow: The heterosexual presumption, homophobias and schools', in D. Epstein (ed.), *Challenging Lesbian and Gay Equalities in Education* (197–230), Buckingham: Open University Press.

Foucault, M. (1972), *The Archaeology of Knowledge*, (A.M. Sheridan Smith, Trans.), London: Routledge.

Gee, J.P. (1996), *Social Linguistics and Literacies: Ideology in discourse*, Oxon: RoutledgeFalmer.

Grace, A.P. & Wells, K. (2005), 'The Marc Hall prom predicament: Queer individual rights v. church institutional rights in Canadian public education', *Canadian Journal of Education, 28*(3), 237–70.

Griffin, C. (2000), 'Absences that matter: Constructions of sexuality in young women's friendships', *Feminism & Psychology, 10*(2), 227–45.

Hesse-Biber, S.N. (2007), 'Feminist research: Exploring the interconnections of epistemology, methodology and method', in S.N. Hesse-Biber (ed.), *Handbook of Feminist Research: Theory and praxis* (1–26), Thousand Oaks: Sage.

Hewson, L. (31 July 2009), 'Having a ball', *Otago Daily Times*, 22.

Hinson, S. (1996), 'A practice focused approach to addressing heterosexist violence in Australian schools', in L. Laskey & C. Beavis (eds), *Schooling and Sexualities: A practice focused approach to addressing violence in Australian schools* (241–58), Deakin: Deakin Centre for Education and Change.

Holland, J., Ramazanoglu, C., Sharpe, S. & Thompson, R. (1998). *The Male in the Head: Young people, heterosexuality and power*, London: Tufnell Press.

Human Rights Act (1993): www.legislation.govt.nz/
Johnson, J.M. (2002), 'In-depth interviewing', in J.F. Gubrium & J.A. Holstein (eds), *Handbook of Interview Research: Context and method*, Thousand Oaks: Sage.
Kehily, M.J. (2002), *Sexuality, Gender and Schooling: Shifting agendas in social learning*, London: RoutledgeFalmer.
Kehily, M.J. & Nayak, A. (1997), '"Lads and laughter": Humour and the production of heterosexual hierarchies', *Gender and Education*, 9(1), 69–87.
Le Brun, C., Robinson, E., Warren, H. & Watson, P.D. (2004), 'Non-heterosexual youth: A profile of their health and wellbeing: Data from Youth 2000', Auckland: University of Auckland.
Lewis, J. (27 May 2008), '18 pupils stood down at St Hildas', *Otago Daily Times*, 5.
Mac An Ghaill, M. (2000), 'Rethinking (male) gendered sexualities: What about the British heteros?', *Journal of Men's Studies*, 8(2), 195–212.
Marriage (Definition of Marriage) Amendment Act (2013): www.legislation.govt.nz/
Martino, W. (1999), '"Cool boys", "party animals", "squids" and "poofters": Interrogating the dynamics and politics of adolescent masculinities in school', *British Journal of Sociology in Education*, 20(2), 239–63.
Martino, W. (2000), 'Policing masculinities: Investigating the role of homophobia and heteronormativity in the lives of adolescent school boys', *Journal of Men's Studies*, 8(2), 213–38.
Maykut, P. & Morehouse, R. (1994), *Beginning Qualitative Research: A philosophical and practical guide*, London: Falmer.
McCullough, M. (11 June 2009), 'Off to the ball ... but what if you want to take your same-sex partner?' *Otago Daily Times*, 1.
Nairn, K. & Smith, A.B. (2003), 'Taking students seriously: Their rights to be safe at school', *Gender and Education*, 15(2), 133–49.
Neumann, W. (2006), *Social Research Methods: Qualitative and quantitative approaches*, Boston: Pearson Education.
New Zealand Post Primary Teachers' Association (2012), 'Affirming diversities in the school community guidelines': www.ppta.org.nz/index.php/resources/publications
Painter, H. (2009), 'How safe?: How safe and inclusive are Otago secondary schools? Ae ranei he haumaru, he wahi whāi kit e katoa ngā kura tuarua o Otago?' A report on the implementations from the 'Safety in our schools – Ko te harumaru i o tatuu kura' action kit: He purongo ūruhi i ngā tuanaki a te kete mahi 'Safety in Our schools – Ko te harumaru i o tatu kura', Dunedin, NZ: OUSA Queer Support.
Quinlivan, K.A. & Town, S. (1999), 'Queer pedagogy, educational practice and lesbian and gay youth', *International Journal of Qualitative Studies in Education*, 12(5), 509–24.
Renew, S. (1996), 'Acting like a girl: Lesbian challenges to the construction of gender and schooling', in L. Laskey & C. Beavis (eds), *Schooling Sexualities: Teaching for a positive sexuality* (151–85), Victoria: Deakin Centre for Educational Change, Deakin University.
Rossen, F.V., Lucassen, M.F.G., Denny, S. & Robinson, E. (2009), *Youth '07: The health and wellbeing of secondary students in New Zealand: Results for young people attracted to the same or both sexes*, Auckland: University of Auckland.
Rout, B. (1992), 'Being staunch: Boys hassling girls', in S. Middleton & A. Jones (eds), *Women and Education in Aotearoa 2* (169–80), Wellington: Bridget Williams.
Sedgwick, E. (1993), 'How to bring your kids up gay' in M. Warner (ed.), *Fear of a queer planet* (69–79), Minnesota: University of Minnesota Press.
Smith, G. (May 2008), 'School formal a glamorous event', *Maniototo Leader*, 10.
Smith, L.A. (2006), 'Un/silencing lesbian and bisexual students: Some women's experiences of how their high schools met their needs', Master's thesis, University of Otago, Dunedin.

Smith, L., Nairn. K. & Sandretto, S. (2015). 'Complicating heteronormative spaces at school formals in New Zealand', *Gender, Place and Culture*. DOI: 10.1080/0966369X.2015.1034245

Tay, K. (2 September 2007), 'For whom the belles toil', *Sunday Star Times*, C6.

United Nations (1989), *United Nations Convention on the Rights of the Child*: www.ohchr.org/en/professionalinterest/pages/crc.aspx

Vincent, K. & Ballard, K. (1997), 'Living on the margins: Lesbian experience in secondary school, *New Zealand Journal of Educational Studies, 32*(2), 147–61.

Warner, M. (1993), 'Introduction', in M. Warner (ed.), *Fear of a Queer Planet* (vii–xxix), Minnesota: Minnesota University Press.

Watson, S. (1996), 'Heterosexing girls: "Distraction" and single-sex school choice', *Women's Studies Journal (Special Issue: Educating Sexuality), 12*(2), 115–27.

Weitz, R. (2001), 'Women and their hair: Seeking power through resistance and accommodation', *Gender & Society, 15*(5), 667–86.

Wyss, S. (2004), '"This was my hell": The violence experienced by gender non-conforming youth in US high schools', *International Journal of Qualitative Studies in Education, 17*(5), 709–30

# 7.
# 'Picturing' heteronormativity in secondary schools

## Louisa Allen

Critical sexualities literature (Plummer 2008) has established that schools *are* heteronormative spaces. That is, they are spaces in which heterosexuality is constituted as the 'default' of human sexuality and subsequently 'normal', while lesbian, gay and bisexual identities are cast as 'abnormal other' (Warner 1993). The occurrence of this phenomenon has been documented through various spheres of education, from early childhood (Blaise 2005; Gunn 2011) to primary (DePalma & Atkinson 2009; Renold 2005), secondary (Allen 2007a; Dalley & Campbell 2006; Quinlivan & Town 1999) and within higher education (Epstein, O'Flynn & Telford 2003; Mayo 2007). Heteronormativity is understood to be overtly and covertly expressed in these educational contexts (Ferfolja 2007) and made visible through a plethora of practices. These inhere in institutional policy and at the level of classroom pedagogy via a silence around lesbian, gay, bisexual, transgendered and intersex (LGBTI) issues. Within school policy documents for instance, reference to equity for LGBTI is missing or lags behind inclusion of other issues such as racism (Epstein, Hewitt, Leonard, Mauthner & Watkins 2007; Ferfolja 2007). In the curriculum, LGBTI identities and interests are also often omitted (Hillier, Turner & Mitchell 2005) or their inclusion is configured negatively as 'other' or 'pathological'. Commenting on the inclusion of homosexuality in UK-based schools, a participant in Ellis and High's (2004) research said, 'It was mentioned more like an illness than a way of life' (221). In one of its most blatant forms, heteronormativity is also seen to underpin overt acts of homophobia in classrooms and playgrounds (DePalma & Jennet 2012). The incidence of homophobic verbal and/or physical abuse is an effect of heteronormativity that has received considerable media attention and proven a rallying point for inclusion of sexual diversity issues in social forums.

Conceptually, heteronormativity is not only used as a noun. When employed as a noun, homophobic abuse is labelled 'heteronormative' or schools are deemed 'heteronormative' spaces. In this sense, heteronormativity is understood as having a tangible effect or product. However, within the existing literature heteronormativity is also employed as a verb, a 'doing' that is less tangible with multiple facets and means of acting. From this perspective heteronormativity is productive and articulated as, 'the mundane, everyday ways that heterosexuality is privileged and taken for granted as normal and natural' (Martin 2009, 190). This meaning is invoked by DePalma and Atkinson (2010) when they define it (drawing on Donelson & Rogers 2004, 138) as the 'organizational structures in schools that support heterosexuality as normal and anything else as deviant' (1670). Within existing research these organisational structures are typically understood as discursive. They comprise a collection of normalising discourses that constitute sex and gender as a binary serving to 'privilege and legitimize heterosexual desire and gender, at the expense of other gendered and sexual identities' (Cullen & Sandy 2009, 143). These discourses mobilise what Butler (1990) conceptualises as the heterosexual matrix: the idea that for bodies to be intelligible, 'there must be a stable sex expressed through a stable gender (masculine expresses male, feminine expresses female) that is oppositionally and hierarchically defined through the compulsory practice of heterosexuality' (151). The matrix describes 'a socially constructed conflation of sex/gender/sexuality' (DePalma & Atkinson 2010, 1670) which scaffolds the operation of heteronormativity and enables it to perform specific regulatory effects. At school, this means the regulation of female and male bodies and subjectivities to conventionally distinct and binary gendered performances in which these constituted opposites are sexually attracted.

While the focus of research on heteronormativity in schools has been predominately discursive in terms of identifying the presence of these normalising meanings, how these discourses are embodied constitutes a more recent concern. These insights have been gleaned from feminist, post-structuralist and queer theory work around gender and sexuality in the classroom (Nayak & Kehily 2006; Renold 2005; Youdell 2005). What this research reveals is the way in which heterosexuality as 'normal' is embodied in the gendered and sexual performances of students through the constitution of particular types of masculinities and femininities. For instance, Renold (2000) describes the way girls in an English primary school were invested in, and drew social currency from, 'the production of their bodies as heterosexually desirable commodities' (310). This investment was evidenced in their choice of clothing deemed attractive to the opposite sex (e.g. miniskirts and high heels) and the perpetual monitoring of their bodies in terms of somatic 'ideals' of femininity (e.g. worrying about their weight and dieting). Understanding how heteronormativity is embodied through students' gendered and sexual performances has produced new knowledge of its configurations and scope.

This chapter seeks to extend this important work, by examining the way heteronormativity inheres and is produced in unexplored dimensions of schooling. In articulation with an identified 'spatial turn' in the social sciences (Kalervo, Gulson & Colin 2007), and renewed concerns with materialisation (Bennett 2010), this chapter investigates the ways in which sexual meanings are (re)produced through, and at, the intersections of bodies and spaces at school. Existing studies of heteronormativity at school tend to explore its operation through methods that rely on text as talk, or through the analysis of school policies (Ellis & High 2004; Myers & Raymond 2010; Painter 2009; Sexton 2012). However, to investigate spatial, embodied and material dimensions of schooling it was necessary to employ visual methods. Through an analysis of photos taken by participants, it is argued that both spatial and corporeal (i.e. bodily) dimensions of school life are institutionally regulated to centre heterosexuality as 'normal'. Yet, students' engagement with school spaces and corporeal modalities involve a constant negotiation of these forms of institutional regulation. That is, while student bodies and schooling spaces are designated for specific (heteronormative) purposes, young people disrupt these meanings through their corporeal engagements in and with them.

The chapter begins by conceptualising the relationships between bodies and space to establish the theoretical foundations for the photo analysis undertaken. Following an explanation of the research methodology, four photographs are analysed to illuminate ways in which heteronormativity is (re)produced and disrupted.[1] In contrast to a history of educational research which takes gay, lesbian and bisexual students and their experiences of discrimination as the sole object of investigation (Sears 1992), this chapter works 'queerly' (Jagose 1996). By 'queer' I refer to the theoretical landscape emerging in the late 1980s and early 1990s, characterised by the work of

---

1 Faces in these photos have been deliberately obscured to ensure de-identification. We regret the subsequent poor quality of these informal diary photos.

Butler (1990), Sedgwick, (1990), Jagose (1996), Halberstam (1998) and Fuss (1989). Queer theory is concerned with the destablisation of identity categories, particularly those of gender and sexuality (Beasley 2005). In this chapter, however, it is not the sexual or gender identity of students that makes this work 'queer': both self-identified lesbian and straight subjects feature in photos. What is queer about this work is that it is an investigation of the 'normal' or, more specifically, how the heteronormal is performed and disrupted at the intersection of bodies and space at school. In a queer attempt to destabilise identity categories, 'who' engages in these performances (in terms of whether students identify as lesbian, gay, bisexual or straight) recedes, in order to foreground 'how' heteronormativity is performed and disrupted. This does not dismiss the idea that there may be a (tenuous) relationship between identity and heteronormativity (see Allen 2010). Instead I employ Warner's (1993) proposition that '"queer" defines itself against the normal rather than the heterosexual' (xxvi).

## Conceptualising the relationship between bodies and space at school

In thinking about how heteronormativity operates at school this chapter articulates with a recent 'spatial turn' in the social sciences. The late twentieth century has witnessed a resurgence in acknowledging the role of 'space' in the production of meanings about, and possibilities for, social life (Kalervo, Gulson & Colin 2007). Although the uptake of these ideas has been slower in education than other disciplinary areas (McGregor 2004), there is increasing recognition of the way space is implicated in 'who we can be and become' at school (Paechter 2004, 307). O'Donoghue's (2007) research in Ireland mobilises this theme through his examination of the way 10- and 11-year-old boys learn to articulate and perform masculinities in particular places at school. He illustrates this phenomenon by way of a student named James, who capitalises on a concrete corner of the playground to bully other boys in his performance of 'tough' masculinity. Through this example it is possible to see how the playground's material features and an area beyond teacher surveillance serve to enable James' particular performance of masculinity. O'Donoghue (2007) argues all learning is 'emplaced', and physical spaces are deeply politicised and actively participate in supporting, furthering and shaping or disrupting meanings and performances of masculinities. One aim of this chapter is to apply this conceptualisation of space as 'politicised' to an understanding of how heteronormativity is implicated with/in the mundane spatial arrangements of schooling.

Such an analysis necessitates a particular understanding of the ontology of space, bodies and their relation. Historically, within Western thought, space has been understood as a backdrop for people and action, a neutral container for social relationships that is homogenous, transparent and static (Morgan 2000). From this perspective, space is a tangible entity independent from the actors and actions occurring within it. This Newtonian view (Agnew 2005) has been criticised for its failure to acknowledge the mutability of space and ways it can be actively constituted through, productive of, and permeated with, social relations and power (Brown, Browne & Lim 2009). This facility is seen in the way that the things people do in a space can qualitatively change its nature. One example is 'gay parades' and 'pride marches', which transform what geographers of sexualities conceptualise as the heteronormative space of the street, into a 'gay space' (Valentine 2001). From this perspective, space is in a perpetual state of *becoming*, a contested site, made and remade (and sometimes undone) (Crang 2005) by the actions of people. Within this framework it is people who are seen to have agency in relation to space, that is, they are the ones who 'make' it. Although the meanings and functions of spaces are considered fluid, space does not contain any agency of its own (i.e. independent of people). A recognition of space as a site of possibility for agency in its own right is subsequently denied. What might be seen as problematic about such an immutable spatial materiality is that the potential to change any inequalities it scaffolds are limited (to people).

To suggest spaces might be agentic I draw on Bennett's (2010) thoughts around material agency into articulation with spatial theory outlined in the previous paragraph. Characterising her work as concerned with a political ecology of things, Bennett posits materiality (or things) as possessing a kind of 'Thing-power'. Rather than seeing things as 'dead', inanimate objects, Bennett reconfigures them as 'vibrant matter'. She describes this vibrancy as 'the curious ability of inanimate things to animate, to act, to produce effects dramatic and subtle' (Bennett 2010, 6). Conventionally, 'things' (or materiality) are only seen to have agency when humans *do something with* or *to* them. The idea that materiality might have an agency of its own, separate from human action (although not totally divorced from it), is a prevalent idea in social theory and feminist philosophy (Barad 2003; 2007). Bennett (2004) concedes, 'Thing-power materialism is a speculative onto-story, a rather presumptuous attempt to depict the nonhumanity that flows around but also through humans' (349). It is not possible to explore Bennett's ideas more fully here (for details see Bennett 2004; 2010). However, for further explanation of her ideas in relation to space, sexualities and schooling see Allen (2013; 2014).

Theoretically, this chapter attempts to apply Bennett's notion of vibrant matter, 'that things can have a laudable effect on humans' (Bennett 2004, 348) in conceptualising the realm of schooling space. I want to argue that rather than being an inert backdrop to the action of human subjects, space at school is mutable and therefore always becoming. This becoming is not simply as a consequence of the actions of humans, but *in interaction* with them, a relationship that acknowledges space and matter as vibrant. In the analysis of photos in this chapter, the way certain material features of schooling spaces actively shape and lend themselves to particular sexual and non-sexual meanings will be explored. Subsequently, the chapter contributes to an understanding of space as constitutive of, and constituted through, students' embodied actions. In this way, space is conceptualised as an *in process materiality*.

## Methodology

To capture embodied and spatial elements of schooling and their implication in the production of heteronormativity, a visual methodology involving photo-diaries and photo-elicitation was used. Participants were given a 24-exposure disposable camera and asked to take photos, over seven days, of how they learned about sexuality at school (see Allen 2011a for more details). Once the films were developed, participants engaged in an individual photo-elicitation interview of approximately one hour. This involved photo-diarists choosing a handful of photos and explaining how these reflected what they learned about sexuality at school. Poring over photographs together foregrounded rich data about embodied and spatial aspects of schooling that might have gone unnoticed in traditional text-based methods. The advantage of cameras is that they can 'convey real, flesh and blood life' and are able to depict how objects and bodies are materially positioned in relation to each other (Becker, cited in Rose 2007, 238). These photos from diarists and their comments about them that are analysed in this chapter.

This was a small-scale exploratory study involving 22 Year 12 and 13 students from two North Island schools. In New Zealand, decile rankings indicate the extent to which a school draws its students from low socioeconomic communities, with decile 1 schools containing the highest proportion of these students and decile 10 the lowest (verbatim, Ministry of Education 2004). Fern College (FC) was mid-decile and Kowhai College (KC) was high decile. In total, 12 participants self-identified as European, six as Māori, two as Pasifika and two as African. All participants were volunteers and the research was granted ethics approval from the University of Auckland Human Subjects Ethics Committee (see Allen 2009). All references to participants and schools are pseudonyms. For more details about the photo-diary method and analysis of images see Allen (2011a; 2011b).

## Performing heterosexuality as normal

A common image across diaries depicted groups of (typically) five or more students 'hanging out' together during break times. These students congregated in outdoor spaces such as the covered walkway between classes, seats or walls adjacent to classrooms, or milled around building corners designated as their usual 'hang-out'. Damian, who had taken a photo typifying this scene (Figure 7.1), explained the significance of these spaces and their collection of bodies for learning about sexuality. In response to my question, 'where do you think students get most of their knowledge about sexuality from?' he replied: 'I'd say mostly it will come from just walking around school and seeing what's going on with couples like that and then sometimes we learn it from class but more of it would be outside of the class and just your own experiences with what you see and what you do' (16 years, Māori/European, FC). Other participants also noted the importance of peer groups in learning about sexuality outside of formal class time. Rosalind described how lunchtime conversations among peers provided an opportunity to hear other people's experiences of sexuality and relationships, and were more 'relaxed' and 'straight up' than formal sexuality education. Emphasising this point she explained, 'I've learned so much from asking other people and listening to these conversations' (18 years, European, FC). The congregation of peer groupings outside the classroom during break-times provided opportunities for participants to learn unofficially about sexuality and relationships. That peers are an important source of information for young people is not a new finding (Measor, Tiffin & Miller 2000). That such learning habitually occurs in congregating groups of students outside the classroom, in terms of both physical and temporal space, is.

Figure 7.1. Hanging out.

By concentrating on the intersections of body and space it is possible to see the embodied and spatial dimensions of this learning. For instance, a distinguishing feature of many of these groupings was that as well as individual members in conversation with each other, they would contain one or more 'couples'. Coupledom was expressed physically through intimate contact with someone else, such as kissing, hugging or sitting on another's knee. For instance, in Damian's photo (Figure 7.1), there is a couple to the mid-right of centre: the male student has his hand on the female student's bottom as they stand kissing each other. The heteronormative context of schooling, where to be sexually attracted to the opposite gender signals appropriate masculinity and femininity, means that being part of a couple confers peer-group status (Myers & Raymond 2010). Intimate physical contact between male and female students marked these students as desired/desiring, with some participants considering this an enviable position. Shelley and Tom, who elected to undertake their photo-elicitation interview together, were two such students. When asked to choose their favourite image, Tom selected one of a male/female couple standing outside a classroom in an embrace and the following discussion ensued:

Tom: [I like] this one [photo] because these two have been together for like three years and like they're still hugging and like still kissing and still obviously in love like after that long you know ...
Louisa: Are they friends of yours?
Tom: Yeah they're good friends of mine.
Louisa: Is that typical to be going out for three years?
Tom: Not in high school.
Shelley: There are a few cases but ...
Tom: Definitely been going out for three years, but like most people go out for a couple of months and then move on to the next one sort of thing but those two everybody knows that they've been together for like years now and like everybody knows that it's not like, they always hang out together, like they're always together, they're not ever sick of each other.
Louisa: Is it kind of like a model relationship that others want to follow, is that what you were going to say, it's what you'd like a relationship to be like?
Tom: I guess like I've heard people say 'oh I wish my relationship was like theirs'.
Louisa: So do you reckon other people learn stuff about sexuality when they see these two together?
Tom: Because everybody says in high school things aren't for real and stuff like I guess seeing them people realise that it can be, that there is such a thing as love when you're young ...
(Tom: 18 years, European, FC; Shelley: 17 years, Māori, FC)

Observing couples around school provided some students with a model for what relationships could/should be like. The physical presence of entwined male and female bodies offered an embodied expression of presumed heterosexuality that was idealised by other students. Analysing the embodied and spatial arrangements of these photos reveals a seeming mundaneness to this 'coupledom'. In Figure 7.1 for instance, the couple engaged in a sexually charged embrace are surrounded by those who appear indifferent to their actions. No one seems to be paying attention to them; instead students are steeped in conversation, watching other student interactions or – like the young women in the foreground – eating an apple. These heterosexual performances appear to enjoy what DePalma and Atkinson (2009) characterise as 'simple visibility'. In the absence of other embodied representations of sexuality as anything but heterosexual, they

Figure 7.2. Boys hugging.

form part of the everyday experiences of school life where their repetition marks them as unremarkable. In this way, such embodied expressions of sexuality are both constitutive of heteronormativity and a manifestation of its operation in schooling spaces.

In contrast to the abundance of photos of opposite gender 'couples', equivalent pictures expressing embodied sexuality of same-gender couples (or even where boys touched each other) were rare. One such image (see Figure 7.2) shows two male students with arms and legs exaggeratedly wrapped around each other in a hug as they stand facing the camera. Explaining this image, Crystal described these two boys as 'just showing what good friends they were and how secure they were about their sexuality' (17 years, European, KC). Crystal's comment is made here against the backdrop of schooling as a heteronormative space. There is a farcical quality to the picture generated via the theatrical nature of the embrace and smirks on the young men's faces. Endeavouring to probe this aspect of the photo further, I asked Crystal the following:

*Louisa: So they are kind of having a laugh there as well aren't they, in a way?*
*Crystal: No, they're not. You see guys occasionally hug and stuff but not like girls. Girls link arms or sometimes hold hands and stuff but guys*

*wouldn't, so they're [the boys in the photo] just showing that they can, they're guys and they're still close friends.*

For Crystal, this photo illustrates that while girls are able to express physical affection for each other and not be labelled lesbian, young men at her school generally cannot be physical in this way as they risk being seen as homosexual. Such embodied interactions within the heteronormative space of school are subsequently always read as indicating homosexual identity. Her reading of the image is that these young men disrupt these dominant meanings of masculinity in the schooling space by showing they can embrace each other *and* not be gay. As she states, they are 'secure' in their heterosexuality.

It might be argued this embodied depiction of young men serves to support rather than disrupt schools as heteronormative spaces. While the boys are physically intimate, Crystal's insistence that in reality they are not gay serves to reinstate the 'normalcy' of heterosexuality. Similarly, the young men's own embodiment also undertakes this work. Their smirks and exaggerated 'staged hug' seek to confirm their heterosexuality least their actions be misinterpreted as homosexual. Humour has been identified as a key strategy for consolidating normative masculinities (Dalley-Trim 2007; Kehily & Nayak 1997). For instance, young men might engage in an activity deemed 'homosexual', such as walking 'effeminately', and employ humour (such as an overly exaggerated swagger) to deflect thoughts that this signals actual homosexual identity. Humour acts here as a buffer between symbolic homosexuality and a personally lived homosexual identity in order to maintain 'heterosexual-integrity'. The 'comic' edge to these young men's corporeal positioning achieves the same result. By 'humorously' acting out their comfort of same-gender bodily intimacy, they distance themselves from homosexuality to reclaim heterosexual identity. It is therefore possible to see how heteronormativity is perpetuated through these young men's embodied actions. Despite what Crystal tells us about these young men's serious intentions as representative of non-normative masculinity, their corporeal positioning captured via visual methods jostles to recuperate normative heterosexuality. It is only possible to discern the meaning of these young men's embodied actions via their contingency upon schooling space as heteronormative.

## Disrupting heteronormativity at the intersection of body and space

While the pictures so far described can be seen to reinscribe schooling space as heteronormative, in this section I explore two photographs that go some way to disrupt this. The first (Figure 7.3) was taken by Lucinda, of her two friends who are known to be 'out' lesbians at school. In this photo the two young women are seen in a tight embrace, one standing behind the other nuzzling her head into her girlfriend's shoulder. When I asked Lucinda why she had taken this photo she indicated that by seeing this couple at school, other students were learning 'that it doesn't matter whether you're lesbian or straight because you have different relationships at school' (16 years, African, FC). Lucinda's photo offers an important political statement given participants across both schools largely insisted, as Imogen did, 'I don't think there are any [same-gender] relationships going on in this school' (17 years, European, KC). As indicated in the analysis of Figure 7.1, most spaces at Fern College featured embodied expressions of heterosexuality. When gay, lesbian or bisexual relationships were acknowledged, they were recognised as unlikely to be public or as openly visible as heterosexual couples. Expressing this sentiment, Gerard explained,

Figure 7.3. Same-gender desire.

*I don't know anybody at, I know there are homosexual people at this school but I don't know if they're in relationships. Since I've been here I've probably seen two lesbian relationships and in fact one of the same girls was in both relationships when I think about it. Other than that they keep that pretty under cover (16 years, Māori, FC).*

Given the apparent invisibility of same-gender relationships in the temporal spaces of schooling, this photo poses a disruption to its heteronormative landscape. This rupture is achieved by depicting desire between two women whose smiles (obscured) indicate obvious pleasure from their physical intimacy. Expanding her discussion, Lucinda revealed these young women have been subject to sustained verbal and physical harassment from other students for being lesbian, culminating in a lunchtime brawl in which Lucinda was embroiled. Although this narrative invokes homophobic discrimination and abuse, embodied features of this photo tell another story. The clasp of these young women's hands, fingers indistinguishably intermeshed, exudes female same-gender desire despite the designation of their school as heteronormative space. It is through an analysis these young women's corporeal positioning within the material space of schooling that such an interruption to heteronormativity can be discerned.

Another photo that also undertakes this work appeared more frequently across photo-diaries and depicted a male and female student talking to each other (see Figure 7.4). These photos often exuded a staged feel, conveyed via a lack of spontaneity in subjects' bodily positioning. For instance, in Figure 7.4 the students' stances appear exaggerated because of the theatrical placement of their hands on their hips. Leo, who had taken a series of these photos, described them in this way, 'So this one [pointing to Figure 7.4] is just basically the same as this one [pointing to a previous photo], it just shows a girl and a boy talking but nothing sexual is going on' (18 years, European, KC). Leo described the premeditated nature of this photo and the fact he had asked his friends (who were not a couple) to pose as if 'just talking to each other'. When asked why he had wanted to depict this he said, 'if you are talking to the opposite sex then people always think that it's sexual and this shows that it isn't always.'

One feature of schools as heteronormative spaces is that relations between opposite genders are always posited as potentially sexual. Epstein and Johnson (1994) characterise this as the 'heterosexual presumption',

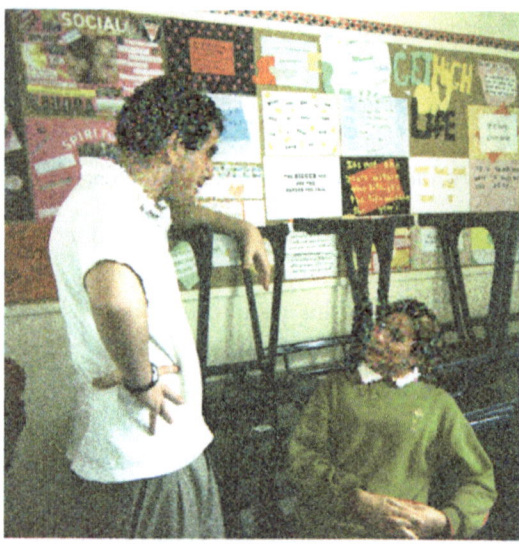

Figure 7.4. Just talking.

the taken-for-granted assumption that everybody will be, or should be, heterosexual (198). This assumption is architecturally embedded in schools in the separation of male and female toilets in order to maintain students' modesty. The idea that female and male students should be sexually attracted to each other is fortified at secondary school as the biological maturation of student bodies is conflated with awakening and intensifying this desire. Aware of this presumption, the prevalence of these 'just-talking' images can be read as students' critical commentary on the heteronormativity of schooling space. In representing opposite-gender students as engaging non-sexually, photo-diarists resist the notion that young people *should be* and *are always* attracted to each other. Leo self-identified as heterosexual and appeared to frame his opposition to heteronormativity in relation to its positioning of young people as always sexually motivated. Yet, this political message opens space for acknowledging that opposite-gender students may not necessarily be sexually attracted, because they are same-gender attracted.

## Concluding thoughts

While previous studies have illuminated the ways in which heteronormativity is discursively sustained at school, this chapter explores how it is maintained through spatial and embodied relations. Through a reading of student embodiment depicted through visual methods, it is possible to see how heteronormativity inheres at the intersections of bodies and space. For instance, the corporeal positioning of student bodies at lunchtime while 'hanging out' with a group of friends reveals the ways in which heterosexual coupledom is rendered 'normal' and 'desired'. While such forms of spatial embodiment scaffold heteronormativity, others contest it. Such disruptions are manifest in the anomalous image of same-gender female desire as captured by Lucinda. Despite evidence in the existing literature of schools as heteronormative spaces, student bodies can interrupt these meanings through their corporeal engagements in/with these spaces.

What is particularly interesting is that all but one of these photos are taken outside the classroom. Leo's picture (Figure 7.4) is qualitatively different from the other images in its premeditation. Here the classroom location intensifies a sense of transgression in the delivery of a political message, because it is a space symbolic of institutional heteronormativity. A marginal favouring of outside spaces is a pattern consistent across all photos with 143 of the 279 taken capturing outside spaces. In extending our understandings of the role of space as implicated in the production of sexual meanings, it might be argued that outside spaces offer better material conditions for young people's expressions of sexuality. In Figure 7.1, where students 'hang out' during break-time, the roof of the outdoor walkway enables students' 'coupled moments' to be sheltered from duty-teacher surveillance. The enclosed classroom space means teachers have a more encompassing view of students, while outside students are dispersed, rendering sexual acts less detectable.

Outside spaces also engender freedom from desks so bodies can lounge and make contact more easily. Classrooms are purpose-built spaces designated for learning, while outside areas are coded more ambiguously. For instance, while outside spaces may signify a learning space, they are not dedicated to this purpose (e.g. the netball courts may be variously used for eating lunch or a fire evacuation meeting point). As a consequence of the way educational spaces are seen to be 'properly' devoid of sexuality (see Allen 2007b), students may experience a greater sense of freedom (generated by there literally being more space outside) to express sexuality. One way of theorising this capacity is to conceptualise it as a kind of agency inherent in the material conditions of space which students mobilise for their own purposes.

# References

Agnew, J. (2005), 'Space: Place', in P. Cloke & R. Johnston (eds), *Space of Geographical Thought: Deconstructing human geography's binaries* (81–96), London: Sage.

Allen, L. (2007a), 'Keeping students on the straight and narrow: Heteronormalising practices in New Zealand secondary schools', *New Zealand Journal of Educational Studies*, 41(2), 311–32.

Allen, L. (2007b), 'Denying the sexual subject: Schools' regulation of student sexuality', *British Educational Research Journal*, 33(2), 221–34.

Allen, L. (2009), '"Caught in the act": Ethics committee review and researching the sexual culture of schools', *Qualitative Research*, 9(4), 395–410.

Allen, L. (2010), 'Queer(y)ing the straight researcher: The relationship(?) between researcher identity and anti-normative knowledge', *Feminism and Psychology*, 20(2), 147–65.

Allen, L. (2011a), '"Picture this": Using photo-methods in research on sexualities and schooling', *Qualitative Research*, 5(11), 487–504.

Allen, L. (2011b), 'The camera never lies?: Analysing photographs in research on sexualities and schooling', *Discourse: Studies in the Cultural Politics of Education*, 32(5), 761–77.

Allen, L. (2013), 'Behind the bike sheds: Sexual geographies of schooling', *British Journal of Sociology of Education*, 34(1), 56–75.

Allen, L. (2014), 'Tau(gh)t bodies: Student sexual embodiment and schooling', in K. Fitzpatrick & R. Tinning (eds), *Health Education: Critical perspectives* (89–105), London, Routledge.

Barad, K. (2003), 'Posthumanist performativity: Toward an understanding of how matter comes to matter', *Signs: Journal of women in culture and society*, 28(3), 801–31.

Barad, K. (2007), *Meeting the Universe Halfway: Quantum physics and the entanglement of matter and meaning*, Durhman, NC: Duke University Press.

Beasley, C. (2005), *Gender and Sexuality: Critical theories, critical thinkers*, London: Sage.

Bennett, J. (2010), *Vibrant Matter: A political ecology of things*, Durham: Duke University Press.

Bennett, J. (2004), 'The force of things: Steps toward an ecology of matter', *Political Theory*, 32(3), 347–72.

Blaise, M. (2005), *Playing It Straight: Changing images of early childhood*, London: Routledge.

Brown, G., Browne, K. & Lim, J. (eds) (2009), *Geographies of Sexualities: Theory, practices and politics*, Farnham: Ashgate.

Butler, J. (1990), *Gender Trouble: Feminism and the subversion of identity*, New York: Routledge.

Cullen, F. & Sandy, L. (2009), 'Lesbian Cinderella and other stories: Telling tales and researching sexualities equalities in primary school', *Sex Education*, 9(2), 141–54.

Crang, M. (2005), 'Time: Space', in P. Cloke & R. Johnston (eds), *Space of Geographical Thought: Deconstructing human geography's binaries* (199–220), London: Sage.

Dalley, P. & Campbell, M. (2006) 'Constructing and contesting discourses of heteronormativity: An ethnographic study of youth in a francophone high school in Canada', *Journal of Language, Identity, and Education*, 5(1), 11–29.

Dalley-Trim, L. (2007), 'The boys' present ... Hegemonic Masculinity: A performance of multiple acts, *Gender and Education*, 19(2), 199–217.

DePalma, R. & Jennett, M. (2012), 'Homophobia, transphobia and culture: Deconstructing heteronormativity in English primary schools', *Intercultural Education*, 21(1), 15–26.

DePalma, R. & Atkinson, E. (2010), 'The nature of institutional heteronormativity in primary schools and practice-based responses', *Teaching and Teacher Education*, 26, 1669–76.

DePalma, R. & Atkinson, E. (2009), *Interrogating Heteronormativity in Primary Schools: The No Outsiders project*, Stoke on Trent: Trentham.
Donelson, R. & Rogers, T. (2004), 'Negotiating a research protocol for studying school-based gay and lesbian issues', *Theory into Practice, 43*(2), 128–35.
Ellis, V. & High, S. (2004), 'Something more to tell you: Gay, lesbian or bisexual young people's experiences of secondary schooling', *British Educational Research Journal, 30*(2), 213–25.
Epstein, D., Hewitt, R., Leonard, D., Mauthner, M. & Watkins, C. (2007), 'Confronting homophobia in UK schools: Taking a back seat to multicultural and antiracist education', in L. van Dijk & B. van Driel (eds), *Challenging Homophobia: Teaching about sexual diversity* (75–83), Stoke on Trent: Trentham.
Epstein, D. & Johnson, R. (1994), 'On the straight and narrow: The heterosexual presumption, homophobias and schools', in D. Epstein (ed.), *Challenging Lesbian and Gay Inequality in Education*, Buckingham: Open University Press.
Epstein, D., O'Flynn, S. & Telford, D. (eds), (2003), *Silenced Sexualities in Schools and Universities*, Stoke on Trent: Trentham.
Ferfolja, T. (2007), 'Schooling cultures: Institutionalizing heteronormativity and heterosexism', *International Journal of Inclusive Education, 11*(2), 147–62.
Fuss, D. (1989), *Essentially Speaking: Feminism, nature and difference*, London: Routledge.
Gunn, A. (2011), 'Even if you say it three ways, it still doesn't mean it's true: The pervasiveness of heteronormativity in early childhood education', *Journal of Early Childhood Research, 9*(3), 280–90.
Halberstam, J. (1998), *Female Masculinity*, London: Duke University Press.
Hillier, L., Turner, A. and Mitchell, A. (2005), 'Writing themselves in again, 6 years on: The 2nd national report on the sexual health & well-being of same-sex-attracted young people in Australia', Melbourne: Australian Research Centre in Sex, Health & Society, La Trobe University.
Jagose, A. (1996), *Queer Theory: An introduction*, New York: New York University Press.
Kalervo, N., Gulson, S. & Colin, S. (2007), 'Knowing one's place: Educational theory, policy, and the spatial turn', in N. Kalervo, S. Gulson & S. Colin (eds), *Spatial Theories of Education: Policy and geography matters* (1–16), New York: Routledge.
Kehily, M. & Nayak, A. (1997), 'Lads and laughter: Humour and the production of heterosexual hierarchies', *Gender and Education, 9*, 69–87.
Martin, K. (2009), 'Normalizing heterosexuality', *American Sociological Review, 74*, 190–207.
Mayo, C. (2007), 'Queering foundations: Queer and lesbian, gay, bisexual, and transgender educational research', *Review of Research in Education, 31*, 78–94.
McGregor, J. (2004), 'Editorial', *Forum, 46*(1), 2–5.
Measor, L., Tiffin, C. & Miller, K. (2000), *Young People's Views on Sex Education*, London: RoutledgeFalmer.
Ministry of Education (2004), 'School deciles' : www.minedu.govt.nz/print_doc.cfm
Morgan, J. (2000), 'Critical pedagogy: The spaces that make the difference', *Pedagogy, Culture and Society, 8*(3), 273–88.
Myers, K. & Raymond, L. (2010), 'Elementary school girls and heteronormativity', *Gender and Society, 24*(2), 167–88.
Nayak, A. & Kehily, M. (2006), 'Gender undone: Subversion, regulation and embodiment in the work of Judith Butler', *British Journal of Sociology of Education, 27*(4), 459–72.
O'Donoghue, D. (2007), '"James always hangs out here": Making space for place in studying masculinities at school', *Visual Studies, 22*(1), 62–73.
Paechter, C. (2004), 'Space, identity and education', *Pedagogy, Culture and Society, 12*(3), 307–08.
Painter, H. (2009), 'How safe?: How safe and inclusive are Otago secondary schools? Ae ranei he haumaru, he wahi whāi kit e katoa ngā kura tuarua o Otago?' A report on

the implementations from the 'Safety in our schools – Ko te harumaru i o tatuu kura' action kit: He purongo ūruhi i ngā tuanaki a te kete mahi 'Safety in our schools – Ko te harumaru i o tatu kura', Dunedin, NZ: OUSA Queer Support.

Plummer, K. (2008), 'Studying sexualities for a better world? Ten years of sexualities', *Sexualities: Studies in culture and society, 11*(1/2), 7–22.

Quinlivan, K. & Town, S. (1999) 'Queer as fuck? Exploring the potential of queer pedagogies in researching school experiences of lesbian and gay youth', in D. Epstein & J. Sears (eds), *A Dangerous Knowing: Sexuality, pedagogy and popular culture* (242–56), London: Cassell.

Renold, E. (2000), '"Coming out": Gender, (hetero)sexuality and the primary school', *Gender and Education, 12*(3), 309–26.

Renold, E. (2005), *Girls, Boys and Junior Sexualities: Exploring children's gender and sexual relations in the primary school*, Abingdon: RoutledgeFalmer.

Rose, G. (2007), *Visual Methodologies: An introduction to the interpretation of visual materials* (2nd edn), London: Sage.

Sears, J. (ed.), (1992), *Sexuality and the Curriculum: The politics and practices of sexuality education*, New York: Teachers College Press.

Sedgwick, E. (1990), *Epistemology of the Closet*, Berkeley: University of California Press.

Sexton, S. (2012), 'Queer Otago secondary students' views of their schooling environment', *New Zealand Journal of Educational Studies, 47*(1), 93–105.

Valentine, G. (2001), *Social Geographies: Space and society*, Harlow: Pearson Education.

Warner, M. (1993), *Fear of a Queer Planet: Queer politics and social theory*, Minneapolis: University of Minnesota Press.

Youdell, D. (2005), 'Sex–gender–sexuality: How sex, gender and sexuality constellations are constituted in secondary schools', *Gender and Education, 17*(3), 249–70.

# 8.
# Sexuality, education and diversity

## Katie Fitzpatrick

Sexuality education in New Zealand schools, somewhat surprisingly, continues to be a controversial topic. Recent commentary in the *New Zealand Herald* suggests that even the idea that young people might be taught about sex and sexuality in formal education still shocks some people (Fitzpatrick 2013; Tapaleao 2013; Young 2013). The topic has, however, been a formal part of New Zealand curriculum policy since the 1990s. The policy document *Health and Physical Education in the New Zealand Curriculum* (Ministry of Education 1999, henceforth MOE), introduced sexuality education as a mandatory part of schooling. While no clear specifications were given about how much time schools should spend on the subject, from then on it was required across year levels (see also MOE 2002). Sexuality education was positioned as a key area of learning and part of health and physical education, a status that was maintained in the most recent New Zealand curriculum (MOE 2007; 2015).

Sexuality education is described in the 2015 sexuality education guide:

*Sexuality education encompasses learning about physical development, including sexual and reproductive knowledge, gender identity, relationships, friendships, whānau and social issues (MOE 2015, 4).*

The national curriculum conceptualises sexuality education as more than just human biology, extending learning to include feelings, relationship negotiation, gender identity and sexual decision-making. It also separates sexuality education from learning about abuse and victimisation. This differentiation has the potential to allow for a wider view of teenage (especially girls') sexualities, beyond discourses that conceptualise sexuality as risky and girls as 'victims' of boys' desires (Fine 2003). However, this conceptualisation emanates from a decidedly Western epistemology. This is evident in health education more broadly, as Hokowhitu (2014) argues: colonisation of Aotearoa/New Zealand resulted in 'the subjugation of local indigenous knowledges within and by western rationalism'. He also notes that this resulted in 'the enforced degradation of one health system, and the imposition of medical discourses via epistemological colonisation' (33). Unsurprisingly, an Education Review Office (2007a; 2007b) report observed that schools were not meeting the needs of diverse students in sexuality education programmes, stating that only 20 per cent and 25 per cent of schools respectively were effective at including Māori and Pasifika understandings of sexuality/gender in the curriculum and therefore meeting the needs of Maori/Pasifika students. Allen (2001; 2004; 2005) has long argued for young people's perspectives to more directly inform sexuality programmes in schools, but there are few studies that explicitly address the perspectives of students from Māori and Pasifika backgrounds.

Of interest here are the ways that young people navigate sexuality at school in relation to their own cultural worldviews. How do they navigate, resist and take up dominant messages about sexuality in schools? In this chapter I argue that young people's perspectives need to be considered in debates around sexuality, and I share some insights from an ethnographic study with South Auckland youth. First, I argue that understanding the cultural fields of sexuality in schooling, in connection with young people's cultural worlds, is important. In the second section I employ the theoretical tools of Pierre Bourdieu to explore this. In the third section I briefly introduce the study methods and participants. The remainder of the chapter is dedicated to sharing these young people's perspectives of sexuality and sexuality education.

## Understanding sexuality and field

Bourdieu's (1990) notion of 'field' provides a theoretical framework for understanding sexuality education in New Zealand schools. According to Bourdieu, a field is a site of cultural production. While the boundaries of such cultural sites are both contested and uncertain, each field, nevertheless, has recognisable cultural practices, or what Bourdieu termed a 'logic of practice'. Such a logic of practice is 'specific and irreducible to those that regulate other fields' (Bourdieu & Wacquant 1992, 97). Individual fields can then be told apart via differences in the logic of practice. Part of the logic of practice of any field pertains to the forms of capital that are recognised and rewarded. Fields are, thus, 'characterised by their own distinctive properties, by distinctive forms of capital' (Thompson 1991, 15). Capital is an articulation of status within a field and, according to Bourdieu (1986), exists in three forms:

> ... as economic capital, which is immediately and directly convertible into money and may be institutionalized in the forms of property rights; as cultural capital, which is convertible, on certain conditions, into economic capital and may be institutionalized in the forms of educational qualifications; and as social capital, made up of social obligations ('connections'), which is convertible, in certain conditions, into economic capital and may be institutionalized in the forms of a title of nobility (242).

In the field of schooling in New Zealand, certain forms of capital are explicitly evident. Institutionalised cultural capital can be seen in the National Certificate in Education Achievement (NCEA), the formal qualification system in senior high school. Within this system, numeracy and literacy are awarded a special place; students cannot gain the qualifications without completing the numeracy and literacy components. These subjects are also specifically measured and reported on via national standards in all primary schools (Thrupp & Easter 2012). I argue that health education – and sexuality education as its sub-set – has little capital value in schools. Indeed, both areas occupy a marginal and uncertain place in the curriculum. Paechter (2000) argues that this is largely a result of health education's status as a 'body subject'. Body subjects (like physical education, health and dance) are relegated in a Cartesian discourse to lower-status forms of education than so-called 'academic' subjects like English and mathematics (Middleton 1998; see also Fitzpatrick 2013).

Sexuality education is also viewed in problematic ways in wider New Zealand society. As is evident in the aforementioned media commentary, it is a controversial school subject because it is so closely linked to cultural values and norms. It interrupts the logic of practice of some communities because it challenges the assumption that sexual matters have no place in schooling. Such a logic of practice requires silence around issues of sex and sexuality, especially in public educational sites. Every field is, however, a site of both contestation and conformity to the logic of practice (Bourdieu 1990), and sexuality education exists at a crossroads between liberal and conservative views of the body and sexual behaviour.

Sexuality discourses that circulate in New Zealand society have their roots in our colonial history, and are invariably based in British epistemologies that were, and continue to be, underpinned by Christian discourses of the body, sex and gender. Complex and different across and between communities, such discourses sought to regulate and repress sexuality (see Kamitsuka 2010) rather than celebrate it.

Sexuality education content consistent with the New Zealand curriculum (MOE 2007; 2015) in some ways challenges these discourses by introducing an overtly liberal approach to matters of the body. It tends to be underpinned by the belief that young people have a right to knowledge, and the assumption that sexuality is a normal part of human development. However, such assumptions are in conflict with one colonising force: the Christian church (Aspin & Hutchings 2007). Churches are, of course, not the only sites where sexuality is contested. For example, Moloney and Kirman (2005) argue that the general social field in New Zealand is homophobic and so tends to reinforce narrow and exclusionary messages about sex and sexuality. They observe that 'fear, abhorrence and hatred of gays and lesbians is residual within certain constituencies in New Zealand … [and] talk of ever-increasing tolerance for sexual minorities is contradicted by the ever-present reality of discrimination' (17). These narrow and exclusionary messages are inevitably reflected in school programmes and environments. Crucially, in public discourse, gender is inextricably connected to sexuality in what Youdell (2005) calls the sex–gender–sexuality constellation. Such a constellation, she argues, constitutes sex, gender and sexuality in particular ways 'that open up possibilities and set limits for "who" a student can be' (250). She argues that within the constellation

> *the female body is already feminized, the feminine is already heterosexual, the hetero-feminine is already female. Sex–gender–sexuality, then, are not causally related; rather, they exist in abiding constellations in which to name one category of the constellation is to silently infer further categories (256).*

In schools then, as in other sites, gender and sexuality are tied together in complex ways. Schools are sites of surveillance and regulation upon multiple levels, including bodies, gender and sexuality. Notions of sexuality are frequently silenced (Fine 2003), particularly those that disrupt the social dominance of heteronormativity (Atkinson & DePalma 2009). Sexuality education may appear in official curriculum policy, but it is contentious and the sexualities of students are subject to scrutiny and policing. Drawing on recent studies in New Zealand schools, Allen (2007) argues that 'schools are heavily invested in a particular sort of student that is "ideally" non-sexual' (222).

## Colonisation and sexuality

The non-sexual student aligns with views of schooling as 'rationalist' academic space. Aspin and Hutchings (2007) point out that rationalist approaches to sexuality were imposed on Māori in New Zealand via colonisation and in line with Christian traditions; the same can be said for the experience of various Pasifika peoples. Indeed, Aspin and Hutchings (2007) argue that narrow and fearful views of sexuality (including sexual diversity) are a direct product of colonisation; prior to colonisation, Māori notions of sexuality were not predicated on current norms:

*[T]oday it is clear that there are powerful colonizing forces at work attempting to sever the links between historical and contemporary Māori sexuality by downplaying the importance of sexual diversity in historical Māori society ... When we lay such claims against the evidence, it becomes obvious that these claims are based on imposed Western views rather than historical fact (Aspin & Hutchings 2007, 418).*

Bhabha (1994; see also Gilroy 2000) suggests that people caught in colonial contexts are not (only) victims to these kinds of imposed discourses, although they are the subjects of them. Drawing on the notion of hybrid identities, he shows how individuals who live with multiplicity enact forms of resistance to power, particularly colonial power relations. While Bhabha (1994) argues that individuals do not have a unified singular self that is subject to, or a victim of, outside oppressive forces, he acknowledges that identities are created within particular contexts. A hybrid identity is, at once, a result of the power relations and a response to them:

*Hybridity is the sign of the productivity of colonial power, its shifting forces and fixities; it is the name for the reversal of the process of domination through disavowal (that is, the production of discriminatory identities that secure the 'pure' and original identity of authority) (Bhabha 1994, 159).*

According to Bhabha, moments of response disrupt the dominant discourses and 'disarticulate the voice of authority'; a hybrid response, then, is a survival strategy – a way to assert agency in situations where others may see no room for agency (Bhabha, interview with Mitchell 1995, 82).

Tupuola (2004) argues that Pasifika youth in New Zealand actively resist essentialised and homogenised notions of self. Rather, she suggests they draw on a range of global, youth and local cultures to form complex individual identities. Such identities are explored further below. In the next section I introduce a study that sought the perspectives of a group of Māori and Pasifika[1] youth in South Auckland, at a school I call 'Kikorangi High School'.

## An ethnographic study

Kikorangi High School is a suburban secondary school in Otara, South Auckland, with approximately 1100 students and 75 teachers. Allocated a decile one ranking (the lowest socioeconomic category available on the scale of 1–10) by the New Zealand Ministry of Education, the school comprises almost wholly Pasifika and Māori students.[2]

Having taught health and physical education (PE) at the school between 1999 and 2004, I returned in 2007 to conduct a critical ethnography of how young people engaged in health and PE classes. According to Thomas (1993), critical ethnography is 'conventional ethnography with a political purpose':

> *Critical ethnography is a way of applying a subversive worldview to the conventional logic of cultural inquiry. It does not stand in opposition to conventional ethnography. Rather, it offers a more direct style of thinking about the relationships among knowledge, society and political action* (Thomas 1993, vii).

In the context of this study, this involved interrogating and paying attention to issues of injustice, power relations and the way culture, ethnicity, gender, sexuality and other 'identity markers' such as religion intersected in the lives of these young people. In order to examine these issues, I spent time during the year in four different Kikorangi classes with Year 12 and 13 (16–18-year-old) students of health education and PE. At this level of schooling, few subjects are compulsory and students choose their preferred options. All four classes were formal, academic senior high-school subjects,

---

1. I draw together both Māori and Pasifika in this study. I do so, not in order to collapse identity positions and ethnicities, but rather in connection with the youth in this study who, as explained further below, identified in complex ways with their Pasifika and/or Māori cultural heritages. Several students in this study identified as both Māori and Pasifika, as well as with a specific Pacific ethnicity.
2. Student breakdown by ethnicity shows a clear majority of Pasifika students at the school: Samoan (48 per cent), Cook Islands Māori (21 per cent), Tongan (11 per cent) Niuean (4 per cent). Māori comprise 12 per cent, Pākehā/European 1 per cent and Indian 1 per cent. Fewer than 1 per cent identify otherwise. These figures obscure students who identify with multiple ethnicities, however.

assessed for NCEA. Each class met for four hours per week, apart from the Year 12 PE class, which met for eight hours. On average, I spent three days a week at Kikorangi and participated in over 300 hours of classes.

I kept a reflective journal throughout the year, and conducted extensive research conversations with students and their teachers,[3] using a critical approach. Some of these conversations took the form of focus-group discussions with four to six students, while others were individual interviews. The range of topics varied greatly during the year but included general discussions about health and PE classes, the school environment, sexuality and relationships, gangs and drugs, perceptions of the community and school, as well as racism and discrimination. In this chapter I focus only on one aspect of the study, relating to sexuality in the school (see Fitzpatrick 2013 for the full study).

Building relationships was a key part of my approach. While school leaders and members of the community knew me as a former teacher at the school, I consciously built relationships with the students in order to establish mutual trust. Cammarota and Fine (2008), Madison (2012) and others (e.g. Carspecken 1996) argue that meaningful, long-term and reciprocal relationships should form the basis of any ethical approach to social research. This was especially important as I am Pākehā, and therefore from a different cultural background to the students. I formed ties with students and teachers, not only by attending classes and through the research discussions, but also by attending outdoor education camps, 'hanging out' with students during lunchtime and regularly exchanging text messages. Throughout the study I used a process of checking meaning and interpretation with students, and have ongoing relationships with several of these young people.

In analysing the resulting research data, I used students' stories and conversations in articulation with social theory to construct narratives. These are more evident in other publications emanating from this study (see Fitzpatrick 2013), but the quotations here come from many conversations with students over a period of time. Short dynamic episodes involving activities, conversations, jokes, classes and discussions with students provided especially cogent contexts to form into narratives and to weave into theorised discussion (Clandinin & Connelly 2000; McDrury & Alterio 2003).

---

3   In this chapter I draw only on research materials from students in the study.

While many students were part of the wider study, in this chapter I focus specifically on a few Year 12 and 13 students. The young people whose voices inform this piece are: Harriet (16, Niuean and Māori); Matt (17, Samoan); Sione (17, Samoan and Cook Islands Māori); Alex (17, Cook Islands Māori); and Moses (17, Cook Islands Māori and Samoan).

## Heteronormativity and school

As discussed earlier in this chapter, school is undoubtedly a space where sexuality is regulated. Despite this, students in the study held open and informal discussions about intimate relationships during classes and breaks. Harriet, for example, explained:

> *You know, sometimes in class it's all about the 'mingling', like who got mingled with who at the party on the weekend ... they [friends] distract you, talking about gossip and TV and boys, especially boys – what he said and she said and he did.*

Harriet's observation that such discussion is distracting is important and I return to discussion of it below. Her observation that her girlfriends talk about boys a great deal is a clear example of sexuality assumptions underlying all discussions of intimate relationships. All the relationship discussions I was party to were framed, first and foremost, by 'compulsory heterosexuality' (Rich 1986; Morris-Roberts 2004) or heteronormativity. This is a societal assumption that all people are heterosexual unless specifically identified as gay, lesbian, bisexual or queer. Students in the study assumed in the first instance that all intimate relationships were heterosexual.

Butler (1999) theorised sexuality in relation to the 'heterosexual matrix'. Sexual orientation and desire in this matrix cannot be divorced from notions of sex and gender. She explained that '"masculine" and "feminine", "male" and "female" exist *only* within the heterosexual matrix; indeed, they are naturalized terms that keep the matrix concealed and, hence, protected from a radical critique' (Butler 1999, 141, emphasis in original). The matrix, then, collapses sex, gender and sexuality. That the female body is at once both feminine and heterosexual becomes a 'naturalised' assumption, an unquestioned reality (Youdell 2005). Drawing on this same assumption, Harriet automatically aligned the girls' discussions of intimacy with heterosexual relationships.

Heterosexuality then is the norm and homosexuality is an 'othered' identity, one that is marginalised and often positioned as deviant (Epstein & Johnson 1998). Such dominant notions of sexuality create a dichotomy between gay and straight that ignores more fluid and contested sexual identities. This is not to suggest that the labels 'gay' and 'lesbian' were unused by students at Kikorangi or considered taboo; on the contrary, they were used in specific ways to name and marginalise. While we were walking across the field at school one day, Harriet pointed to a boy from another class and commented to me, 'I think he's gay.' Although this statement was not necessarily derogatory, it was consciously used to establish a point of difference and make a judgment about the boy's sexuality. This evaluation was based on appearance and/or dispositions rather than on any actual knowledge about sexual behaviour or orientation. Even though Harriet actively expressed her support for gay rights during class discussions, vocally affirming anyone's right to 'be themselves', her use of the term 'gay' was not neutral, despite her not intending it to be negative. Presumed sexual orientation was used as a category, to identify otherness. In all of the discussions I had with students, there was a silent, assumed heteronormativity, much like I experience in other social settings.

While 'gayness' can be named and marginalised, heterosexuality is often invisible, a powerfully normative discourse that does not require naming. Foucault (1978) points out how such silence actually conveys a great deal of meaning:

> *Silence itself – the things one declines to say, or is forbidden to name, the discretion that is required between different speakers – is less the absolute limit of discourse, the other side of which is separated by a strict boundary, than an element that functions alongside the things said, with them and in relation to them in the overall strategies (27).*

While students like Harriet purposely named gay relationships or possible 'gayness', heterosexuality was presumed (Epstein & Johnson 1998). Crowley (1999) argues that when homosexuality is named it often evokes disgust, hatred and difference, even if these are not felt or meant by the speaker. Another student, Matt, talked about the prestigious boys' school in the South Island of New Zealand that he had attended before coming to Kikorangi. He commented that he felt no pressure to be in a relationship at Kikorangi, unlike at his previous school where 'you had to have a girlfriend and, if you didn't, they [other students] just thought you were gay'. Matt thought it ridiculous that being in a heterosexual relationship was required as proof of not being gay. Nevertheless, he acknowledged that being called 'gay' by students at his previous school was humiliating. Students also used the word 'gay' as a negative adjective. Alex described one lesson taught by a relief teacher as 'so gay', by which she meant boring, stupid and not worthy of her attention.

The sexual dichotomy of homosexual/heterosexual is a Western construct: 'Lesbian is a Western term, implicated in Western history and politics ... the homosexual is a Western construction' (Elleray 2004, 175). Māori and Pasifika students' cultural contexts offered alternative, non-Western views of sexuality. In Māori, for example, the word takatāpui is used to describe 'non heterosexual forms of expression' (Aspin & Hutchings 2007, 422). In Samoan culture, the term fa`afafine is used to describe an identity that has no articulation in Pākehā terms:

> *Fa`afafine – literally 'in the way of a woman' – is the Samoan term for anatomically male individuals who adopt behavioural attributes associated with female gender. The Tahitian and contemporary Hawaiian equivalent is mahu; the Tongan, fakaleiti (Wallace 2003, 140).*

Wallace (2003) argues that Western notions of sexuality and gender, imposed on other cultural articulations, fail to understand such a diversity of gender identities. He states that 'Fa`afafine ... are not to be understood in relation to European categories of identification such as gay, transvestite or transsexual ... Fa`afafine are not homosexuals' (139). While Kikorangi youth talked in heteronormative terms and used the term gay to 'other',[4] their cultural worldviews also disrupted such categories. Sione, for example, explained that 'being a fa`afa[fine] is fine, it's acceptable in my culture'.

Māori and Pasifika notions of sexuality, overlapping with Western notions, can take apart and expose the heterosexual matrix in new ways. Such an overlapping of fields, as Bourdieu (2005) suggests, can allow for transformation. Elleray (2004) argues that:

> *In so far as Māori are necessarily bicultural – both tangata whenua (indigenous peoples) and Westerners, saddled with the task of translating themselves between those two designations – so the Māori lesbian may be both part of a community of Māori women attracted to one another, and part of the Western gay and lesbian movement (177).*

---

4   To mark someone as different or not belonging.

Kikorangi students then could draw on both Western and Māori/Pasifika understandings of gender and sexuality. Further complicating this, however, is how bodies and sexualities coexist in the intersections between not only Western, but also Western Christian, notions of sexuality.

## Considering the body

Sione's conflict about whether to get a traditional Samoan pe`a (tattoo) is an example in this regard. While his grandmother wanted him to be tattooed, Sione felt uncertain about whether pe`a aligned with his Christian value of 'purity'. He later explained how he experienced this conflict between his Samoan cultural practices and the church he attended:

> *My culture influences me by the choices I make, there's a tradition for Samoans, my grandma told me that one day I have to get one of those tattoos – pe`a ... I think should I get one of those and I really want to continue the tradition and stuff but I have to decide ... it relates back to the Christian thing, like for Christians your body has to be pure and you're not allowed to have anything on your body and that goes for tattoos and stuff, and it makes me think. Should I go with the tradition or should I go with the Christian thing?*

Many Samoan churches observe fa`a Samoa (Samoan cultural ways and protocols), however, so questioning of the church's teachings is closely related to questioning of cultural values and practices. Fleras and Spoonley (1999) observe that Pasifika youth who are born in New Zealand are actively negotiating cultural practices and beliefs. Referring to Samoan churches, they argue:

> *The centrality of the church is also an issue for Samoan communities. There is a substantial investment in the authority and structures of the church, and yet the influences of the secular world contrast with the discipline and involvement of a church that is dedicated to strict religious observance and the maintenance of traditional religious and cultural values (211).*

Part of this religious observance concerns the 'purity' of the body as well as a split between body and soul. Christian traditions uphold the sacredness of the body and are concerned about the pollution of the body by base desires associated with sex and sexuality (Kamitsuka 2010). The tradition of Samoan pe`a predates the Christian missions in the Pacific and is a rite of passage that celebrates the body and its adulthood, its readiness for 'the demands of life'. It denotes high status and the ability to endure pain (Wendt 1999). Wendt states, 'the tatau for men and malu for women were considered clothing, the most desired and highest-status clothing anyone could wear. When warriors went into battle with their penis sheaths and tatau they were "clothed", fully clothed, fully armoured' (400). He explains the term pe`a:

> *The common name for tatau is pe`a, flying fox ... If you look at the tatau frontally, the male genitals, even with a penis sheath, look like the pe`a's head, and the tatau spreading out over the thighs and up toward the navel and outward looks like its wings outstretched. The expression is "Faalele lau pe`a!" – Let your flying fox fly! Show how beautiful and courageous you've been in enduring the pain of the tatau, parade it for all to see. The sexual connotations are also very obvious (402).*

Sione's view of his body was conflicted at the intersection of fa`a Samoa traditions and church teachings. But this very intersection also allowed him insight into these different ways of knowing and gave him a context for questioning and reflecting on his bodily choices. Aspin and Hutchings (2007) argue that:

> [T]he application of Western concepts of sexuality to indigenous ways of looking at the world ignores some of the realities of the lives of indigenous peoples. This is significant for schools to consider as frequently 'little or no consideration is given to the fact that indigenous peoples may not view Western concepts of sexuality as appropriate descriptors of their particular form of sexual expression and identity' (423).

Sione's questioning of bodily practices surrounding pe`a is an example of a more fluid identity as 'a response to the social/material world as well as an accommodation, manipulation and gentle rebuff of the traditional identity' (McIntosh 2005, 46). McIntosh argues that for Māori youth, a 'fluid identity plays with cultural markers such as language ... custom and place and reconfigures them in a way that gives both voice and currency to their social environment' (46). She observes that this often means young people engage in a 'fusing of different ideas and practices from a diversity of cultural backgrounds to articulate [an] identity that is strongly grounded in its particular social landscape' (46).

Likewise, Tupuola (2004) argues that many Pasifika youth 'seem to identify with multiple identities and seem to explore their personal identities through a social–cultural lens' (96). Such a lens may in fact result from the multiple fields these young people are experiencing. In Sione's case, he was able to reflect on the differing cultural contexts he was immersed in and bring a thoughtful and knowledgeable approach to his decision. This in some ways shows his conscious approach to the field in a Bourdieuian sense. As McNay (1999) highlights, 'Bourdieu does not deny the possibility of reflexive self-awareness nor the attendant potential for politically motivated change' (106). Sione's awareness of the different fields, and the conflict he experienced at the intersection of these, is a form of social and political awareness; such awareness can potentially become a form of such resistance and disavowal. The story of another student, Moses, was also prescient in this regard.

## Moses

Moses was 16 and his girlfriend, also a Kikorangi student, was 15. When she became pregnant in the school holidays the couple decided to have the baby, although this decision went against her family's wishes. Moses explained that, at the time, 'we were kinda scared about how our families would react ... my girlfriend's family wanted an abortion, but we wanted the baby, so they couldn't stop us.' The couple had already discussed plans to have children after they left school, and Moses staunchly defended their right to have the child despite other people's assertions that they were too young. His determination to have the baby was partly because his own father was dying of kidney failure: 'My dad was the happiest [about my daughter] because he wants to see my kids before he passes, so that the family is complete.'

When his girlfriend became pregnant Moses found the pressure of school increasingly difficult to manage. He was determined to finish school and 'get a good job', because he did not want his daughter to see him 'work in a factory', but the financial and emotional pressures were huge:

> *I try to work hard [at school] but it's just the thought of baby ... 'cause baby just pops into my head and I start daydreaming and it's hard to concentrate. Money is a big issue ... I have to work and miss school and buy baby's nappies and stuff ... money's a big thing ... My dad, his pay's not high. After bills and shopping all that he's left with is about $40. [At the end of the week], I have $100, so I give $60 to him and then I'm left with $40, and that goes to baby's nappies.*

Despite these pressures, when the baby arrived Moses expressed joy at being a parent: 'Being a dad changed my life ... I want to be the best dad ever and make her [my daughter] happy.' He explained that the support from family members was significant; his girlfriend's parents helped financially and looked after the baby during the day so that he and his partner could both continue to attend school. Although his girlfriend's family initially wanted an abortion, 'once they saw baby they were all happy and smiley'.

Moses' commitment to his family and his new daughter was strong. Although school success was important to him, family came first. Shortly before the birth, Moses told his teacher that he could not attend his class outdoor education camp because the baby was due. Moses' teacher was concerned about him missing key assessment opportunities at camp and suggested 'maybe you can come for some of the time, it's worth 15 credits [toward the NCEA]'. A classmate, Tu, burst out laughing when the teacher said this. He held his hands out like scales to sarcastically weigh up 'baby: 15 credits – life: 15 credits'. He was showing how ridiculous the idea of school achievement was in light of the most significant event in Moses' life, the birth of his daughter. The class laughed in agreement; achievement at school hardly warranted comparison with such an event. While the teacher was concerned with the accumulation of educational capital, the cultural and social family context was much more important to Moses than the arbitrary cultural rules of school.

Moses' experience is not uncommon in South Auckland, which has a higher teenage pregnancy rate than other regions. The teen pregnancy unit at Kikorangi was just another part of the school and was openly accepted by staff and students. Seeing pregnant girls at school was part of the everyday routine. However, Breheny and Stephens (2007) explain that in society, teenage parenting is 'typically framed ... as a social problem through association with psychological dysfunction, poor parenting and socioeconomic disadvantage' (334). In the general social field in New Zealand, this is certainly the case. For instance, Statistics New Zealand (2003) reports:

> *Teenage childbearing is generally considered a poor life choice. It is widely acknowledged that the responsibilities of early parenthood have long-lasting effects on the socio-economic wellbeing of the women and children involved. This results in part from interrupted education; failure to attain educational potential; reduced earning potential; reduced career prospects; and, more generally, simply being emotionally and socially unprepared for childrearing (9).*

Drawing on this field, Moses might have felt ashamed and regretful. Within his Cook Island family, however, the birth of a child was a cause for celebration and a reason for his father to rejoice. Moses also admitted there was an enormous challenge between school and fathering but was positive about being a father – which, for him, was where the real capital lay.

Aspin and Hutchings (2007) point out that indigenous cultures tend to view sexuality in a more holistic light:

> *In order to arrive at a complete understanding of sexual identity it is important to recognize the multiple strands that make up one's sense of identity. For indigenous people, the cultural aspects of one's identity are just as important as the sexual aspects (423).*

Moses viewed his new baby as an important addition to the family, a continuation of family and culture. In this, the baby was a cause for celebration, not a source of angst about teenage sexuality or the problems of teen parenting as espoused in policy.

Like Sione, Moses experienced conflict at the intersection of fields when his girlfriend became pregnant. While his teachers and parents wanted him to continue with school, his new role as a father changed how he viewed these fields; he drew on his cultural background and perspectives to actively negotiate these contexts. In the final section, I reflect on how the experiences of these young people can and should impact on how we view sexuality education programmes in New Zealand schools.

## Conclusion

I began this chapter by pointing out that, despite years of curriculum presence, sexuality education in New Zealand schools remains marginalised and contentious. Few schools also effectively connect with Māori and Pasifika youth in the programmes that do exist (Education Review Office 2007a; 2007b). I suggest that current programmes may be failing to connect with Māori and Pasifika students because they do not pay enough attention to young people's cultural worldviews or the complex articulation of the social fields they inhabit.

The intersections between students' cultural perspectives of sexuality and the framing of sexuality within the curriculum actually provide an excellent opportunity for school programmes to better meet the needs of diverse youth. Sione's conundrum concerning pe`a, for example, might provide a perfect starting place for learning about how sexual and gender identities and decisions are intertwined with cultural beliefs and religious beliefs and implicated with New Zealand's colonial history. A study of this kind can begin to unwind assumptions about 'naturalised' heteronormativity and Western cultural perspectives, allowing students to question and critique dominant notions of what is normal and, therefore, acceptable. Likewise, Moses' experiences draw our attention to the complex multiple environments that young people are negotiating every day. The young people in this study were actively resisting normative notions of sexuality and gender, even while immersed within discourses of heteronormativity in their school environment and peer groups. As I argue elsewhere (Fitzpatrick 2014; Fitzpatrick & Tinning 2014) there is great potential for sexuality education, as a part of school-based health education, to address this kind of complexity. The latest national sexuality education guide may provide a starting point for this. It will only happen if we are fully cognisant of the contemporary dilemmas young people are facing (and actively negotiating) at the intersection of youth culture, ethnicity, gender and schooling.

## Acknowledgement

Sections of this chapter have previously been published in *Critical Pedagogy, Physical Education and Urban Schooling* (2013, New York: Peter Lang).

## References

Allen, L. (2001), 'Closing sex education's knowledge/practice gap: The reconceptualization of young people's sexual knowledge', *Sex Education*, 1(2), 109–22.
Allen, L. (2004), 'Beyond the birds and the bees: Constituting a discourse of erotics in sexuality education', *Gender and Education*, 16(2), 151–67.
Allen, L. (2005), '"Say everything": Exploring young people's suggestions for improving sexuality education', *Sex Education*, 5(4), 389–404.
Allen, L. (2007), 'Denying the sexual subject: Schools' regulation of student sexuality', *British Educational Research Journal*, 33(2), 221–34.
Aspin, C. & Hutchings, J. (2007), 'Reclaiming the past to inform the future: Contemporary views of Māori sexuality', *Culture, Health and Sexuality*, 9(4), 415–27.
Atkinson, E. & DePalma, R. (2009), 'Un-believing the matrix: Queering consensual heteronormativity', *Gender and Education*, 21(1), 17–29.
Bhabha, H. (1994), *The Location of Culture*, New York: Routledge.
Bourdieu, P. (1986), 'The forms of capital', in J. Richardson (ed.), *Handbook of Theory and Research for the Sociology of Education*, (241–58), Westport, CT: Greenwood.
Bourdieu, P. (1990), *The Logic of Practice* (R. Nice, trans.), Malden, MA: Polity.
Bourdieu, P. (2005), 'Habitus', in J. Hillier & E. Rooksby (eds), *Habitus: A sense of place* (2nd edn, 43–50), Aldershot, UK: Ashgate.

Bourdieu, P. & Wacquant, L. (1992), *An Invitation to Reflexive Sociology*, Cambridge, UK: Polity.
Breheny, M. & Stephens, C. (2007), 'Individual responsibility and social constraint: The construction of adolescent motherhood in social scientific research', *Culture, Health and Sexuality*, 9(4), 333–46.
Butler, J. (1999), *Gender Trouble: Feminism and the subversion of identity*, London: Routledge.
Cammarota, J. & Fine, M. (2008), 'Youth participatory action research: A pedagogy for transformational resistance', in J. Cammarota & M. Fine (eds), *Revolutionizing Education: Youth participatory action research in motion* (1–12), New York: Routledge.
Carspecken, P. (1996), *Critical Ethnography in Educational Research: A theoretical and practical guide*, New York: Routledge.
Clandinin, D.J. & Connelly, F.M. (2000), *Narrative Inquiry: Experience and story in qualitative research*, San Francisco, CA: Jossey-Bass.
Crowley, V. (1999), 'Witches, faggots, dykes and poofters: Moments of danger and the realms of subjectivity', in D. Epstein & J.T. Sears (eds), *Dangerous Knowing: Sexuality, pedagogy and popular culture* (210–25), London: Cassell.
Education Review Office (2007a), *The Teaching of Sexuality Education in Years 7–13*, Wellington: Author.
Education Review Office (2007b), *The Teaching of Sexuality Education in Years 7–13: Good practice*, Wellington: Author.
Elleray, M. (2004), 'Weaving the wahine takatāpui: Mirimiri and Tahuri', in L. Alice & L. Star (eds), *Queer in Aotearoa New Zealand* (175–86), Palmerston North: Dunmore.
Epstein, D. & Johnson, R. (1998), *Schooling Sexualities*, Buckingham, UK: Open University Press.
Fine, M. (2003), 'Sexuality, schooling, and adolescent females: The missing discourse of desire', in M. Fine & L. Weis, *Silenced Voices and Extraordinary Conversations: Re-imagining schools* (38–67), New York: Teachers College Press.
Fitzpatrick, K. (2013), *Critical Pedagogy, Physical Education and Urban Schooling*, New York: Peter Lang.
Fitzpatrick, K. (11 November 2013), 'Quality sex education vital for schools', *New Zealand Herald*: www.nzherald.co.nz
Fitzpatrick, K. (2014), 'Critical approaches to health education', in K. Fitzpatrick & R. Tinning (eds), *Health Education: Critical perspectives* (173–89), London: Routledge.
Fitzpatrick, K. & Tinning, R. (eds), (2014), 'Considering the politics and practice of health education', in K. Fitzpatrick & R. Tinning (eds), *Health Education: Healthism and neoliberal bodies* (1–13), London: Routledge.
Fleras, A. & Spoonley, P. (1999), *Recalling Aotearoa: Indigenous politics and ethnic relations in New Zealand*, Auckland: Oxford University Press.
Foucault, M. (1978), *The History of Sexuality, Vol. 1: An introduction*, New York: Pantheon.
Gilroy, P. (2000), *Against Race: Imagining political culture beyond the color line*, Cambridge, MA: Harvard University Press.
Hokowhitu, B. (2014), 'If you are not healthy, then what are you? Healthism, colonial disease and body-logic', in K. Fitzpatrick & R. Tinning (eds), *Health Education: Critical perspectives* (31–47), London: Routledge.
Kamitsuka, M. (2010), *The Embrace of Eros: Bodies, desires and sexuality in Christianity*, Minneapolis, MN: Fortress.
Madison, D.S. (2012), *Critical Ethnography: Method, ethics, and performance* (2nd edn), Thousand Oaks, CA: Sage.
McDrury, J. & Alterio, M. (2003) *Learning Through Storytelling in Higher Education: Using reflection and experience to improve learning*, London: Kogan Page.

McIntosh, T. (2005), 'Māori identities: Fixed, fluid, forced', in J.H. Liu, T. McCreanor, T. McIntosh & T. Teaiwa, *New Zealand Identities: Departures and destinations* (38–51), Wellington: Victoria University Press.

McNay, L. (1999), 'Gender, habitus and the field: Pierre Bourdieu and the limits of reflexivity', *Theory, Culture & Society*, 16(1), 95–117.

Middleton, S. (1998), *Disciplining Sexuality: Foucault, life histories, and education*, New York: Teachers College Press.

Ministry of Education (1999), *Health and Physical Education in the New Zealand Curriculum*, Wellington: Author.

Ministry of Education (2002), *Sexuality Education: Guidelines for principals, boards of trustees and teachers*, Wellington: Author.

Ministry of Education (2007), *The New Zealand Curriculum*, Wellington: Author.

Ministry of Education (2015), *Sexuality Education: A guide for principals, boards of trustees and teachers*, Wellington: Author.

Mitchell, W.J.T. (1995), 'Translator translated: Interview with cultural theorist Homi Bhabha', *Artforum*, 33(7), 80–84.

Moloney, P. & Kirkman, A. (2005), 'Introduction: Mapping the sexual landscape', in A. Kirkman & P. Moloney (eds), *Sexuality Down Under: Social and historical perspectives* (9–28), Dunedin: University of Otago Press.

Morris-Roberts, K. (2004), 'Colluding in "compulsory heterosexuality"? Doing research with young women at school', in A. Harris (ed.), *All About the Girl: Culture, power, and identity* (219–30), London: Routledge.

Paechter, C. (2000), *Changing School Subjects: Power, gender and curriculum*, Buckingham, UK: Open University Press.

Rich, A. (1986), 'Compulsory heterosexuality and lesbian existence', in A. Rich, *Blood, Bread and Poetry* (23–75), London: W.W. Norton.

Tapaleao, V. (17 June 2013), 'Sex report slams Kiwi lessons', *New Zealand Herald*: www.nzherald.co.nz

Thomas, J. (1993), *Doing Critical Ethnography*, Newbury Park, CA: Sage.

Thompson, J.B. (1991), 'Editor's introduction', in P. Bourdieu, *Language and Symbolic Power* (J.B. Thompson, ed.; G. Raymond & M. Adamson, trans.; 1–31), Malden, MA: Polity.

Thrupp, M. & Easter, A. (2012), *First Report: Researching schools' enactments of New Zealand's national standards policy*, Report commissioned by New Zealand Educational Institute Te Riu Roa: www.educationaotearoa.org.nz/storage/ea-magazine-files/2012/autumn/RAINS%20Final_2012-02-23.pdf

Tupuola, A-M. (2004), 'Pasifika edgewalkers: Complicating the achieved identity status in youth research', *Journal of Intercultural Studies*, 25(1), 87–100.

Wallace, L. (2003), *Sexual Encounters: Pacific texts, modern sexualities*, Ithaca, NY: Cornell University Press.

Wendt, A. (1999), 'Afterword: Tatauing the post-colonial body', in V. Hereniko & R. Wilson (eds), *Inside Out: literature, cultural politics, and identity in the new Pacific* (399–412), Maryland: Rowman & Littlefield.

Youdell, D. (2005), 'Sex–gender–sexuality: How sex, gender and sexuality constellations are constituted in secondary schools', *Gender and Education*, 17(3), 247–70.

Young, Audrey (12 November 2013), 'Govt eyes school lessons to stop rape', *New Zealand Herald*: www.nzherald.co.nz

# 9.
# Acknowledging and working double binds
The im/possible work of a high school
Queer–Straight Alliance

## Kathleen Quinlivan

In this chapter I explore the ways in which a high school Queer–Straight Alliance (QSA) negotiates the paradox of developing a queer curiosity within the normalising culture of a New Zealand high school. I begin by outlining the development and recent growth of the QSA model within New Zealand schools and communities. I argue that Derrida's (1992) notion of the double bind is helpful in both understanding and negotiating how a QSA can interrupt heteronormativity, finessing the often contradictory work they can undertake in schools. Following that I outline the methodology of the Tui High School case study that forms part of a broader research project exploring QSAs as sites of learning in New Zealand high schools. I use data from the case study to explore the ways in which both adults and students acknowledge and actively work the double binds that characterise the im/possible work of the QSA at Tui High School.

## The development of New Zealand Queer–Straight Alliances inside and outside schools

In the past decade in New Zealand cities and towns there has been an unprecedented explosion in the growth and development of community and school-based diversity groups increasingly known as QSAs. This development can be linked to the growing visibility of queer youth through the expansion of national queer community-based organisations, such as Rainbow Youth in Auckland; and local social and support networks for lesbian, gay, bi-sexual, transgender and queer (LGBTQ) youth, such as Q'topia in Christchurch. Most recently, Rainbow Youth has established a national queer youth network called Curious.[1]

---

1   See www.curious.org.nz

Adopted from the North American school-based Gay–Straight Alliance (GSA) model, which emerged as part of the Massachusetts Safe Schools Program in 1988, New Zealand QSAs are open to youth of all genders and sexualities; they tend to be of a less formal nature than their North American counterparts and occur within the broader community as well as schooling contexts (Quinlivan, Goulter & Caldwell 2010). Depending on the culture of the school and the philosophies of students and staff within the group, a school-based QSA can (often simultaneously) play paradoxical roles in engaging with the predominantly heteronormative culture of the school (Quinlivan 2013a). It can provide peer-supportive spaces for students who might otherwise feel socially isolated; and it can also operate proactively to destabilise normative constructions of sexuality, gender and difference (Mayo 2006; 2009; 2013; Quinlivan 2013b).[2] Such paradoxes can make the work QSAs undertake within schools challenging. Furthermore, the notion of queer youth as needing 'support' can be problematic in terms of re-pathologising LGBTQ students as 'abnormal' and 'at risk' in relation to the dominant heterosexual norm, and therefore as 'abject' and 'other' (Rasmussen, Rofes & Talburt 2004; Talburt & Rasmussen 2010; Youdell 2006; 2011). Some QSAs also undertake educational work aimed at developing and maintaining a queerer curiosity (Mayo 2009), allowing for an exploration of sexual and gendered subjectivities as more fluid and temporal for all students (Rasmussen et al. 2004). Working towards problematising the normalcy of heterosexuality while destabilising notions of sexual and gendered normalcies can provide an opportunity to keep open ways of thinking about gender and sexual difference that could benefit all students (Britzman & Gilbert 2004).

The paradoxical roles of QSAs – both providing support and working to unsettle heteronormativity – often sit together uncomfortably within schools (Mayo 2009; Quinlivan 2013a; 2013b). Given the historically normative nature of schooling contexts in relation to youth sexualities and difference, however, it seems inevitable that discourses of liberal inclusion and queer destabilisation will continue to co-exist (DePalma & Atkinson 2009; Nairn & Smith 2003; Quinlivan 2013a; 2013b). I argue that the uneasy (but not always unproductive) tension between the two ways of understanding issues of sexual and gender diversity need to be more fully acknowledged and understood, in order that queer pedagogical work can be

---

2   Although, as Elliott (2012) and Sykes (2011) note, the operation of some QSAs can privilege normative white middle-class sexualities.

more thoughtfully – perhaps even productively – 'worked' in schools (Nairn & Smith 2003; Quinlivan 2013b). Other educationalists disagree, viewing as less than ideal the tendency for queer research on youth sexualities in schools to be underpinned by liberal models of inclusion (Rasmussen 2010; Talburt 2009; Talburt & Rasmussen 2010). Drawing on the work of Edelman (2004), these educationalists query the extent to which notions of social transformation centring on the child can eliminate the marginalisation of sexuality and gender expression. This is especially the case, Talburt (2009) argues, given the role that the state and its institutions play in regulating becoming, pleasure and desire for youth.

Rather than choosing one approach, I suggest we need to explore the productive possibilities of liberal notions of inclusion, queerer modes of curiosity and normative destabilisation operating together. Such an approach acknowledges that tensions will inevitably exist between strategies for engaging with issues such as sexual diversity. Derrida (1992) openly recognises such tensions and their possibilities in his notion of the 'double bind' or 'aporia'.

## Acknowledging and working double binds

Developed in the context of theorising identity and concerns about racism and nationalism, Derrida's (1992) notion of aporia was his response to the tension between paying attention to the valuing of difference while also valuing the laws of agreement about difference that demand universality. The notion challenges simple concepts of resolvability and singular responses. It recognises the double-edged and contradictory nature in which divergent responsibilities can create tensions when engaging with difference. Rather than simplifying such dilemmas, Derrida argues for recognising and embracing the mutually implicated double binds or aporias that emerge when such contradictions arise. Moving away from common-sense understandings and easy consensus, Derrida suggests that acknowledging the impossibilities of engaging with difference is crucial to what we see as being possible (Egea-Kuene 2001). Developing a sensitivity to the ways in which double binds in education underlie the work of QSAs in schools is important in calling into question taken-for-granted assumptions and actions about difference and their consequences (Allen 2008), and when considering educational ethics (Edgoose 2001).

In undertaking queer research in schools, I have found Derrida's (1992) concept of the double bind useful in understanding the tensions that can emerge between discourses of liberal recognition and queer destabilisation (DePalma and Atkinson 2009; Nairn & Smith 2003; Quinlivan 2013a; Talburt & Rasmussen 2010; Youdell 2009). Explicating the intertwined ways in which often contradictory discourses of liberal recognition and queerer notions of destabilisation operate within schools can provide an opportunity to more thoughtfully acknowledge, understand, and even productively negotiate these paradoxes. In this chapter I show the ways in which these mutually intertwined discourses underlie the im/possible work of the QSA at Tui High School, and consider the affordances and the challenges of how the staff and students engage with them.

## Methodology

The Tui High School case study is part of a wider research project funded by the New Zealand AIDS Foundation and the University of Canterbury. The broader project documents case studies of QSAs as sites of learning across a range of New Zealand secondary schools and community contexts (Quinlivan et al. 2010). An ethnographic case study methodology recognises and accounts for the extent to which QSAs have developed idiosyncratically in response to the range of different school cultures and community contexts in which they are situated.

Tui High School is a co-educational decile 6 high school[3] located in the suburbs of a New Zealand provincial centre. In terms of ethnicities, 78 per cent of the student roll are Pākehā (New Zealand European), 15 per cent Māori, 1 per cent Pasifika and 6 per cent were described as 'other'. Tui High School is strong in its arts programmes, particularly the performing arts, a fact noted by both the students and teachers I interviewed. Historically the school has a well-established and robust student-led tradition, and a social justice orientation. The school's QSA has been in existence for 11 years and is therefore well established. Since its inception, many school-based QSAs have subsequently been established in the area. A dedicated student-run drop-in centre in the town supports and networks the efforts of the local school-based QSAs, and provides a venue where members get together to socialise and plan joint events and activities.

---

3   In New Zealand, schools are ranked into deciles 1 to 10 according to the socioeconomic status of the community from which the children are drawn, with 1 being the lowest. Tui High School is placed in the middle of the scale.

Between 15 and 20 students aged 13–17 regularly attend Tui High School's QSA. In 2010 qualitative, semi-structured, face-to-face, individual and group interviews were recorded with 13 student members of the group. In order to gather more data related to particular findings, a second follow-up Skype interview was undertaken with two of the students in 2012 (Quinlivan 2014). The majority of students preferred to use temporal personal qualities such as 'nomad', 'passionate' and 'arty' rather than 'identity labels', to describe themselves. Several of the students chose not to define their sexualities or genders; six described themselves as female and two as male students.

Preliminary face-to-face interviews were also undertaken and recorded with the school's (male) principal and (female) guidance counsellor. A (male) social worker who worked with queer youth from various local schools in the wider community was also interviewed. I undertook participant observations and wrote fieldnotes in a range of sites across the school and in the wider queer youth community context. Informed consent was gained from the participants in the case study and pseudonyms have been used to protect the confidentiality of the participants and the school. Where possible I gained feedback from several participants on the analysis of the project's findings. The excerpts below are from the following: Jack, 51 years, principal; Sarah, 50 years, school counsellor; Lucy, Clark, Adam, Jeff and Rose, members of the QSA at Tui High School. Clark, Adam and Rose were 18 at the time they were interviewed, and Jeff was 15. Lucy was interviewed twice, once in 2010 when she was 16 and again in 2012 when she was 18.

## Acknowledging and working the double binds: Reinscribing and challenging deficit discourses

The QSA students and the staff acknowledge and, to some extent, 'work' the inevitable double binds that characterise their work at Tui High School. As previously explained, one of these is the inescapability of drawing on deficit constructions of queer youth as a rationale for the QSA's work (DePalma & Atkinson 2009; Nairn & Smith 2003; Quinlivan 2013a; Talburt & Rasmussen 2010; Youdell 2009). Comments from Tui High School's principal, Jack, illustrate this bind. His statement frames young people who do not conform to heteronormative understandings of sexuality as in need of the support that the school's QSA offers them:

> [For] the young people ... that go through questioning their sexuality ... it's really difficult ... they see themselves outside the norm and ... they

*can't understand why they are feeling this way and all sorts of things ... I think from that perspective it's really important that they get this support and that ... there is a place here for them.*

While providing a supportive environment for students is important, it also runs the risk (perhaps inevitably) of reinscribing deficit understandings of queer youth. For those attending the group, however, it is important to remember that such double binds can also be re-worked. Although on the one hand Jack reiterated deficit discourses, in conversation with me it became clear that he also recognised and actively worked this double bind. He re-framed meeting the social and emotional needs of students as a priority that schools need to address, and challenged all schools to show the ways in which they are caring for their students:

*The QSA is having quite a ... prominent profile. [Some elements] of our community ... say ... don't send all your kids to Tui High School because they are all gay ... [In terms of] the marketing of the school ... we need to think carefully about that. But we would not step away from supporting things like [the QSA] and that's because we see it as important. I'd say it's not my problem actually, it's yours at the moment ... I'd say ... well, we are just looking after our students in our school as we see fit and appropriate ... you should be thinking about what you are doing.*

The school counsellor, Sarah, also acknowledged the extent to which the QSA could be seen to reinforce deficit assumptions about queer sexualities. However, she strongly asserted that because the QSA is an alliance between students of diverse sexualities, it avoids the support-group label. Sarah suggested that as a student-led group the QSA sets its own agenda; counselling support, which can be gained elsewhere, is not part of the group's role:

*Yeah, you are fighting against the 'problem' [the deficit label] ... [But] I think that diversity groups can [fight] that if they are an alliance. [The QSA] builds an alliance between gays and straights ... That's the key of diversity groups ... it's to be a gay–straight alliance, not a support group. The whole philosophy is just ... poles apart ... a support group [would] have to have a teacher that was running them and looking after them ... No, we don't want that. We won't have that here ... and kids can access their support, like I see so many, they don't access it through the QSA, they access it where they need to.*

As the QSA is student-led, the QSA students believe it challenges any notions that members of the group are somehow in need of support. Lucy, a QSA leader, emphasised the extent to which the student-driven culture of the group provided a space for acceptance of difference and self-expression, a willingness to listen, and openness to peer suggestions for group activities:

> *Yeah, it definitely makes it more interesting rather than going, say, in other school groups ... [where] people just sit and talk and often they're controlled by ... adults and things. It's an environment where everyone can be who they are and express themselves how they want ... and everyone's welcome to bring ideas in (Lucy, 2010).*

Rather than frame members of the QSA as having a deficit, Lucy emphasised the ways in which participation in the group encouraged the development of personal confidence and leadership skills, both for her peers and herself:

> *... you see people grow. I came along to the group with a few friends and was a bit intimidated at first, but I kept going back and then the next year when I was a senior student I felt a bit more included and was able to get more involved with the practical stuff. I think I just kept on getting more and more empowered and excited by it all. I became a leader and I was part of setting up [the coalition of school-based QSAs in town], and now I am setting up QSA Network Aotearoa, so I did just keep on growing and getting more and more inspired and getting more ideas about how we could make things better (Lucy, 2012).*

In this section I have shown the ways in which a double bind characterises the work of the QSA at Tui High School. It appears that drawing on deficit constructions of queer youth has a certain inescapability. At the same time, however, the aporia can be seen as productive, since deficit constructions of queer youth are challenged by principals, counsellors and students alike.

Lucy's comments draw attention to developing students' personal skills as well as to the social justice orientation of the QSA at Tui High School. Next I explore this and other roles that the QSA played within the school.

## Productive double binds: The social justice and support roles of the QSA

As indicated earlier, educationalists have critiqued the ways in which research in schools, which describes itself as queer, often problematically reinforces queer youth as deficit, and in the process reproduces heteronormalcy (Talburt 2009; Talburt & Rasmussen 2010). It could be considered that the political and support roles that QSAs often play are illustrative of tensions between queer political activism and a more liberal approach to inclusion, which can fail to problematise heteronormativity (Mayo 2006; 2009; 2013; Quinlivan 2013b). However, I suggest that such critiques have the unfortunate effect of reinforcing a polarising liberal/queer, either/or binary, which fails to do justice to the complexities of working against heteronormativity within the pervasively normalising cultures of most schools. This is particularly unhelpful when it comes to considering what it might mean for QSAs to undertake work to widen understandings of sexuality, gender and difference within schools (Quinlivan 2013a). In talking with students and staff involved with the QSA at Tui High School, it became apparent that the group played multiple roles within the school, often simultaneously and complementarily. On the one hand the group organised a raft of activities to challenge the politics of heteronormativity as a social justice issue; on the other, in undertaking this work, it provided a supportive context for students.

Several of the students saw that the QSA played an important political role in educating people about discrimination and its effects. Rose emphasised the educational role the group played in challenging prejudice, and the way in which the QSA's influence had spread to other schools in the town:

> [The QSA model] is ... spreading elsewhere which is raising more awareness [and providing] ... education and support, which is really good ... I've seen so many horrible things happen because of people who don't understand ... and ... I think it's really important that ... people are educated ... and stop being prejudiced, and discriminating and ... abusing people. I think it's just really unfair to be judged for who they are and treated differently so ... that's why I think it's really important that people understand.

Many other students I spoke to emphasised the importance of the support role that the QSA provided, stressing the significance of an accepting environment that is less constrained than the largely heteronormative cultures of their peers. Clark explained that the QSA played an important role in enabling him to accept himself and experience the support of friends:

> *[The QSA] is really cool because it ... is a place in school where you can be yourself. You don't have to hide ... who you really are. And ... most of the other people who are there are in the same boat so they know what you are going through ... most of them have been through what I've been through as well ... So it's a good place just to talk, make friends, where you can fit in.*

Enabling young people to feel accepted and valued for themselves is not to be underestimated and, when combined with social justice orientations, need not perpetuate deficit constructions of queer youth. In addition, it seems important to note that the needs, views and desires of the students themselves can shift and change over time. Clark emphasises how participation in the group has enabled him to develop his own confidence and recognise the need to work for social change more widely:

> *[The QSA] has helped me to open myself out – like I am so much more open with myself now ... and it's just ... like I was saying before with going and having that place where you can say what you want to say and not being judged ... In [the QSA] I wanted to help more than just people in the school. I want it to go out further into the world so it can just open up other people's lives and make them feel comfortable with who they are.*

Despite my own framing of support and political action as two separate roles, the group's leader Lucy firmly reiterated the need to understand these functions of the QSA as complementary and intertwined:

Kathleen: *So you know how [the QSA] seems to operate in terms of both support and kind of politically, which is the one of those that appeals to you the most?*

Lucy: *Yeah, both, definitely, kind of ... I think they come together ... if you've got the group to support people well that's all very well, but if you're not doing anything to actually try and stop the problem that it's taking the need to support, and, I don't know, you're not really fulfilling your support purpose in a way and ... I think they come together very well (Lucy, 2010).*

Rather than framing the support and social justice roles of the QSA as an either/or double bind, these data speak to the interconnected and productive ways in which the paradoxes of the two roles can be productively 'worked' within a school.

While the multiple activities of the QSA within Tui High School were impressive (Quinlivan, in press), it is also important to recognise that some of the students had different views about the roles of the group. Next, I explore the nature of these challenges.

## Productive dissensus: Negotiating double binds within the QSA

In many ways the hopes and dreams of the QSA students and the staff who support them at Tui High School resonate with Jose Esteban Munoz's (2009) notion of a queer utopia as an educated hope – the dreams of an emergent group dwelling in the region of a critically hopeful 'not yet'. Both in terms of social justice and support, they are working beyond the heteronormative here and now towards a vision of a world that accepts and values difference. In moving towards such anticipatory spaces of hope, Munoz helpfully reminds us that hopes can (and will perhaps inevitably) disappoint, but that such disappointment needs to be risked. I suggest that part of risking disappointment involves an openness towards recognising and engaging with dissensus. The QSA student members and associated staff all acknowledged they often had different opinions about the direction of the QSA; in some cases its modus operandi was not embraced with equal enthusiasm by all.

The strength of visual and performing arts programmes at Tui High School provided a context within which QSA members explored forms of expression that challenged the heteronormativity of the here and now, and enabled pleasurable and astonishing glimpses of a queer futurity (Munoz 2009). Educationalists also note the extent to which aesthetic expression can engender subjective and social reconstruction through providing an affective and relational educational space, within which young people can challenge social norms and re-vision themselves and their worlds (Greene 2001; Hickey-Moody 2012; Verner-Chappell 2010). Jeff, a 15-year-old QSA member, captured the pleasure and beauty of the activist aesthetics that characterised many of the group's events, describing the QSA as 'butterflies starting a tornado'.

Lucy also suggested that aesthetic expressions group members engaged in at school, such as theatre, could provide expansive and generative spaces for re-thinking social and cultural norms:

> [A]t Tui High School we've got a really good arts and drama department ... self-expression and creativity ... it's a good way to ... make people think about things in ways they haven't before ... I think that's the big part of theatre anyway ... that speaks to people so much more than being told (Lucy, 2010).

Over the course of the conversations I had with a range of group members, however, concerns emerged about the efficacy of the aesthetic theatrics used by the QSA to get their messages across. In particular, students queried the extent to which such approaches perpetuated narrow stereotypical representations of queerness and ran the risk of trivialising what they understood to be serious social justice issues. Perhaps this suggests that framing and engaging in dissensus, as I advocated earlier, can be a challenging prospect. The possibilities for acceptance and inclusion within liberal rights mandates, valued by Rose and Adam, appear to be compromised by what they perceived as narrow, stereotyped and frivolous depictions of sexual difference signified by the activities of the QSA:

> [I]f ... you want acceptance ... and you want to try to get people thinking that [not] everyone, like all gay people, fall under a certain stereotype for example, then following that stereotype isn't going to help. It's just going to make people think all gay people are like that. If you flaunt that ... (Rose).

> ... I think the whole point of the whole queer [project] is to fit in with society. I just feel that, the hula-hooping and the ... dancing ... it's just distancing us like, more and more away from [that] ... (Adam).

For Rose and Adam, there appears to be a clash between the provocative 'in your face' 'camp' activist aesthetics of the QSA such as hula-hooping, which were undertaken with the intention to challenge and destabilise heteronormativity, and the liberal demands for equality that Rose and Adam value. While other members of the QSA may disagree, Rose felt that the QSA's playful performative activist theatrics may detract from what she saw as the more serious messages that the QSA would wish to promote:

> [I]f we just do something that's so outrageous then people are going to just see it as outrageous and probably won't look into why we're doing it. Like ... with the hula-hooping thing, like it's fun and it's ... for a good cause, but ... people are just gonna see people hula-hooping and they're not gonna consider issues with that. So I think it needs to be more ... educational activities.

Other views about the pros and cons of the membership and directions of the QSA also emerged over the course of the interviews with students. Several expressed concern about the lack of racial diversity among group members, and the messages this sent about the group. One member, Jessica, drew my attention to the fact that the QSA was primarily attended by Pākehā students, which had the problematic effect of equating queerness with white homo-normative privilege (Elliott 2012; Kumashiro 2001; Mayo 2009; 2013; Sykes 2011). She noted the group was aware of the issue and was considering how to address it.

The tension between radical activist aesthetics and liberal demands for inclusion that the QSA members drew my attention to – the extent to which the group could address issues of race as well as sexuality and gender – provides an illustration of Derrida's (1992) notion of the double bind. Such dilemmas, Derrida suggests, will inevitably arise as a matter of course in such situations. Rather than see such aporias as dilemmas to be hidden, ignored or glossed over, Derrida suggests that they be anticipated, accepted and engaged with openly as a matter of course. What I found encouraging and very hopeful as I spoke to the students about their work, and in their feedback on this chapter, was their openness to acknowledge and explore the inevitable double binds that characterised their work, and their willingness to acknowledge the tensions they faced. Recognising that double binds will inevitably characterise the work of engaging with difference not only acknowledges the complex nature of the work; it also has the potential to frame dissensus as a productive opportunity rather than a failure or an obstacle to be overcome.

Participation in the research project provided an opportunity to openly acknowledge and discuss the challenges members of the QSA faced in their work. In this way dissensus was framed as productive and generative space for the students (and associated staff), rather than a limitation. In some cases the discussion led to the recognition that student leaders would bring differing strengths and enthusiasms to their work within the QSA; as the leadership changed on a yearly basis, the focus would also change. Given the shifting membership of the QSA, it is inevitable that the group will develop organically over time to reflect the aspirations of its members, who will continue to discuss and debate the pros and cons of the QSA's multiple roles within their school.

## Conclusion

In this chapter I have explored the affordances of Derrida's (1992) notion of the double bind in order to understand and engage more with the complex work undertaken by the QSA at Tui High School. Drawing on student and staff data generated within a school-based case study, I have argued that open acknowledgement of the ways the group will often be pulled in contradictory and competing directions holds the potential to enable such challenges to be more carefully and thoughtfully negotiated. Both the principal and the counsellor at Tui High School showed how they simultaneously utilised and challenged deficit discourses in staking a claim for the work of the QSA within the school. Student members of group provided examples of how they moved beyond polarising binaries that pit queer activism against liberal notions of inclusion. They explained how they juggled the often-contradictory demands of social justice and support, suggesting that it may be helpful to frame these as complementary rather than oppositional. Finally, the students and the staff actively demonstrated the value of productive dissensus. They acknowledged the tensions between radical activist aesthetics and liberal approaches to inclusion, and also considered intersections of the politics of race, sexualities and genders.

Rather than viewing tensions as failures and limitations, Derrida's notion of the double bind challenges us to consider paradoxes and contradictions more as important opportunities for critical engagement and problem-solving. The work of the QSA members, and the staff who support them in challenging heteronormativity within Tui High School, provides a powerful site of learning: it demonstrates that students can make a difference within their school and the wider community. The group also provides a context within which the students can critically consider the affordances and possibilities that inform their initiatives and, in the process, become better equipped to more thoughtfully negotiate and 'work' the inevitable challenges they will face.

## References

Allan, J. (2008), *Re-thinking Inclusion: Philosophers of difference in practice*, Dordrecht: Springer.

Britzman, D. & Gilbert, J. (2004), 'What will have been said about gayness in teacher education?', *Teaching Education*, 15(3), 81–96.

DePalma, R. and Atkinson, E. (2009), 'Outing queer into practice: Problems and possibilities', in R. DePalma and E. Atkinson (eds), *Interrogating Heteronormativity* (1–6), Stoke on Trent: Trentham.

Derrida, J. (1992), 'Force of law: The mystical foundations of authority', (M. Quaintance, trans.), in D. Cornell, M. Rosenfield and D. Carlson (eds) *Deconstruction and the Possibility of Justice* (3–67). New York: Routledge.

Edelman, L. (2004), *No Future: Queer theory and the death drive*, Durham, NC: Duke University Press.

Edgoose, J. (2001), 'Just decide: Derrida and the ethical aporias of education', in G. Biesta & D. Egea-Kuehne (eds), *Derrida and Education* (119–33), London: Routledge.

Egea-Kuehne, D. (2001), 'Derrida's ethics of affirmation: The challenge of educational rights and responsibility', in G. Biesta & D. Egea-Kuehne (eds), *Derrida and Education*, (186–208), London: Routledge.

Elliott, K. (2012), 'The right way to be gay: How schools structure sexual inequality', in E. Meiners & T. Quinn (eds), *Sexualities in Education: A reader* (158–66), New York: Peter Lang.

Greene, M. (2001), *Variations on a Blue Guitar. The Lincoln Center Institute Lectures on Aesthetic Education*, New York: Teachers College Press.

Hickey-Moody, A.C. (2012), *Youth, Arts and Education: Reassembling subjectivity through affect*, London: Routledge.

Kumashiro, K. (2001), 'Queer students of color and anti-racist, antiheterosexist education: Paradoxes of identity and activism', in K. Kumashiro (ed.), *Troubling Intersections of Race and Sexuality: Queer students of color and anti-oppressive education* (1–25), Lanham: Rowman & Littlefield.

Mayo, C. (2006), 'Pushing the limits of liberalism: Queerness, children and the future', *Educational Theory*, 56(4), 469–87.

Mayo, C. (2009), 'Access and obstacles: Gay–straight alliances attempt to alter school communities', in W. Ayers, T. Quinn and D. Stovall (eds), *Handbook of Social Justice in Education* (319–31), New York: Routledge.

Mayo, J.B. (2013), 'Critical pedagogy enacted in the gay–straight alliance: New possibilities for a third space in teacher development', *Educational Researcher*, 42(5), 266–75.

Munoz, J.E. (2009), *Cruising Utopia: The then and there of queer futurity*, New York: New York University Press.

Nairn, K. & Smith, A. (2003), 'Taking students seriously: Their rights to be safe at school', *Gender and Education*, 15(2), 133–49.

Quinlivan, K. (2013a), 'The methodological im/possibilities of researching sexuality education in schools: Working queer conundrums', *Sex Education: Sexuality, society and learning*, 13(1), 556–69.

Quinlivan, K. (2013b), 'Disrupting heteronormativity: A high-school queer–straight alliance?', in N. Higgins & C. Freeman (eds), *Childhoods: Growing up in Aotearoa New Zealand* (249–61), Dunedin: Otago University Press.

Quinlivan, K. (2014).'"Butterflies starting a tornado": The queer "not yet" of a New Zealand school-based queer straight alliance as a utopic site of learning', in E. Meyer and D. Carlson (eds), (272–83), *Handbook of Sexualities Education*, New York: Peter Lang.

Quinlivan, K., Goulter, M. & Caldwell, F. (2010), *Diversity Groups as Sites of Learning in New Zealand School and Community Contexts*, Auckland: New Zealand AIDS Foundation.

Rasmussen, M.L. (2010), 'No Outsiders and "the eternal sunshine of the spotless child"', *Journal of LGBT Youth*, 8, 210–14.

Rasmussen, M.L., Rofes, E. & Talburt, S. (2004), 'Introduction', in M.L. Rasmussen, E. Rofes and S.Talburt (eds), *Youth and Sexualities: Pleasure, subversion and insubordination in and out of schools* (17–39), New York: Palgrave MacMillan.

Sykes, H. (2011), 'Hetero- and homo-normativity: Critical literacy, citizenship education and queer theory', *Curriculum Inquiry*, 41(4), 419–32.

Talburt, S. (2009), 'Toys, pleasure and the future', in R. DePalma and E. Atkinson (eds),

*Interrogating Heteronormativity*, (85–94), Stoke on Trent: Trentham.
Talburt, S. (1999), 'Open secrets and problems of queer ethnography: Readings from a religious studies classroom', *International Journal of Qualitative Studies in Education*, 12(5), 525–39.
Talburt, S. and Rasmussen, M. (2010), '"After queer" tendencies in queer research', *International Journal of Qualitative Studies in Education*, 23(1), 1–14.
Verner-Chappell, S. (2010), 'Young people talk back: Community arts as a public pedagogy of social justice', in J. Sandlin, B. Schutz & J. Burdick (eds), *Handbook of Public Pedagogy: Education and learning beyond schooling* (318–26), New York: Routledge.
Youdell, D. (2006), *Impossible Bodies, Impossible Selves: Exclusions and student subjectivities*, Dordrecht: Springer.
Youdell, D. (2009), 'Lessons in praxis: Thinking about knowledge, subjectivity and politics in education', in R. DePalma & E. Atkinson (eds), *Interrogating Heteronormativity* (35–49), Stoke on Trent: Trentham.
Youdell, D. (2011), *School Trouble: Identity, power and politics in education*, New York: Routledge.

# 10.
# (Trans)gender diversity, cisnormativity and New Zealand education cultures

A dialogue

James Burford, Joey MacDonald, Sam Orchard
& Philip Wills

**Chorus:** Who are we? We are a collective of kin-by-choice, passionately entangled with trans*[1] and gender-diverse communities in Aotearoa/New Zealand. Collectively, we have known each other since 2010, although some among us have known each other longer. We became connected by the kinds of weavings that bring queer communities together in small cities like Ōtepoti–Dunedin. Between us is a richness of experience, including: lives and activisms that contend with systems of class, race, colonisation and gender; queer/trans* youth and community work; diversity practice within higher education and mental health sectors; queer/trans* cultural production; trans* community leadership and governance; three Master's degrees concerned with experiences of sexual and gender diversity (Burford 2010; MacDonald 2012; Orchard 2011); as well as important encounters with being taught to teach, being teachers, and being taught.

We are writing this chapter in order to contribute to a much-needed conversation between trans* and gender-diverse community, and education stakeholders in New Zealand. Our intention is critical-activist, and we seek a mix of outcomes from our writing. In the first case, we hope to call stakeholders to consider the ways that normative education cultures reproduce unsafe environments and unsatisfactory outcomes for too many trans* students, teachers and family/whānau members. We hope to challenge researchers in particular to consider trans* experiences of education to be not only a worthwhile research interest, but one that merits urgent

---

1   Trans* is a signifier for a number of distinct, yet connected non-normative gender identities. Using the * at the end of 'trans' reminds us that a number of words might follow it (such as feminine, masculine, gender or sexual). We expand upon this further in later sections of this chapter.

consideration. Coupled with our desire to critique is a desire to contribute to the positive transformation of New Zealand's education cultures. To that end, we offer resources (both conceptual and practical), which might provide some helpful points for realising change.

In this collection about educational cultures in New Zealand, we wish to acknowledge the continuity of the oldest educational cultures in this place: Māori ways of being and knowing. As a part of honouring this, we want to greet our elders, indigenous and immigrant, especially those who have struggled to keep alive possibilities of sexual and gender diversity. We welcome you. We also greet the members of our communities who have shaped our thinking and been present for the many discussions that led to, and sustained, this project. Thank you, and welcome.

As writers in this dialogue, we do not claim to be representative of trans* and gender-diverse communities in New Zealand. Our words emerge from our femme, queer, genderqueer, transman, Māori and Pākehā[2] bodies, and the various political investments these positions orient us toward. They do not come from intersex bodies, or working-class bodies, as well as any number of other positions of social disadvantage. In initiating this conversation with education stakeholders, we simultaneously call for more engagement with diverse trans* perspectives on education in New Zealand. Before we begin, we have something to say about how we have written and represented this chapter.

*We struggled.*

It wasn't that we had nothing to say – far from it. Rather, *we couldn't agree on what to write, and how it should be written – and we didn't want to have to agree in order to speak in one voice.* In response to this dilemma, we chose to write a dialogue. In so doing we hope to disengage ourselves from normative logics of academic representation and their focus on coherence and linearity. We have patched together unruly fragments, allowing our voices to be sometimes harmonious, and other times jangling in disagreement. At all times, however, we are connected. Our text itself emerged from an extended series of conversations via videoconference and email, that took place from mid-2012 until early 2014. Our discussions happened in fits and starts – sometimes gaining momentum, and other times ebbing as alternative

---

2   A Māori language word for New Zealanders of European descent.

commitments took precedence. At the end of this time-period we brought our pieces of text into one conversation.

While we envisaged this conversation as being one we primarily have among ourselves, we occasionally address 'you', the reader, to acknowledge your proximity to this exchange, and to call on your response. This chapter will raise more questions than we can answer. We hope readers find our provocations, as well as the tools we share, useful for their own practices.

## Animating affects

*Jamie*: Of all the conversations we had during this project, it feels like two of the most frequent were *why* we are writing, and how we *feel* about it. I recall that we initially positioned ourselves as undertaking an 'intervention', which might address the seeming marginalisation of trans* and gender-diverse people in LGBT[3] education research in New Zealand. As the chapter has progressed our motives appear to have become more nuanced, seeking not only a call for accountability, but to proliferate some helpful resources for education stakeholders to use. The ways we have positioned ourselves in relation to this project seem to have been animated by a number of different feelings. Sam, I think you were the first to identify two of those: desperation and rage.

*Sam*: Yeah, I did feel pretty desperate about writing this chapter. This feeling emerged from my context of years of voluntary and professional work as a queer and trans* community worker and mental health advocate, as well as years of being embroiled in higher education. I jumped at this project because I felt desperate about the need for trans-positive change in education cultures. I saw the possibilities of chapters like this to influence education practice. But I also felt desperate *not* to be pulled into yet another exhausting project that would ask for my patience and generosity. The more I thought about this piece, the more conflicted it felt. Writing like this is sticky and difficult work – and perhaps that's why few people have done it.

---

3   Increasingly, education researchers and policy-makers have adopted acronyms like 'LGBT' in order to attempt to speak more inclusively about queer and trans* communities. However, I think it is important to ask questions about the effects of such terminology. Trans* scholar Dean Spade (e.g. Spade 2004) has coined the term LGBfakeT to acknowledge the ways that trans* perspectives are often conflated with, and then subsumed by, gay, lesbian and bisexual accounts.

In writing I have also felt rage. *Do we have to constantly explain how painful it is to be excluded?* My desperation about the failure of allies (including many gays and lesbians) to stand alongside us and/or create space for trans* participation, often turns into fury. I manage to work with these feelings in the hope that connecting with readers might create the transformative change we desperately need.

*Philip*: When you first suggested writing this, Jamie, I was missing the beautiful queer community we had formed in Dunedin. I was taking post-grad education papers and was desperately lonely intellectually, and especially for the company of other bravely gendered people. Adrienne Rich (1986) describes the vertigo of looking in the mirror of your culture and not seeing yourself there. I experienced this at university. I read studies that addressed the needs and experiences of men *and* women, girls *and* boys, but, in my classes at least, there was silence about people who complicate these categories. I appreciated, deeply, the work that Māori scholars had done and were doing to make space for our history and our realities as Māori students; sadly, this space did not extend to the diversity of our sexual or gendered selves. Speaking into this void was ultimately too difficult and I dropped out of university soon after we began this project. I was really excited, gleeful even, about the possibility of showing up in an academic context – in this chapter – with a *team*. I wanted to say: 'See! Look! I make sense. I exist, to these people, I am real.' Also, I really wanted an excuse to talk more with you three, Jamie, Sam and Joe. I wanted to share my sense of our friendship as a fertile intellectual space, a setting where I have learned some of the most important lessons about how to live in this world as a trans* person.

*Joe*: Like Philip, I wanted to engage with my kin. I saw that the four of us writing in solidarity might heal some of the wounds inflicted by my own participation in the education system. I also connect with Sam's image of 'pushing shit up a hill' – this is the feeling I have sometimes, as a person heavily invested in queer and trans* advocacy. It's the feeling I notice when I am facilitating a workshop and yet another person looks me up and down and enquires, with great relish: 'So, what surgeries have you had?'[4] I wanted to have an opportunity to reflect on the way I do not find myself participating wholly – bringing my whole self – in formal educational cultures, and to tie

---

4   For further discussion about trans micro-aggressions, see Nordmarken (2014).

this to the way these cultures fail to hold others accountable for their trans* negativity. As we have been talking I keep wanting to think about 'education in community' instead of schooling. Why? Because the former has proven more conducive for my learning, creativity and healing.

*Chorus*: Why we have published these reflections? Two reasons are clear to us. The first is that we wish to introduce ourselves, and gesture towards why this area of knowledge matters greatly to us. Our second intention in making our feelings visible is to put our feelings into practice. We have shared how we felt in the hope that it will *move* you, our reader. Perhaps our desperation for trans* perspectives to be in dialogue with education stakeholders will resonate with you, prompting you to stand in solidarity with us. It could be that our anger is catching. You might find yourself furious about the unsafe educational cultures that many trans* people negotiate, and implement the practical steps we introduce later. Maybe some combination of the optimism, thrill, love and compassion that has drawn us together and sustained us as we have written will linger with you, and inform your own practice. We invite you to locate the passions that this dialogue stirs in your own body, and to take them forward.

## Words …

*Jamie*: This section is about the words we use as we talk to and about the communities at the centre of this chapter. Rather than introduce these in a conventional sense, we would like instead to weave in a comic that Sam has illustrated (opposite), which can also act as a helpful resource for educators to use with their colleagues and students. Sam's comic illustrates the complexity, fluidity and political nature of terminology. Contemplating language that might group together all gender non-normative identities and expressions is a necessarily challenging and troubling enterprise. Within New Zealand community development practice, health and research we see a number of terms in circulation. A common one is trans*. As explained earlier, the asterisk serves as a placeholder for any words that might follow (e.g. masculine, or gender). Trans* may also be used to speak about identities that do not start with the prefix 'trans' but are spoken about within a trans* 'umbrella' (such as genderqueer or non-binary). However, alternative composite terms are in circulation in New Zealand, such as 'gender diverse' (Burford, Lucassen, Penniket & Hamilton 2013) and 'transgender' (Clark et al. 2014).

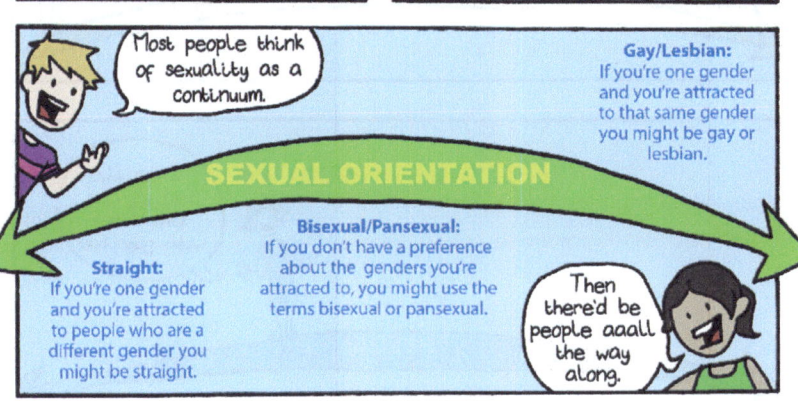

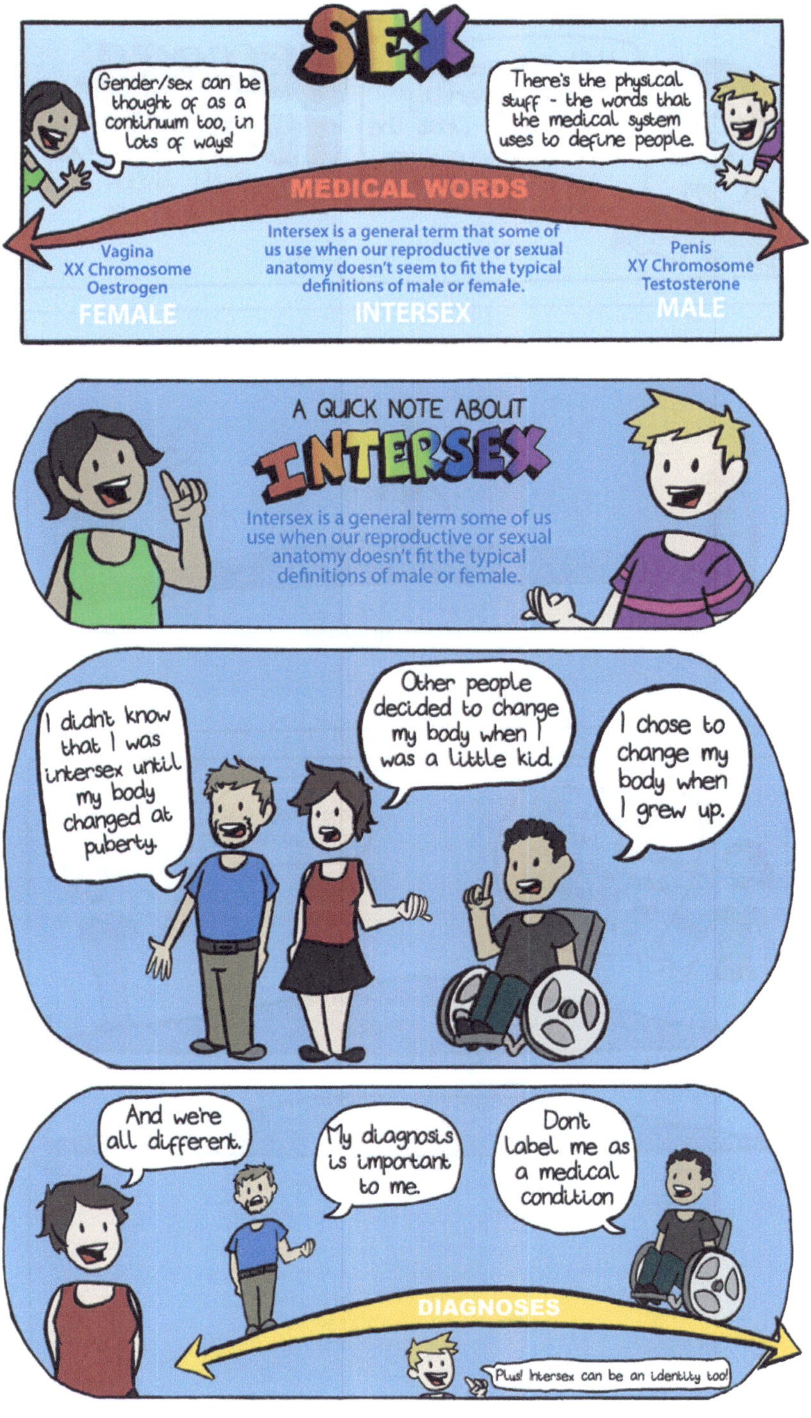

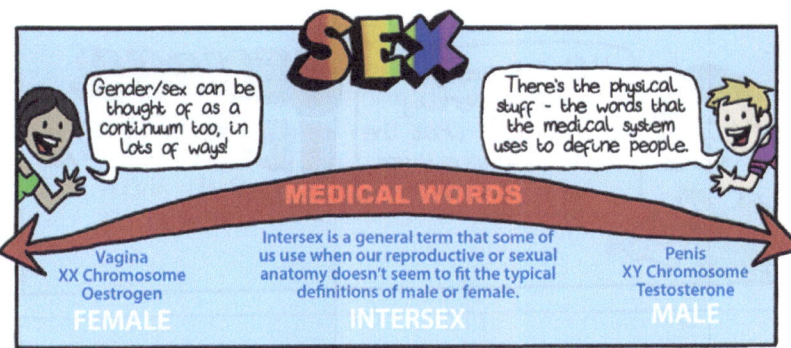

### Woman
People down this end might use words like 'girl', 'woman', 'lady' or 'sister'.

For most people down this end you would use pronouns like 'She' or 'Her'.

### Gender Queer/Androgynous Bigendered or Non-Gendered

People here may use words like Gender Queer, Androgynous, Bigendered or Non-gendered. This might be because:
- They feel like neither a man nor a woman,
- They identify as both, or
- Their gender identity is fluid and changes.

Use gender-neutral words like 'person'. Ask people what pronoun they prefer and be aware it may change. Some people prefer 'he' or 'she' while others may ask you to use 'they' or new pronouns like 'Zhe' or 'Hir'.

### Man
People down this end might use words like 'boy', 'man', 'bro' or 'dude'.

For most people down this end you would use pronouns like 'He' or 'His'.

Transgender and transsexual people can be found at all parts of this continuum

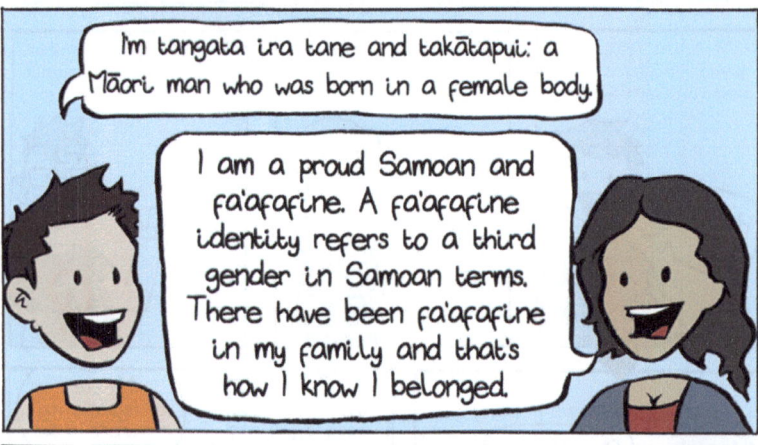

Words and pictures by Sam Orchard. Copyright 2015. www.roostertailcomic.com

*Joe*: Another key term we wish to introduce to this chapter is 'cisgender' (Baril & Trevenen 2014; Serano 2007). This term can be contrasted with transgender.[5] The simplest explanation of these concepts is that trans* people's gender identity is not congruent with the sex we were assigned at birth (male or female, since these are the only two options available for birth certificates in New Zealand). A cisgender person, in contrast, is someone who *does* experience congruence with the sex they were assigned at birth. For example, if someone is assigned female at birth and identifies as a woman, that person might be described as cisgender. Cisgender is a helpful concept because it lets us talk about the particularity of being a person whose assigned sex is congruent with their gender identity. It avoids the notion of 'normal gender' and makes cisgender experience visible, meaning it ceases to be an invisible norm against which 'those weird transgenders' are defined. Care is needed when using such words, however, as the borders between them are permeable. The risk at the individual level is that these terms might be used to police people's identities or experiences, to say who is 'really transgender' or who is 'really cisgender'. There will always be people who are both and neither, because trans* and cis, while useful concepts, cannot cover the complexity of gender identity and expression. One of the clear advantages of understanding the term cisgender is that we are then able to grasp the concept of cisnormativity. This moves us into discussions about wider systems of value, power and privilege on a structural level.

*Jamie*: Cisnormativity can help us to examine the social and institutional reproduction of cisgender privilege and transgender disadvantage. It is defined by Baril and Trevenen (2014) as 'the oppression experienced by transsexual and transgender people in a society that identifies and represents cisexual/cisgender people as dominant, normal and superior' (391). As a concept, cisnormativity takes up a similar analytic route to 'heteronormativity'. If heteronormativity is used to examine the ways in which heterosexuality is institutionally reproduced as normal, natural and highly valued, then cisnormativity can help us to trace the institutional

---

5   The origins of these terms stem from the Latin prefixes *trans*, meaning 'across from', and *cis*, meaning 'on the same side of'. The term cisexual/cisgender arose to prominence in Serano's (2007) *Whipping Girl* as a way of marking the norm of congruence between assigned sex and gender identity and expression. The use of the term 'cisgender' performs a similar function to the naming of 'heterosexuals', rather than leaving this as an unexpressed norm.

reproduction and high value attributed to cisgender embodiment and experience. We can use the concept of cisnormativity as a lens to examine how assumptions about gender embodiment and identity shape education practice, policy and research. I argue that education researchers, practitioners and policy makers who approach sex, sexuality and gender would benefit from using the concepts of heteronormativity and cisnormativity *together*. This will enable those informed by anti-heteronormative politics to consider as well the pervasive impacts of cisgender norms in education, and to discern ways of resisting these.

The concept of cisnormativity gives us greater analytic purchase than others in public circulation, like 'transphobia'. Transphobia is less helpful because it individualises a pattern of action, rendering it as an irrational fear located in some 'bad' or 'unenlightened' individuals – rather than something that is systemic. The use of transphobia has the effect of flattening the scope of analysis; it conceals the complex ways that trans* and gender non-normative people are continually decentred and devalued in society. Using cisnormativity allows stakeholders to explore alternative conjunctions of words, like 'institutionalised cisnormativity', for example. Re-positioning the injustices perpetuated upon trans* people as institutional recognises that communities like schools and universities need to take responsibility for the overt and subtle ways they reproduce transgender disadvantage. This must not mean that individuals get off the hook over their (in)actions that contribute to unsafe educational cultures in this country, as if *only* the institution is responsible, and not the people within it (Ahmed 2012). Instead, we need to deploy cisnormative critique in such a way that we can hold individuals, institutions and communities accountable.

*Philip*: I want to pause here. When we talk about words, we cannot forget about the colonisation of Aotearoa. Along with everything else, colonisation has been a process of imposing European norms of gender and sexuality. This has been documented in relation to sexuality (Aspin 2013) and to the social roles and status available to wāhine Māori[6] (Mikaere 2003). Without delving into the question of how my tūpuna Māori[7] may have expressed

---

6   'Wāhine Māori' can be translated as 'Māori women'; my intention in not translating it is to indicate the possibility that what it means to be a Māori 'woman' is not reducible to what can be known through the English language, or through a European conceptual frame.
7   'Tūpuna Māori' can be translated as 'Māori ancestors'.

their genders, it is becoming clear to me that I cannot assume the system of gender they lived with was binary, static or patriarchal.[8]

I want not only to challenge the dominant gender system; I want to acknowledge, strengthen and protect the gender system indigenous to this land and, likewise, the ways of being and doing gender that exist in the Pacific. I want to find ways of building solidarity between us. In order to do this, I think that we are going to have to think carefully about the logic of a trans* umbrella. I have personally found it helpful to have terms that signal a shared exclusion from the dominant gender system, and for me 'transgender', 'trans' and/or 'trans*' have often played that role. These are also the terms that frame much research, healthcare, social services, community-building and activism; as such they provide concrete incentives for us to identify with them. For these reasons, among others, it is important that inclusion within the ambit of 'trans*' is an option for non-European people. On the other hand, if we non-European people are forced to interpret our lives through an imposed gender framework, even a progressive one like 'trans*', we lose a lot of personal and collective strength. In particular, we lose the opportunity to define ourselves primarily in relation to our land and to our indigenous communities.

I want to signal the existence of indigenous identities that diverge from colonial norms of gender and sexuality, without closing the conceptual gate on who we might be, or how we might describe ourselves. As we have conversations we might listen for Māori who describe themselves as takatāpui, whakawāhine or whakatāne, and for the presence of Pacific people who identify as mahu, from Tahiti and Hawai`i; vaka sa lewa lewa, from Fiji; palopa, from Papua New Guinea; fa`afafine, from Samoa and American Samoa; akava`ine from the Cook Islands; fakaleiti/leiti, from Tonga; and fakafefine, from Niue.[9] On the other hand people might prefer to use English words like gay, homosexual, queer, queen, butch and so on,

---

8   My thinking around this owes a huge debt to Kim McBreen and b. binaohan. See for example McBreen's talk, 'The mātauranga continuum, gender and sexuality' (2013): http://starspangledrodeo.blogspot.co.nz/2013/06/the-matauranga-continuum-gender-and.html; and the blog post by b. binaohan (2012), 'trans/gender 101: how white people could discuss IAOPOC genders without being shitty': http://share.biyuti.com/post/37197929376

9   This list is taken from a speech delivered by Phylesha Brown-Acton at the 2nd Asia Pacific Outgames (2011), in which she argues that including Pacific people under the acronym LGBTI is inappropriate. As she notes, the list is far from exhaustive: www.pridenz.com/apog_phylesha_brown_acton_transcript.html

with meanings that may differ from the predominant European usage – or simply not specify an identity.[10]

As part of existing in gender-diverse communities I am constantly listening to the words people use to describe themselves, and constantly looking for resonance between us. Words are part of this process, as is the willingness to be with mystery, incoherence and creativity.

## Cisnormativity in New Zealand education cultures

*Jamie*: As we explained earlier, cisnormativity is a concept that helps us to understand the systematic valuing of cisgender people, and the corresponding devaluing of trans* and gender-diverse people. There is an urgent need to account for the ways that this system is woven throughout education cultures in New Zealand. In order to begin examining this, I turn to a number of published reports that remain, in my view, under-considered within academic accounts of education in this country.

We can look to examples like *Safety in our Schools – Ko te haumaru i o tatou kura* (NZ AIDS Foundation, Rainbow Youth, & OUT THERE 2004). This action-kit was created as a result of collaboration between the New Zealand AIDS Foundation, the national queer/trans* youth organisation Rainbow Youth, and former youth development project OUT THERE. *Safety in our Schools* was developed to assist boards of trustees,[11] principals and staff to create more inclusive learning environments for queer/trans* students. It drew together relevant legislation, policy documents and available research, and concluded by outlining a number of recommendations for changing school cultures. In 2009 the Otago University Students' Association's (OUSA) queer support coordinator commissioned a follow-up report written by Holly Painter, entitled *How Safe?*. This research generated mixed-methods data to determine the extent

---

10 For an anthropological account of the complexities of the term takatāpui, see David Murray (2004). For examples of a diversity of Māori approaches to gender and sexuality see Hutchings and Aspin (2007).
11 In New Zealand schools, boards of trustees consist of parent representatives, the principal, and staff and student representatives, who are responsible for 'the governance and the control of the management of the school. The board is the employer of all staff in the school, is responsible for setting the school's strategic direction in consultation with parents, staff and students, and ensuring that its school provides a safe environment and quality education for all its students. Boards are also responsible for overseeing the management of personnel, curriculum, property, finance and administration' (www.nzsta.org.nz/board-as-governors/, para 3).

to which Otago secondary schools had implemented the recommendations produced by the earlier report. Painter (2009) found a complex picture of positive developments and troubling challenges that remained unaddressed.

Examining the recommendations of *Safety in our Schools* provides a snapshot of the pervasive operation of cisnormativity in the New Zealand education system (see NZ AIDS Foundation, Rainbow Youth, & OUT THERE 2004, 26–29). For example, we can read cisnormativity in the difficulties students have in sharing their preferred identification and pronouns, and the challenges that school communities have in respecting these. We can see it in the physical features of the education environment, such as inaccessible bathrooms and changing facilities for many trans* and gender-diverse staff and students. Cisnormativity is in operation when trans* students are unable to access sports teams and physical education classes, or lack access to uniforms that are in alignment with their gender identities. Cisnormativity is visible in the invisibility of positive trans* role models in education cultures in New Zealand. In my view, *Safety in our Schools* tells an important story. For a decade now, a community-based action plan has existed that has provided recommendations to education stakeholders to help them to improve school environments for trans* students. The fact that there is an urgent need to repeat every single recommendation an entire decade on is exasperating.[12]

*Philip*: The New Zealand Human Rights Commission's (2008) report *To Be Who I Am – Kia noho au ki tōku anō ao* highlights a consistent series of issues for education stakeholders to take account of. In addition to those Jamie introduced, there is discussion of the flow-on effects of cisnormativity in this report. These include student alienation, disruptive behaviour and absenteeism, which are frequently treated as discipline issues rather than read as indicators of the systemic operation of cisnormativity that creates cycles of alienation. The report suggests that the challenges gender-diverse students experience around participating in activities, such as team sports, excludes these young people from support networks that their peers are able to rely on. It highlights boys' schools as an area of particular concern, both historically and currently. It gives some examples of straightforward,

---

12 For a recent set of guidelines, see the Post Primary Teachers' Association's (2012) document, 'Affirming diversity of sexualities and gender identities in the school community: Guidelines for boards of trustees and principals': www.ppta.org.nz/resources/publications

affirming responses from schools and school counsellors, as well as peer support among trans* students. At the tertiary education level, it raises issues of documentation, architecture, and a general disinclination to discuss the individual needs of trans* and gender-diverse students.

*Jamie*: Recent academic approaches to gender diversity in the New Zealand education system are a welcome addition to what remains a rather slim body of work. One example is the work of the Youth'12 research group, which has used nationally representative survey data to examine the health and wellbeing of secondary students who report being transgender. If the reports we introduced earlier highlight the way cisnormativity operates in New Zealand education cultures, this study might be read to assess the depth of its effects on students. In a recently published paper, Clark and colleagues found that of 8166 responding students, 1.2 per cent reported being transgender, 2.5 per cent reported being unsure about their gender, and 1.7 per cent did not understand the question (Clark et al. 2014). In general, the authors found that students represented in these three groups had 'compromised health and well-being relative to their non-transgender peers' (1). It is helpful to examine the results of this study closely. For example, students who responded in the three categories mentioned had greater risk of experiencing violence directed towards them, and more concerns about personal safety: 'more than half were afraid someone at school would hurt and bother them, and nearly one in five transgender students reported bullying at school on a weekly (or more frequent) basis' (3–4). Mental health was another significant concern. Approximately 40 per cent of the transgender students 'had significant depressive symptoms, had harmed themselves, and had been unable to access healthcare when they needed it' (4). Alarmingly, one in five transgender students had attempted suicide in the previous 12 months. The study called for schools, health services and communities to 'consider that transgender youth represent an important population that has specific needs' (1).

*Philip*: Together, these resources make distressing reading. When the climate in New Zealand educational institutions is so unwelcoming and invisibilising, not to mention dangerous, it is important that educators do not wait for students to make themselves known as trans* or gender diverse before thinking about challenging cisnormativity. The point is that educational cultures will have to change before it is safe for us to be ourselves.

*Chorus*: We would like to make several practical recommendations for educators who wish to make educational cultures more equitable for trans* people:

1. Please assume that there is at least one trans* or gender-diverse person in every class you teach.
2. Please don't assume that you will know who that person is. Some of us present ourselves as binary gendered, some do not.
3. Do not perpetuate or tolerate negative environments. Examples include staying silent when people call each other 'tranny' as an insult, or addressing groups of people as 'you girls' or 'you boys' when there are people in that group whose gender identities have not been disclosed to you.
4. Be attentive to, and supportive of, the words we use to identify ourselves, the pronouns we use and the types of clothing we wear to express our gender identities.
5. Engage with resources that already exist. Read the reports that we introduced earlier. Implement their recommendations. Learn from existing interventions like Rainbow Youth's work, which brings educators and storytellers into secondary schools to speak to students about sex, sexuality and gender diversity (Burford et al. 2013). Look too at the work of OUSA Queer Support and its Queer Friendly Staff Network, which has undertaken diversity training with academic and general staff across Otago University. These are but a few examples of an increasing number of available resources.
6. Advocate for the creation of proactive support for trans* students. Unitec's recent (2014) announcement that it will offer two annual scholarships for trans* students is an excellent example of this (Street 2014).
7. It is okay to make mistakes. Please keep trying.

## Emerging questions for transgender studies of education in New Zealand

*Jamie*: There remain a number of questions that need to be considered for future research, policy and practice concerning transgender issues in education in New Zealand. In particular, there are absences in knowledges about trans* students, trans* teachers and trans* family members/whānau, and more detailed analyses than we have been able to offer of the way that cisnormativity is threaded across, and reproduced by, the education system itself. There is a need to account for and expand upon existing gender diversity practices that are taking place across the education system, some of which we gestured to previously.

A trans* studies approach prompts challenging questions about the working categories that often structure educational research. For example, what is the effect of education research that offers two sex/gender categories for participants to select from? Or research practices that assume (often binary) gender identity, and accompanying pronouns, based upon gender presentation? How much more accurate and useful could this information be, if researchers enabled participants to self-select gender identity? I can recall numerous occasions where I have declined to participate in research projects because I was frustrated by the need for participants to identify their sex (male *or* female). I would have been a potentially enthusiastic participant had the choice of gender identity and pronoun been offered. This example is an incredibly common way that cisnormativity is reproduced in education research itself. The effects of cisnormativity do not only cause hurt and feelings of marginalisation (as Philip explained earlier); they also contribute to the systematic failure to collect data on the experiences of trans* populations in education. This, in turn, creates challenges in developing effective responses to the issues we have outlined.

Another issue to grapple with is visibility. The narrative that we have presented in this chapter is that trans* people's negotiations of education cultures are under-documented in New Zealand. This is an important story, and should galvanise further work. However, it is possible to discern 'presences' as well as absence. For example, while we were writing this piece, a number of accounts of transgender young people and schooling emerged in the mainstream media. While we would identify much of this reporting as negatively oriented, shallow and ill-informed, it nevertheless represents a certain kind of knowledge about trans* experiences of schooling that I think is worth charting and analysing. As Sam and Philip will discuss below, however, our positions on this matter are not identical. We had different responses to the idea of drawing on these texts, and could not agree on the political or educative value of doing so.

In thinking about how to respond to particular kinds of invisibility, I found myself drawn back to thinking about earlier activisms around HIV/AIDS. Do those of us working to create change for trans* people in education need to think about shocking and shaming education stakeholders into some kind of response? Perhaps. I think one way forward for trans* studies of education in New Zealand would be to begin to curate what Ann Cvetkovich (2003) calls 'archives of trauma', to make visible what is, for many trans* people, the daily grind of education. This kind of work could be achieved, as I have alluded to above, by examining already public accounts like newspaper articles, or projects like Sam's Master's thesis – which illustrated the complexity of queer and trans* lives (Orchard 2011). It could also be accomplished by generating new texts, through methods such as oral history.

*Sam*: I struggle with the issue of visibility. On the one hand, as a comic artist I spend a lot of time telling stories that celebrate the positive parts of trans* and queer life in New Zealand. I developed this tactic in direct response to the media's insistence on scandalising and problematising our existence.[13] However, I also see merit in tactics that 'shock and shame'. In 2012 I was involved in a national awareness and fundraising campaign for Rainbow Youth called WTF, which stood for both 'What the fuck?' and 'Where are the funds?'[14] This campaign filmed a message from celebrities and community members to raise awareness of the ongoing prevalence of negative statistics about queer and trans* New Zealanders, and called for people to donate to organisations that work directly on these issues. We used 'shock and shame' tactics to illustrate the huge amount of work that needs to be done to support our communities.

For me, there remain ethical questions about how to enact these tactics. There is a tension between playing into the mainstream media's representation of queer and trans* people as broken (the old 'mad, sad or bad' idea), and accurately depicting the consequences of the systematic devaluing of trans* lives, and pushing for further support for our communities.

*Philip*: I also think these questions of representation are really important. Trans* people have been silenced, but also made visible in really distorted ways, as Sam pointed out. When it comes to visibility, how do we increase our self-determination, both in terms of what we share and who we share it with? I also wonder about being seen and being known. I know that even when we are visible we may be so in ways that are confusing for some. As

---

13  For more on this, please see these comics: www.roostertailscomic.com/comic/why-comics/ and www.roostertailscomic.com/comic/why-comics-part-two/

14  See the video: www.youtube.com/watch?v=2D_4JwQ2Fug

Joe said in one of our conversations: 'I know it is confusing for many people, cis and trans*, that I am a femme transmasculine person who is taking testosterone and wearing skirts and dresses most of the time. Other people's confusion, out in the public world, frequently manifests as rude staring or verbal violence. How do we avoid the expectation that we explain ourselves definitively, or the false promise that doing so will make us safe?' As many trans* people know, visibility can mean the opposite to safety in institutions and communities that are permeated by cisnormativity. We need to reserve the right to remain invisible.

*Joe*: I think this discussion speaks to the need to carefully consider the ways we wish to approach trans* scholarship in education studies in New Zealand. We need to think about the ethics of trans-education research. In particular, we should ask how people who do not live in trans* communities can undertake such research ethically. How can we ensure that trans* people have first-person authority over their embodiment, experience and narratives (Bettcher 2009; MacDonald 2013)?

Speaking generally, I have noticed that, for me, healing happens in relationship. Healing requires the acknowledgment of complexity and messiness. For healing spaces to be enabled in educational institutions, I believe we need to create cultures that allow multiple truths, different ways of embodying transness or cisness, or non-binaryness. We must not force ourselves or others into particular narratives about what it means to be a 'real' or 'good' trans* person. Incoherence is part and parcel of personhood. I feel very attached to both the concepts of incoherence and clarity. I want to be clear that my incoherence is both a challenge for myself, and a source of power. I am proud to be a trans* person. I am proud to be a non-binary person. The times that I feel most understood are moments when my incoherence is (somewhat) understood and (absolutely) valued.

## Conclusion

*Chorus*: In this chapter we have sought both to challenge education stakeholders, and to offer some useful concepts and resources to improve educational cultures in Aotearoa/New Zealand. We hope that our dialogue will not only enable readers to better understand and identify cisnormativity in educational contexts, but will also inspire you to develop ways of resisting it. Starting this chapter was a struggle, and concluding it feels no different.

There is much more we could say, and much more that needs to be said. We farewell you, in the same spirit that we began with:

In desperation
In rage
In hope.

## Acknowledgements

We would like to express our gratitude to our kin, Hana and Aun, for their loving contributions to bringing our collective together. We are also indebted to a number of readers who provided feedback on earlier drafts of this chapter – thank you.

## References

Ahmed, S. (2012), *On Being Included: Racism and diversity in institutional life*, Durham, NC: Duke University Press.

Aspin, C. (2013), 'Hōkakatanga – Māori sexualities', Te Ara – the Encyclopedia of New Zealand: www.TeAra.govt.nz/en/hokakatanga-maori-sexualities/sources

Baril, A. & Trevenen, K. (2014), 'Exploring ableism and cisnormativity in the conceptualization of identity and sexuality "disorders"', *Annual Review of Critical Psychology*, 11, 389–416.

Bettcher, T. (2009), 'Trans identities and first person authority', in L. Shrage (ed.), *You've Changed: Sex reassignment and personal identity* (98–120), Oxford: Oxford University Press.

Burford, J. (2010), '(The) margin(s) speak!: A multifaceted examination of practising "men who have sex with men" development in Bangkok', Master's thesis, Victoria University of Wellington, Wellington.

Burford, J., Lucassen, M., Penniket, P. & Hamilton, T. (2013), *Educating for Diversity: An informative evaluation of the Rainbow Youth sexuality and gender diversity workshops*, Auckland: Rainbow Youth.

Clark, T., Lucassen, M., Bullen, P., Denny, S., Fleming, T., Robinson, E. & Rossen, F. (2014), 'The health and well-being of transgender high school students: Results from the New Zealand adolescent health survey (Youth'12)', *Journal of Adolescent Health*, 55(1), 93–99. DOI: 10.1016/j.jadohealth.2013.11.008

Cvetkovich, A. (2003), *An Archive of Feelings: Truama, sexuality and lesbian public cultures*, Durham, NC: Duke University Press.

Hutchings, J. & Aspin, C. (2007), *Sexuality and the Stories of Indigenous People*, Wellington: Huia.

Murray, D. (2004), 'Takatāpui, gay, or just HO-MO-SEXUAL, darling? Māori language, sexual terminology, and identity in Aotearoa/New Zealand', in W. Leap and T. Boellstorff (eds), *Speaking in Queer Tongues: Globalization and gay language* (163–80), Chicago: University of Illinois Press.

MacDonald, J. (2012), 'A coalitional politics of incoherence: Ethical (trans)masculinities in New Zealand', Master's thesis, University of Otago, Dunedin.

MacDonald, J. (2013), 'An autoethnography of queer transmasculine femme incoherence and the ethics of trans research', in N. Denzin (ed.), *40th Anniversary Studies in Symbolic Interaction* (129–52), Bingley: Emerald.

Mikaere, A. (2003), *The Balance Destroyed: The consequences for Māori women of the colonisation of tikanga Māori*, Auckland: International Research Institute for Māori and Indigenous Education.

NZ AIDS Foundation, Rainbow Youth & OUT THERE (2004), *Safety in our Schools – Ko te haumaru i o tatou kura: An action kit for Aotearoa New Zealand schools to address sexual orientation prejudice*, Wellington: New Zealand AIDS Foundation.

New Zealand Human Rights Commission (2008), *To Be Who I Am – Kia noho au ki tōku anō ao*, Auckland: New Zealand Human Rights Commision.

Nordmarken, S. (2014), 'Becoming ever more monstrous: Feeling transgender in-betweenness', *Qualitative Inquiry*, 20(1), 37–50.

Orchard, S. (2011), 'Family portraits: A collection of stories about queer people in New Zealand', Master's thesis, AUT University, Auckland.

Painter, H. (2009), 'How safe?: How safe and inclusive are Otago secondary schools? Ae ranei he haumaru, he wahi whāi kit e katoa ngā kura tuarua o Otago?' A report on the implementations from the 'Safety in our schools – Ko te harumaru i o tatuu kura' action kit: He purongo ūruhi i ngā tuanaki a te kete mahi 'Safety in our schools – Ko te harumaru i o tatu kura', Dunedin, NZ: OUSA Queer Support.

Rich, A. (1986), *Blood, Bread, and Poetry: Selected prose 1979–1985*, New York: W.W. Norton.

Serano, J. (2007), *Whipping Girl: A transsexual woman on sexism and the scapegoating of femininity*, Berkeley: Seal.

Spade, D. (2004), 'Fighting to win', in Mattilda Bernstein Sycamore (ed.), *That's Revolting!: Queer strategies for resisting assimilation* (47–53), New York: Soft Skull.

Street, D. (26 February 2014), 'Scholarship for transgender students': www.stuff.co.nz/national/education/9764997/Scholarship-for-transgender-students

## 11.
# 'I feel proud of what I've achieved while having a baby so young'

Teenage mothers contest normative constructions of their sexual, social and educational identities

### Jenny Hindin-Miller & Rebeccah Hibbert

Pregnant teenagers are one example of non-normative sexuality in mainstream Aotearoa/New Zealand schools. In heteronormative social contexts, including schools, young women are expected to wait until they are of an appropriate age and in a long-term committed relationship before they have sex (Youdell 2005). They are also expected to finish their education and have a career before starting a family (Harris 2004). Pregnant school-aged young women are constructed as socially deviant because they do not conform to these normative social codes.

As a consequence of their non-normative sexuality, pregnant teenagers are regarded as 'impossible bodies' and 'impossible learners' in the mainstream school system (Youdell 2006). This outsider status means that few pregnant teens remain in mainstream schools after they have given birth. Alternative education providers or Teen Parent Units (TPUs) have been established in New Zealand to respond to the educational and social needs of school-aged parents. This chapter draws on findings from our two research projects (J. Hindin-Miller 2012; R. Hindin-Miller 2012), which show how TPUs are able to successfully challenge and disrupt (hetero)normative constructions of teenage parenthood. The chapter documents young mothers' perspectives on mainstream schools, their turning-point experiences of pregnancy, and their engagement in education at a TPU. The young women's perspectives contest normative discourses of teenage parenthood and the subsequent anticipated negative life-course outcomes for teenage mothers and their children.

## The authors' research studies

Jenny has worked for 15 years with teenage parents and their children. In the 1990s she established Karanga Mai Young Parents' College, New Zealand's second school for teenage parents. Jenny's subsequent PhD research explored the longer-term influence of a TPU on the lives of 10 former students (J. Hindin-Miller 2012). Drawing on participants' narrative accounts, her study became a wider story of the (re)construction of the young women's identities as learners, as mothers and as young women. The negative construction of teenage parenthood in contemporary New Zealand society provided a context for the study. All but one of Jenny's participants had experienced educational exclusion, and the thesis explored how a TPU was able to engage these young women in education and support their multiple identities. Teenage parenthood and engagement in education were life-changing turning points for the young women, which led them to frame their own identities as 'successful' and served to contest dominant constructions of teenage pregnancy.

Rebeccah was working with the Canterbury regional teen parent coordinator when she decided to undertake her Master's degree in education. Her thesis was a case study that explored four young mothers' perceptions of the ways in which their TPU challenged and reframed negative social constructions of teenage motherhood (R. Hindin-Miller 2012). Central to the young mothers' accounts was the unit's culture of success, which differed markedly from their experience of mainstream schooling and contributed to their re-engagement with, and enjoyment of, academic education. Attendance at the unit affirmed the young women's identities as mothers, students, young adults and friends.

## Teen Parent Units: A historical overview

In the 1990s New Zealand's high rates of teenage pregnancy, combined with an increasing focus on youth development and early intervention programmes, led to the establishment of the first iterations of what are now known as TPUs. Fergusson and Woodward's (2000) findings – that pregnant New Zealand teens were 10 times more likely than their non-pregnant peers to leave high school without formal qualifications – gave support to these educational initiatives. In 2004 the Ministry of Education formally agreed to establish policy guidelines and funding for TPUs (Ministry of Education 2004); today there are 23 TPUs in New Zealand and negotiations are under way to establish more. These units enable young parents to continue their education in a supportive environment, with onsite (or neighbouring) childcare facilities and transportation to and from school. They work to support young mothers to construct alternative life course 'scenarios' and to risk new ways of being female (Bullen, Kenway & Hey 2000). The 600 or so parents who are enrolled at TPUs are a small but significant proportion of the approximately 4500 teenage parents who give birth in New Zealand each year (Collins 2010).

Within TPUs the ratio of teacher to students is set at 1:10. Each student has an individual education plan, drawn up to meet her (or his) specific educational needs and goals. In order to offer the full range of secondary school subjects and NCEA qualifications, the curriculum is provided by distance education providers as well as by courses taught at the units. Comprehensive services, provided by the units' staff, assist students to develop a range of personal resources necessary to enhance their own and their children's future health and wellbeing. The units typically employ social workers and nurses, and draw upon strong interagency support from services such as Plunket, Work and Income, and Housing NZ,[1] as well as counselling services, legal and budgeting advisors, and so on (J. Hindin-Miller 2012).

## Setting the scene: NZ societal constructions of teenage motherhood

New Zealand has a relatively high number of teenage mothers, on a par with Britain and, in the OECD, second only to the United States (Wylie 2009). Within the New Zealand context of entitlement to free education until the age of 19, teenage mothers are by definition school-aged, although they are often already disengaged from school when they find themselves pregnant (Burdell 1995; J. Hindin-Miller 2012). Mainstream schools and society at large have difficulty accepting and accommodating teenage mothers because of their non-normative sexuality and non-traditional life-course trajectories. In fact, teenage mothers comprise a socially marginalised subculture on a number of grounds, including class, race, gender and age, all of

---

1   Plunket is a publicly funded organisation that provides support services to families and children under five. Work and Income is a government agency providing employment services and financial assistance. Housing NZ is a government agency that manages state houses and tenancies, providing affordable housing to those in greatest need.

which contribute to the dominant construction of teenage parenthood as 'unacceptable' and 'problematic'.

Teenage mothers have been the focus of negative social, academic and political discourse in Western nations, including New Zealand, for the past 40 years, despite a significant decrease in the teenage birth rate since its peak in the 1970s (Wilson & Huntington 2006). Many societal, political, historical and economic factors have contributed to Western constructions of teenage pregnancy as 'problematic' (Daguerre & Nativel 2006), including changes in traditional family structures, women's roles, and normative adolescent and life-course trajectories (Cherrington & Breheny 2005). In New Zealand, prevailing societal discourse serves to construct teenage parenting as a form of social deviance and a burden on the state (Breheny & Stephens 2007a). Teenage parenthood is also constituted as a form of social exclusion because most school-aged mothers are 'out of school' and isolated from family support.

Public attitudes have been significantly influenced by health research and medical discourses, which focus on the 'risks' and/or 'deficits' associated with teenage parenthood. For instance, New Zealand researchers Woodward, Fergusson and Horwood (2001) argue that young women who become pregnant have higher rates of educational failure, behavioural problems, sexual risk-taking and family dysfunction. Titles of their studies, such as 'Teenage pregnancy: Cause for concern', reflect their deficit construction of teenage mothers (R. Hindin-Miller 2012). Breheny and Stephens (2010) have reviewed the societal impact of research that constructs teenage pregnancy and parenting in deficit terms, concluding:

> *These discourses are deployed compatibly to produce a coherent subject: the financially dependent, ethnic minority member who is psychologically, physically and educationally unprepared for parenthood and whose reproduction produces disadvantage for the individual and the state (318).*

In the next section we consider aspects of this negative construction in more detail.

*Normative adolescent trajectories*
In the past few decades, increased emphasis on the importance of education has resulted in young people in Western societies spending extended years in schooling. Adolescent dependency on family support has been prolonged

and the assumption of 'adult' responsibilities, such as employment and parenthood, has been significantly delayed (Kehily 2007). Lesko (2001) argues that one consequence of this 'slowed-down development' is the denial of young people's sexual maturation and the construction of teenage pregnancy as problematic. Teenage mothers are constituted as deviant because of the physical evidence of their sexuality, which directly challenges the construction of school-aged 'girls' as non-sexual (ibid.). Many schools struggle to accept this display of sexual maturation, preferring pregnant students to leave rather than 'contaminate' other students (Hunter 2007; Lall 2007).

## Changing roles of women and the 'ideal' mother

Changes in women's roles and employment opportunities available to women have transformed traditional family structures in Western societies. Since the 1970s the expected trajectory for young women in countries such as New Zealand has become that embodied by Caucasian, middle-class, educated young women, who spend more years in education, pursue a career and become financially independent before having children (Allen & Osgood 2009).

Since the 1980s, the neo-liberal model of 'good' citizenship, in which both parents in the family work to achieve financial independence, has also challenged traditional family structures (Bullen et al. 2000). Neo-liberal discourses of 'autonomous, individualised and ambitious young women' (Allen & Osgood 2009, 3) have served to devalue the 'at home' mother (Cherrington & Breheny 2005) and constitute the 'ideal' mother as wealthy and in her mid-thirties. Younger mothers, who are statistically more likely to come from working-class or ethnic minority groups, do not conform to this ideal and are vilified primarily because of their resistance to expected middle-class trajectories, rather than because of poor outcomes for themselves and their children (Wilson & Huntington 2006). Regarded as socially deviant 'dole bludgers', teenage mothers have come to be considered significantly disadvantaged in the Western world (Daguerre & Nativel 2006, 1).

## 'Kids having kids'

One result of the social changes in women's roles has been that the average age of first-time mothers in New Zealand has increased from 23.3 years in 1967 to 30.5 years in 2009 (Statistics NZ 2009). This increase serves to highlight the youthfulness of teenage mothers, who have come to be regarded as 'kids having kids' (Hoffman & Maynard 1997) and as 'unfit parents', because they break contemporary 'rules' of age-appropriate development and motherhood (Breheny & Stephens 2007b). This is despite young women aged 17 to 19 having fewer risks in pregnancy and childbirth than women who delay childbearing until their thirties (Daguerre & Nativel 2006). Rather than being seen as making 'a valuable contribution ... to society as mothers', teenage mothers are widely condemned (Breheny & Stephens 2007a, 344). Such constructions impact upon the hopes, aspirations and life choices of teenage mothers, which tend to be more modest than their non-parenting peers (Patterson, Forbes, Peace & Campbell 2010).

## The critique of deficit constructions of teenage motherhood

Despite the prevalence of such deficit discourses about teenage motherhood, our experiences of working with and researching teenage mothers reveal how they actively resist and reject such discourses. All 14 women in our combined studies had been teenage mothers and students of a TPU in New Zealand's South Island/Te Wai Pounamu. The 10 participants in Jenny's study (J. Hindin-Miller 2012) were identified by the pseudonyms Anahera, Andy, Emma, Jade, Kate, Rachel, Sam, Tatiana, Te Huia and Zena. Interviewed in 2010, all but one of Jenny's participants were in their twenties and had left the TPU between one and five years previously. The four participants in Rebeccah's study (R. Hindin-Miller 2012), were identified by the pseudonyms Chelsea, Jane, Lucy and Shelley. Interviewed in 2011, they were all current students of the TPU.

### Participants' experiences of school disengagement

We had many conversations with our participants about their experiences of disengagement in mainstream schooling. Apart from one exception – Anahera, who had enjoyed all levels of schooling – the stories were remarkably consistent, and revealed that the young women were already experiencing the school environment as hostile prior to their pregnancies.

Three predominant themes emerged. The first was the inability of schools to respond appropriately to the young women's individual learning needs. The second was the poor relationships the young women had experienced with teachers, whom they felt were mostly uncaring and uninterested. The third was the frustrating and unsympathetic school context, which reinforced the young women's identities as 'impossible' or unsuccessful learners because they did not conform to normative discourses of acceptable, middle-class, feminine identities (J. Hindin-Miller 2012; Youdell 2006).

With the exception of Anahera, all reported they had hated high school and felt anonymous there. Emma, for instance, said: 'You were just a number.' Several were very capable academically, although their schools had failed to recognise and support their potential. Chelsea had left her mainstream high school when she became pregnant and regarded herself as a failing student. Her subsequent academic success at the TPU transformed her perception of herself as a learner. She commented, 'Now I've had a lot of Excellences. And I've just passed my Tertiary Studies Course with an A+, so that was pretty cool.'

Six participants had readily identifiable learning challenges for which they felt they had received inadequate support. Six had been stood down, suspended or asked to leave school because of their defiance of school rules and structures. For example, Jane said '[I was] a student that was really naughty at school you know, getting expelled and suspended and you know, all the bad stuff.' Seven participants had 'dropped out' of school; six became pregnant while at high school, and nine left mainstream school without any qualifications. Emma stated she had 'hated secondary school and was never there.' She 'dropped out' in her third year without any qualifications.

> *I found every excuse in the book not to go to class. I've never been very good with reading and writing ... and I'd get into trouble when my work wasn't done ... after Year 9 it just got worse and I was like, 'I can't be bothered anymore, I just won't do it!'*

Only five participants achieved their National Certificate in Educational Achievement (NCEA) Level One; Anahera was unique in completing NCEA Level Three (while pregnant).

In common with many other teenage parents, our participants' lack of academic success had contributed to their experience of school as unrewarding (te Riele 2007). Their subsequent academic achievements at the TPU, however, directly challenge the widely-held notion that teenage mothers are less academically able than their peers (Woodward, Horwood & Fergusson 2001).

In their personal lives there was little to encourage the participants to view schooling more positively. The school failure of many of their parents, older siblings and friends reflected their own experiences of school as a hostile environment, characterised by power disparities and inequities as well as institutional control and exclusion. The young women's experiences support Youdell's (2006) argument that:

> [G]ender, sexuality, social class, ability, disability, race, ethnicity and religion as well as popular and sub-cultural belongings … [determine] the 'sort' of student and learner that s/he gets to be, and the educational inclusions s/he enjoys and/or the exclusion s/he faces.

These are the 'identity markers' which, according to Youdell, 'foreclose the possibility of educational "success"' and produce the student as an 'impossible learner' (2006, 2). Shared by many young women who become teenage mothers, these identities appear to be synonymous with school exclusion and failure.

The young women in our studies were predominantly working-class Māori and Pākehā. Almost all were framed by mainstream schools and teachers as failing or impossible learners. While actively resisting the constraints of their schooling experiences, as evidenced in their high rates of truancy and disengagement from school, the young women nevertheless 'took up' this negative framing of their identities. In common with many disaffected early school leavers, the young women decided that school was 'not for them' (Patterson 2011). Their subsequent engagement with education as teenage mothers signalled their resistance to the seeming inevitability of their prior disengagement.

## Participants' experiences of school pregnancies

The young women who became pregnant while still enrolled at high school experienced a range of (hetero)normative school responses to their visible sexuality, which was seen as a challenge to normative codes of socially acceptable 'feminine', 'student' and 'sexual' behaviour. As Shelley explained, 'Well, at [mainstream school] if you said you were having sex with someone they'd call you like a slut or something.' Despite some schools and individual teachers working to support and accommodate pregnant students, others encouraged or pressured them to leave school. Sometimes teachers assisted this departure by enrolling them in alternative forms of schooling, such as the Correspondence School or a TPU. In extreme cases, schools actively removed pregnant students as soon as they could because they perceived them to be sexually immoral and contaminating of other students.

Regardless of the intent of individual schools and teachers, the unique needs of teenage parents prove challenging for mainstream schooling.

Breastfeeding, for instance, poses a visible and uncomfortable 'problem', particularly in a co-educational facility. Most schools are unlikely to be able to assist with transport or provide convenient and accessible childcare, two services necessary to a young mother's continued participation in schooling (Baragwanath 1997; Seitz & Apfel 1999; SmithBattle 2006). TPUs offer both, as integral aspects of their service.

## Participants' experiences of pregnancies that occurred when disengaged from school

The young women who had 'dropped out' or were 'stood down' from school and subsequently became pregnant had little reason not to continue with their pregnancies. Many national and international studies of teenage pregnancy have found that young women from disadvantaged backgrounds, whose educational experiences have been unfulfilling, envisage a narrow range of life choices for themselves. These young women are much more likely than their educationally successful counterparts to continue with their pregnancies, despite negative societal judgements (Bullen et al. 2000; SmithBattle 2006).

## Pregnancy as a life 'turning point'

Several studies report that pregnancy and parenthood are actually positive life 'turning points' for many young women (Hallman 2007; Wylie 2009). This was also a finding of our own research studies. Our participants described how pregnancy impelled them to start thinking about the future rather than simply 'living for the day'. As Emma said, 'You've got someone else to look after now'. Kate also stated, 'I knew I should use this to turn my life around. I knew I needed a change and I should just take it.' For these (and many other) young women, impending motherhood became a focal point around which to 'organise their lives and priorities' (SmithBattle 2006, 131).

In addition to making positive life changes – which for some participants included addressing alcohol and drug abuse or leaving violent relationships – pregnancy and parenthood prompted a transformation in attitudes to education. School qualifications were viewed as a means for creating a better life for their child/ren (J. Hindin-Miller 2012; R. Hindin-Miller 2012; Zachry 2005). This perspective reflects the influence of neo-liberal discourse that frames the 'good mother' as responsible and dedicated to the wellbeing of her infant, while simultaneously working in paid employment. Jade, who was 14 when she became pregnant, explained:

> *I think when you have children it changes you, who you are, because you're thinking about what you're going to do in the future so you kinda put your [negative] feelings aside about school and then you want to do something with your life – so then you come back to school!*

Jade was describing her decision to attend the TPU. Few, if any of the teenage mothers in New Zealand who are fortunate enough to have access to this alternative form of schooling would choose to return to mainstream schools to fulfil their aspirations to gain qualifications. Bullen et al. (2000, 454) argue:

> *Educational interventions ... must help these young women to construct alternative ... scenarios for themselves and their children ... Risking new ways of being female is what is at stake for this cohort ...*

Creating 'alternative scenarios' is the work of TPUs.

## Participants' experiences of the TPU culture

Andy described her experiences of the TPU in the following way:

> *It was your security blanket. You didn't feel any judgement in that environment. No matter what, we were all safe, we were all secure in our place there, you know, and it was comfortable, there was such a strong sense of wellbeing, a sense of family and of belonging, it was just like a second home.*

Andy's statement is reflective of all the participants. The warm, respectful and affirming relationships experienced with teachers and other staff created a sense of family or community for the women and their children. This positive experience was in stark contrast to their sense of alienation in mainstream schools.

> *I don't know what I expected it to be like but I was fresh out of high school and all those horrible teachers who didn't know you apart from your name. I didn't expect that level of ... support to come from teachers ... That was overwhelming, like, 'Wow!' It felt so special to have adults who cared about me in that way ... (Andy)*

The small size of the unit (which had around 30 young women on its roll) and the high teacher-to-student ratio fostered close and nurturing relationships. It also permitted much-needed individual tuition, which was greatly valued by the young women. As Lucy said:

> *It's one-on-one, that's the difference ... you're not stuck in a classroom with 30 other students, you're actually ... sitting there with one teacher eye-to-eye, and ... the teachers really are focused on what you're doing.*

Teachers also worked collaboratively in a main classroom in the unit, which resulted in students and staff being on familiar terms regardless of individual subject choices.

The sense of community experienced by our participants was reinforced by using first names for staff and students, sharing communal eating facilities, reciting daily karakia, and jointly participating in sports, cultural events and other activities, such as singing with children, gardening or going on outings. These cultural practices helped staff and students develop close relationships without the normal structural and hierarchical boundaries present in the conventional school environment. As Lucy and Jade explained:

> *Teachers always have the time to listen to us as well ... if we're struggling, or if we're having a bad day ... or if [we have] exciting news, they always take the time to listen and find out what's going on. (Lucy)*

> *The teachers treat you like equals, they don't treat you like you were a child at school, they treat us like we're adults because we are parents and they're parents as well, so you can kind of relate on those levels as well. (Jade)*

## *The challenge to (hetero)normative constructions of sexual and other identities*

In this safe and nurturing whānau environment the young women felt affirmed and supported in their multiple identities as learners, mothers and women. Negative societal discourses about teenage parenthood and educational failure were strongly contested at the unit. Instead there was positive and optimistic discourse about teenage parenthood and educational achievement, which enhanced the young women's self-confidence and sense of future possibilities. Their status as teenage parents was normalised, affirmed and celebrated, and they were supported to succeed academically in a context where all students were teenage parents and academic success was a normal feature of the unit's culture. As Jane and Lucy stated:

> *All the students are excelling here, like in their schoolwork. [The staff] know we can [succeed]. They have the confidence in us. They've seen it in other students and they know that we can do it, you know, they motivate us. They believe in us. And we can do it! We are women! (Jane)*

> *Mana wahine! We are strong! (Lucy)*

The provision of quality early childhood education services was an integral part of the whānau support offered at the unit. It provided a unique opportunity for close working partnerships between the early childhood teachers and the young women and affirmed their identities as mothers. The on-site location of the centre meant they could visit their children and see or hear them playing while they studied. The young women attributed many positive parenting practices to the influence, guidance and modelling of early childhood teachers. This support was of particular importance for the participants who, like all new mothers, needed the enveloping support of a nurturing whānau to help them flourish in this unfamiliar role (Lawson-Te Aho 2010). As Kate said:

> *That was the best part! You'd go to school, drop the kids off [and] have a really good chat to someone who absolutely loved your child as much as you did ...*

Because the young women and children were immersed in the affirming schooling community and culture, often for a period of three or more years, the unit had a transformative effect on their lives. Daily immersion served to normalise this culture for the young women and their children even though it was, in many cases, very different from the cultural contexts of their homes, relationships and wider society. Emma and Kate made the following comments about the unit:

> *It felt safe, it was so easy, you could go there every day and you'd know that it was always going to be the same ... It was so normal, coming from a life where you never knew, you could get bashed up or something like that ... it was very supportive. (Emma)*

> *When I first started I thought it would be, 'Poor little thing!' but everyone there, it was the one place where I felt I was okay, I was like everyone else, it was like a wee bubble ... You didn't feel like you were abnormal. You didn't feel self-conscious. The group made you feel awesome! (Kate)*

In their national study of the imagined futures of young women attending TPUs, Patterson et al. (2010) found that these alternative school settings provide young mothers 'with the social context in which they can both assert a positive maternal identity, and imagine futures in which their lives, and those of their children, can turn out well' (17). This finding was supported by the young women in our studies and is in stark contrast with medical research, which constructs teenage pregnancy in deficit terms as an impediment to a successful life trajectory. When reflecting on their TPU experiences, participants talked about their growing self-confidence, their less judgemental and more inclusive attitudes toward others, and the social benefits of long-term friendships made at the unit. They described positive transformations in their learning identities, their understanding of the importance of education for their children, their increased self-belief and opportunities, and the impact of these on their life aspirations. They also discussed the support and affirmation they had received as parents in the TPU, the social and educational benefits for their children, and their enhanced capacity to manage life challenges.

## Conclusion: 'I am proud of my achievements! I am a success!'

Of the 10 participants who had already left school at the time of our studies, eight had gone on to tertiary education and had established careers in the fields of education, health, information technology, business management, retail, accountancy and the creative arts. Of the other two, one had been diagnosed with a chronic illness that prevented her from working, and the other was attending Kōhanga Reo with her three children. Several already owned their own homes and none was wholly dependent upon a state benefit. Twelve of the 14 participants were living in committed long-term partnerships, of which four were with the father of their first child. Judging by conventional constructions of success, these young women were manifestly successful. Despite widely accepted negative predictions, and as a direct challenge to normative constructions of ideal femininity, the young women did not appear to have been disadvantaged by becoming teenage mothers.

In the last paragraphs of this chapter we report the young women's perceptions of teenage motherhood, their TPU experiences and their own life success. Chelsea, who is currently a tertiary student said, 'I feel proud of what I've achieved while having a baby so young.' Zena, who was expelled from school in Year 9 and became pregnant at 14, stated: 'I just think being a young mum doesn't stop you from doing what you want to do. Sometimes, being a young mum you can do more than if you weren't a young mum!' The young women reported that their experiences of early parenthood and of the TPU's affirmation of their identities had transformed their lives. Sam, who now works as an IT specialist, reflected on her time at the TPU:

> *I was there at 16 until I was 18. I suppose it influenced me in every way really, coz you kind of grow with it. The way you think about things, the way you see things, the way you see yourself, the way you see learning ... it kind of changed your life ... it was an amazing thing and you were so grateful that you could be there.*

Kate, who now works as a health professional, summed up the transformative influence of her engagement in education at the TPU: 'I feel good about who I am today – I've changed a lot but in a good way. I'm quite happy with my achievements.'

These comments are from young women whom mainstream schooling and societal judgements had constructed as socially deviant, 'impossible learners', and too young to be 'good' mothers. Their lives demonstrate that you can be a teenage parent and a 'good mother'. You can also be educationally successful and a productive and independent member of society, particularly if you receive the support and opportunities offered by affirming educational experiences such as those provided in a TPU.

Our research concludes that TPU educational settings can actively contest (hetero)normative thinking about 'respectable' female behaviour and teenage motherhood.

## References

Allen, K. & Osgood, J. (2009), 'Young women negotiating maternal subjectivities: The significance of social class', *Studies in the Maternal*, 1(2), 1–17.

Baragwanath, S. (1997), 'The education of teenage mothers in New Zealand: A policy vacuum and a practical example of assistance', *Social Policy Journal of New Zealand/ Te Puna Whakaaro*, November (9), 98–105.

Breheny, M. & Stephens, C. (2007a), 'Individual responsibility and social constraint: The construction of adolescent motherhood in social science research', *Culture, Health & Sexuality*, 9(4), 333–46.

Breheny, M. & Stephens, C. (2007b), 'Irreconcilable differences: Health professionals' constructions of adolescence and motherhood', *Social Science & Medicine*, 64, 112–24.

Breheny, M. & Stephens, C. (2010), 'Youth or disadvantage? The construction of teenage mothers in medical journals', *Culture, Health & Sexuality, 12*(3), 307–22.

Bullen, E., Kenway, J. & Hey, V. (2000), 'New Labour, social exclusion, and educational risk-management: The case of "gym-slip mums"', *British Educational Research Journal, 26*(4), 441–56.

Burdell, P. (1995), 'Teen mothers in high school: Tracking their curriculum', *Review of Research in Education, 21*, 163–208.

Cherrington, J. & Breheny, M. (2005), 'Politicizing dominant discursive constructions about teenage pregnancy: Re-locating the subject as social', *Health: An interdisciplinary journal for the social study of health, illness and medicine, 9*(1), 89–111.

Collins, B. (2010), 'Resilience in teenage mothers: A follow-up study', Wellington: Ministry of Social Development.

Daguerre, A. & Nativel, C.E. (eds), (2006), *When Children Become Parents. Welfare state responses to teenage pregnancy*, Bristol: Policy Press.

Fergusson, D.M. & Woodward, L. (2000), 'Teenage pregnancy and female educational underachievement: A prospective study of a New Zealand birth cohort', *Journal of Marriage and the Family, 62*(1), 147.

Hallman, H.L. (2007), Reassigning the identity of the pregnant and parenting student', *American Secondary Education, 36*(1), 80–98.

Hindin-Miller, J. (2012), 'Re-storying identities: Young women's narratives of teenage parenthood and educational support', Doctoral dissertation, University of Canterbury, Christchurch.

Hindin-Miller, R. (2012), '"Today has been about success": Young mothers' understandings of the ways a school for teenage parents supports success', Master's thesis, University of Canterbury, Christchurch: http://hdl.handle.net/10092/7157

Hoffman, S.D. & Maynard, R.A. (eds), (1997), *Kids Having Kids: Economic costs and social consequences*, Washington: Urban Institute Press.

Hunter, C. (2007), 'On the outskirts of education: The liminal space of rural teen pregnancy', *Ethnography and Education, 2*(1), 75–92.

Kehily, M.J. (ed.), (2007), *Understanding Youth: Perspectives, identities and practices*, Thousand Oaks: Sage.

Lall, M. (2007), 'Exclusion from school: Teenage pregnancy and the denial of education', *Sex Education, 7*(3), 219–37.

Lawson-Te Aho, K. (2010), 'Definitions of whanau: A review of selected literature', Wellington: Families Commission.

Lesko, N. (2001), *Act Your Age!: A cultural construction of adolescence*, New York: RoutledgeFalmer.

Ministry of Education (2004), *Education Circular: Teen Parent Units (TPUs) attached to secondary schools*, Wellington: Ministry of Education.

Patterson, L. (2011) *Tracks to Adulthood. Post-school experiences of 21-year-olds: The qualitative component of Competent Learners @20*, Wellington: Ministry of Education.

Patterson, L., Forbes, K., Peace, R. & Campbell, B. (2010), 'Headlines & heartlines: Young New Zealand mothers imagine family, friends and relationships across their life-course', Wellington: Massey University.

Seitz, V., & Apfel, N.H. (1999), 'Effective interventions for adolescent mothers', *Clinical Psychology: Science & Practice, 6*(1), 50.

SmithBattle, L. (2006), 'Helping teen mothers succeed', *The Journal of School Nursing 22*(3), 130–35.

Statistics NZ (2009), 'Median and average age of mother': www.stats.govt.nz/browse_for_stats/population/births/births-tables.aspx

te Riele, K. (2007), 'Educational alternatives for marginalised youth', *The Australian Educational Researcher, 34*(3), 53–68.

Wilson, H. & Huntington, A. (2006), 'Deviant (m)others: The construction of teenage motherhood in contemporary discourse', *Journal of Social Policy*, 35(1), 59–76.

Woodward, L., Fergusson, D.M. & Horwood, L.J. (2001), 'Risk factors and life processes associated with teenage pregnancy: Results of a prospective study from birth to 20 years', *Journal of Marriage and the Family*, 63(4), 1170–83.

Woodward, L., Horwood, L.J. & Fergusson, D.M. (2001), 'Teenage pregnancy: Cause for concern', *New Zealand Medical Journal*, 114(1135), 301–03.

Wylie, S. (2009), 'Meeting the needs of teen parents and their children: Promising practices', Christchurch: Waipuna Youth Social Services.

Youdell, D. (2006), *Impossible Bodies, Impossible Selves: Exclusions and student subjectivities*, Dordrecht: Springer.

Zachry, E. (2005), 'Getting my education: Teen mothers' experiences in school before and after motherhood', *Teachers College Record*, 107(12), 2566–98.

## 12.
# A queer lens on initial teacher education

Vicki M. Carpenter & Debora Lee

Teacher educators are in a unique and powerful position to effect social justice-related change in nationwide classroom and early childhood centre practices. This is because of the influential position they command in the preparation of New Zealand's future teachers. In this chapter we examine initial teacher education (ITE) in one tertiary institution through a queer[1] lens. The changing institutional climate, its people and the policies and processes that related to sexual orientation visibility and inclusion were researched in both 2002 and 2009, and re-evaluated in 2013. Evident through these inquiries was a dynamic between structure and agency; the greater visibility and inclusion of sexual orientation in ITE reflected wider changes in institutional legislation that occurred over this period, as well as teacher educators' desire for change. In the following sections we look briefly at New Zealand's policy and theoretical contexts in relation to social justice, sexual diversity and education. Next, we introduce the institution and discuss our research methods. Following this we compare the findings from 2002 and 2009, and comment on what these say about changes in teacher educators' perceptions and the institutional environment over those seven years. To conclude, we examine the contemporary context, and note that all teacher educators must have a strong commitment to social justice and be inclusive of gender/sexual diversity in their classroom practice.

## The NZ policy context and sexual diversity

It could be argued that New Zealand has liberal queer-related human rights legislation (Vincent & Ballard 1997). In 1986 the Homosexual Law Reform Act decriminalised sex between males aged 16 and older; in 1993 the Human Rights Act was amended to make discrimination on the grounds of 'sexual orientation' (meaning a heterosexual, homosexual, lesbian or

---

1  Queer is used throughout this chapter; our use of the term encompasses lesbian, gay, bisexual and transgender identities.

bisexual orientation) illegal; under an amendment to the Health and Safety in Employment Act (2002), addressing of homophobia in the workplace was made an employer's responsibility; the Civil Union Act 2004 enabled same-gender couples to enter into a formal relationship and have that relationship recognised in law; and in 2013 the Marriage (Definition of Marriage) Amendment Act extended marriage to two people regardless of their sexual orientation or gender identity.

ITE operates within these legislative and cultural frameworks. Despite an evolving and 'accepting' policy context, however, practices that are openly inclusive of non-normative sexual orientations are rare within New Zealand's education system. Historically, societal attitudes to children's and adults' sexualities have been contentious (Surtees 2006); the lingering effects of such attitudes are mirrored in contemporary New Zealand early childhood education and care facilities (ECEC) and schools (Quinlivan 2002; Terreni, Gunn, Kelly & Surtees 2010). As already stated, ITE providers and their faculty members are influenced by, and can influence, the wider education system. ITE is in a unique position: it is able to – and arguably should – challenge taken-for-granted assumptions and prejudices (Robinson & Ferfolja 2002). The legislative framework outlined above ostensibly gives permission to do just that.

There are, however, numerous pressures facing initial teacher educators. For example, ITE curriculum is a contested space. Current neo-liberal policies pressure ITE providers to take more instrumental and technicist approaches to curriculum (Alcorn 1999). As a result, in recent years there has been greater emphasis on teaching content and pedagogical approaches, and less on more 'esoteric' areas such as philosophy and the sociology of education (Kane 2005) – disciplines that offer potential to open hearts, minds and understandings to all forms of diversity and social justice, including sexuality-related issues. The content and delivery of ITE curriculum is central to making the education environment more inclusive and reflective of any current legislation (Robinson & Ferfolja 2002).

## Tertiary environments

ITE is positioned within a wider tertiary environment. A recent study in the United States examined the state of higher education for lesbian, gay, bisexual, transgender (LGBT) faculty members and students (Rankin, Weber, Blumenfeld & Frazer 2010). Over 5000 surveys were completed by queer and straight participants from 50 states. Findings showed that queer staff were less likely than their straight counterparts to feel comfortable with the overall campus climate. They also highlighted how LGBT faculty members and students experienced greater sexual identity-based harassment and discrimination than their heterosexual counterparts. To address such issues the authors recommended inclusive policies, institutional commitment, and the integration of LGBT issues and concerns into curriculum. They also recommended appropriate responses to anti-LGBT incidents or bias; the creation of spaces for civil dialogue between people of all sexual identities; the availability of comprehensive counselling and healthcare; and improved recruitment and retention efforts. No similar study has been undertaken in New Zealand, but the situation here is possibly similar.

## Sexualities and teacher education

This chapter contributes to a body of knowledge examining issues of sexual orientation[2] in ITE (Clark 2010; Ferfolja & Robinson 2004; Robinson & Ferfolja 2002; Sears 2005). International studies demonstrate that sexualities is the area of diversity least likely to be addressed in ITE (Clark 2010; Ferfolja & Robinson 2004; Surtees 2006); yet it is a vital content area because it addresses student wellbeing (Kumashiro 2000).

Heteronormativity (the assumption that everyone is heterosexual) and homophobia (the fear or hatred of homosexuality and LGBTQ people) are central concepts in this chapter.[3] Warner (1993) describes heteronormativity as the discursive practices of compulsory heterosexuality. Heteronormativity is evident both in overt expressions of homophobia, and in the covert presence of unspoken intolerance for diverse (or non-heterosexual) sexualities. It is pervasive in most contexts; its very nature is to stifle 'other' views of the world. The widespread assumption of heterosexuality affects most areas of people's lives (Lee 2010; Warner 1993). In this chapter we are using Jones and Sullivan's (2002) definition of homophobia: 'any negative

---

2   We are using the American Psychological Association's definition of sexual orientation, which generally relates 'to the sex/gender of those to whom one is sexually and romantically attracted' (www.apa.org/pi/lgbt/resources/guidelines.aspx)
3   We acknowledge the theoretical controversies surrounding the terms 'homophobia' and 'heteronormativity' (for instance, see Butler 1991). However, we use these terms because our participants generally used and understood them.

thoughts, feelings or behaviours towards those who are sexually attracted to persons of their own sex' (96).

Teacher educators have a responsibility to confront homophobia and heteronormativity in their classrooms. Kumashiro (2000) maintains it is important to understand that schools are places where harm is done to the sexual 'other', and that this harm is not always the result of acts of blatant homophobia: '[s]ometimes ... the harm results from inactions by educators, administrators, and politicians' (27). Terreni et al. (2010) concur: 'Teachers should aspire to be positive role models for children and demonstrate a commitment to equity, justice and social inclusion' (59). McConaghy (2004) claims that ITE has a legislated responsibility to provide beginning teachers with useful and relevant tools; and New Zealand's *Graduating Teacher Standards* (New Zealand Teachers Council 2007) specifies that beginning teachers must value difference and be able to work effectively within diverse communities.

Australian researchers Robinson and Ferfolja (2001; 2002) argue that homophobia needs to be combatted in ITE before students are released into schools where hegemonic or heteronormative discourses prevail, but assert that teacher educators in general are already acculturated into conservative school norms. They draw attention to some of the dilemmas facing faculty members. For example, if teacher educators are LGBTQ and teach sexuality issues they can be seen as biased, 'pushing their own agenda' (2002, 61) and recruiting for queer sexualities. Straight educators who teach sexualities content may be labelled queer 'by association'.

The potential for ITE to promote critical societal perspectives, including understandings of heteronormativity, often goes unrealised. In an Australian study of ITE, Hatton (1996) maintains that teacher educators and teachers come from a narrow range of social backgrounds; this limits their understandings of inequalities based on class, race and sexualities. She argues that the pluralist or multicultural curriculum objective is given greater attention and priority within diversity programmes in Australian ITE curriculum than sexuality and gender diversity; resources often focus on 'matters of custom, dress, food and so on' (Hatton 1996, 25). Few ITE lessons and resources are used to explore the many variations of sexualities and genders that exist in Australia and the wider international context. Hatton calls for consciousness-raising sessions for teachers and teacher educators to develop sensitivity and critical dispositions; and for resources that assist in developing useful curriculum and pedagogical approaches.

Clark (2010), writing of North American ITE, echoes Hatton:

*While teacher education aimed at issues of diversity is widespread and institutionalized through organizations such as the National Council for Accreditation of Teacher Education (NCATE), the needs of LGBTQ are rarely addressed ... (704).*

In the United States, Sherwin and Jennings (2006) investigated 77 ITE programmes and discovered that 40 per cent did not include sexual orientation in their teaching.

Aside from our own work, we are not aware of any recent research concerning sexual orientation issues in ITE in New Zealand. The largest provider of ITE in New Zealand is in Auckland, the city where our two research projects were conducted. The institutions involved are described in the following section.

## Auckland College of Education, University of Auckland and the merger

In 2002 ITE in Auckland was primarily provided by the 125-year-old Auckland College of Education (ACE). The college had 5025 students and worked closely with local schools and ECEC. In the mid-1990s ACE became a degree-granting institution. While its equity policies explicitly addressed gender and ethnicity, and content around these issues was evident in taught courses, ACE's policies ignored sexual orientation. ITE curriculum courses in health education covered 'sexuality' in a one-off session. Sociology of education courses, which had the potential to include sexual orientation, comprised approximately 15 per cent of the ITE curriculum. None of the generic learning objectives in ACE ITE courses included reference to sexual orientation.

In 2004 ACE merged with the University of Auckland (UofA) and became the Faculty of Education (FoEd). The merger was partially intended to encourage a more critical and academic approach to ITE. While greater emphasis was placed on theory and research, links to teacher practice remained strong and practicum remained integral to ITE curriculum. With subsequent course changes, opportunities arose for health education curriculum and sociology of education courses to become more inclusive of sexual orientation; however, as faculty members involved in lecturing teams for a wide range of courses at the time, we believe the opportunity was missed.

In the broader university at that time the visibility of sexual orientation in equity policies was, at best, tentative. In 2009 the equity policies became two-tiered: groups such as Māori, Pasifika and women, in the first tier, were to have 'programmes developed for them'. Sexual orientation was positioned in the second tier; although it was acknowledged as an equity issue that needed monitoring, no specific policy was drafted. For instance, the rhetoric was: 'Equity groups whose requirements need to be established and monitored include ... gay, lesbian, bisexual, transgender and intersex (GLBTI) staff and students' (McNaughton 2009, 3). Aside from our 2009 study, we are unaware of any other institution-based monitoring or research that has been conducted in this area.

In 2002 and 2009 the teacher educators in the institution were primarily experienced former ECEC, primary and secondary school teachers. Reflecting the workforces from which they were recruited, most were women and Pākehā (New Zealand European). Many came from senior positions in schools and early childhood centres, and tended to be in their 40s or older.[4] With degree-granting status came pressures to 'upskill'; a greater percentage of faculty members in 2009 had Master's or Doctoral degrees,[5] and research played a stronger role in informing ITE.

## Two research studies

Two institutionally funded research studies are discussed here. The 2002 study included both heterosexual and lesbian researchers, and all three researchers were teacher educators. We, the authors, conducted the 2009 research study. We identify as lesbian/queer and teacher educators. As Vicki had worked on the two projects, both sets of raw data were available for this current inquiry.

### 2002 ACE study

The 2002 project investigated faculty members' attitudes to diverse sexualities and the visibility of LGBTQ lecturers on the ACE campus (Fisher, Carpenter & Tetley 2003). A total of 223 faculty members were invited to complete an anonymous paper survey, and 71 responded (a response rate of 31.8 per cent); of these, 17 per cent identified as bisexual (5) or lesbian (7). The

---

4   The mean age of the 223 ACE academic staff in 2002 was between 46 and 50 years; 174 were female and 49 male.
5   See the *University of Auckland Calendar*, 2009, 774–78.

purpose of the study was to examine ACE's policies on sexual orientation, faculty attitudes towards diverse orientation, and the visibility of gay, lesbian and bisexual lecturers.

## 2009 FoEd study

The second study (Carpenter & Lee 2010; Lee & Carpenter 2014) built on the 2002 findings. The purpose of the study was to investigate sexual-orientation visibility and sexual-inclusion practices within ITE in the FoEd. ITE faculty members (144) were invited to complete an online anonymous questionnaire that reproduced some of the 2002 questions. The survey allowed for comments as well as graded responses (using a Likert scale). Thirty-five staff completed the survey (a response rate of 24.3 per cent); six (17 per cent) identified as LGBTQ.

Further to the survey we facilitated two focus-group interviews with faculty members. One group comprised the Rainbow Staff Group (RSG, established in 2004) that included LGBTQ faculty members. As well as being research participants, this group acted as research mentors, through trialling the questionnaire, discussing ethical issues and critiquing the research processes and findings. The second group was 'open' and comprised two faculty members who did not identify as LGBTQ. The themes of inquiry in the interviews included reflections on the initial survey findings; discussions about visibility and inclusion matters for faculty members and students within the FoEd; and an exploration of ways in which the FoEd and its ITE programmes could be more inclusive of sexual diversities.

## Comparisons of findings

As there had been little turnover of core faculty members over the seven years, it is likely that some participants responded to both surveys. Interestingly, although potential participant numbers were almost halved by institutional changes over that time, both surveys attracted a response rate of between 24 and 32 per cent and, in both, 17 per cent of respondents identified as LGBTQ. The reasonable response rates in both projects were perhaps due to a level of trust and support invested in us as colleagues and 'in house' researchers.

We were interested in whether there had been any positive changes regarding levels of visibility and inclusion for non-heterosexual faculty members over the seven years. We were also interested in judging whether the present ITE teaching and curriculum was any more inclusive of sexualities issues. Perusal of both sets of data indicated there had been positive movement. The dominant themes that emerged during data analysis were: 1) visibility and being 'out'; 2) homophobia and heteronormativity; and 3) teaching and curriculum.[6]

### 1. Visibility and being 'out'

'Coming out', or identifying publicly as LGBTQ, was challenging for many teacher educators in both the 2002 and 2009 studies. Unless there was strong evidence to the contrary, heterosexuality was assumed by colleagues. It was therefore more comfortable for some LGBTQ faculty members to work within that status quo. Both studies found non-heterosexual staff were reluctant to share their sexual orientations with either colleagues or students, or both. In 2002 more than half of the ACE bisexual/lesbian respondents had indicated that they did not feel safe being visible on campus, or 'out' with their students or colleagues.

> *Personally, I feel the best option is to keep your private life to yourself so you are not let down by the tokenism offered by the 'politically correct' management of an institution. Many heterosexual people simply pay lip-service to homosexuality, therefore any move made by [my institution] towards acknowledging gay/lesbian staff, I would view with some suspicion. (LGBTQ, survey, 2002)*

In 2009, three of the six LGBTQ respondents were not comfortably open with most of their colleagues; for others there was a provisional 'outness':

> *Although I am happy to be 'out' to most of my colleagues I do not talk openly about my life with many of them. (LGBTQ, survey, 2009)*

> *The Faculty has a middle-class, white, heterosexual ring of confidence around it. (LGBTQ, survey, 2009)*

Only one of the six LGBTQ respondents was prepared to be open with (selected) students regarding her sexual orientation:

> *I'm usually careful, but eventually I come out with some classes. (LGBTQ, survey, 2009)*

---

6   Quotations indicate their sources: 'survey' indicates a survey response, and 'FG' a statement made during a focus group interview. 'Straight' and 'LGBTQ' indicate the self-chosen labels of respondents.

Similarly, many straight faculty members in 2009 were not prepared to be open about their sexualities, but their rationales differed from those of LGBTQ staff. Of the straight faculty, 18 per cent were ambivalent or negative about sharing their sexuality. For these staff however, their sexuality was a non-issue:

*'Open' implies that someone might care about what my sexual orientation is and I don't think it is any of their business. Sexual orientation doesn't come into my professional working life. (straight, survey, 2009)*

*Irrelevant. (straight, survey, 2009)*

As reported previously, Robinson and Ferfolja (2001; 2002) found similar attitudes in their Australian study. Dominant discourses there perpetuated heterosexuality as normal, and constructed non-heterosexuals as deviant and abnormal.

In contrast, in both surveys, some LGBTQ faculty were determinedly 'out'. Their agency was both proactive and visible. Reflecting on the strong and vocal presence of fundamentalist Christian views in 2002, one faculty member said:

*I'm openly gay with students and challenge them to consider their own often Christian unthinking opinion in light of accurate information. (LGBTQ, survey, 2002)*

In 2009 the focus group interview with LGBTQ faculty members allowed for further discussion on the topic of being 'out' with students:

*I'm [coming out to student teachers] very deliberately and I don't actually care much what they think of me, but I care very much that there might be gay/lesbian [or] bisexual students in the class ... it's usually a class that I know pretty well and feel pretty comfortable with but always after that, I 'lose' some students. They are a bit uncomfortable ... (LGBTQ, FG, 2009)*

Kenney (2010) recognises that 'coming out' necessarily means a declaration of 'otherness' that can result in uncomfortable visibility. However, she sees it as a way of making room for LGBTQ: '... space in my classroom, and, I hope, space in my students for the empathy that incites social action' (2010, 72).

A heterosexual faculty member in 2009 expressed concern for LGBTQ students' welfare:

> *We have hundreds of young women coming to these institutions ... and it never occurs to anyone that a certain percentage of those women are gay women, and it worries me because I think they do need some support. (straight, FG, 2009)*

Visibility was recognised in both studies as an issue for LGBTQ faculty members. One lesbian/bisexual lecturer in the 2002 study believed that the health of gay staff was put at risk by a perceived lack of safety:

> *They [faculty members and students] come out quietly, on a one-to-one basis, all lesbian. I have been aware of others, older men, who are gay, not out, and often ill – workplace safety and stress are a real issue and a serious health risk. (LGBTQ, survey, 2002)*

In 2009, similarly, a lesbian faculty member commented on the likelihood of both students and staff having gay family members. She emphasised the silencing of gay men's voices and the possible health consequences for individuals.

In contrast to LGBTQ faculty members, 70 per cent of heterosexual teacher educator respondents in 2009 were happy to acknowledge their sexual orientation with colleagues. A lack of thought about 'mentioning' straight relationships indicates perceptions of 'normality', and the pervasiveness of the heteronormative environment. Some faculty members were aware of the privileges their heterosexual orientation afforded them:

> *... I am part of the mainstream – perhaps this may be different if I wasn't. (straight, survey, 2009)*

> *Since I am the 'default' heterosexual, I rarely think about difficulties in being 'open'. Clearly, speaking about my husband is never a problem. (straight, survey, 2009)*

Allen (2011) believes that in order to effectively problematise heteronormativity, heterosexual educators must critically reflect on the impact of their blatant, and often unconscious, 'outing' of themselves as straight. In comparison, when outside their own communities, LGBTQ subjects are constantly making decisions about whether or not to 'come out' (Morris & Rothblum 1999).

Rationales for LGBTQ silence and invisibility are complex, and undoubtedly include far more reasons (some personal) than the surveys or interviews elicited. The data indicates that, for whatever reasons, some

LGBTQ faculty members in both projects remained quiet about their identities. Arguably the conservative nature of the teaching profession and education in general fed into individuals' assumptions and expectations. LGBTQ silences and invisibilities, in both studies, demonstrate that both ITE environments were heteronormative and therefore probably unsafe workplaces for some.

## 2. Homophobia and heteronormativity

The word 'homophobia' was used by LGBTQ and straight respondents alike in both research studies, while, the term 'heteronormativity' was rarely used. We think this is because the concept of heteronormativity is better understood and utilised by queer researchers. Notwithstanding this, our reading of responses from both sets of surveys pointed to heteronormativity being rife.

> *Homophobia is around but my colleagues, on a one-to-one [basis], are usually very supportive of my lifestyle. (LGBTQ, survey, 2002)*

> *There is some support but visibility remains an issue. I think the environment remains a heteronormative one. (LGBTQ, survey, 2009)*

In 2002 and 2009 teacher educators were aware of the negative effects of homophobia.

> *I left secondary teaching 25 years ago because I was not able to be open about my sexuality and survive in the staffroom. It's easier at this level [tertiary] ... I'm not sure that being open about my lesbianism would help me! We've come a long way but there's still a need for this questionnaire and that speaks volumes. (LGBTQ, survey, 2002)*

Seven years later a faculty member was hesitant to use homophobia to describe what she experienced:

> *I don't know about homophobia as such ... it felt like an uneasy tolerance and I know that's a form of homophobia ... nothing nasty or vindictive or anything. It's just that behind-your-back-type behaviour that you wouldn't really expect in a professional institution. (LGBTQ, survey, 2009)*

More assertive responses to homophobia were provided by other LGBTQ participants:

> I've been up-front on numerous occasions with students, stating: 'I find your language and attitude offensive. As a gay man I object very strongly to your comments, and would ask you not to engage in such a manner in future.' (LGBTQ, survey, 2009)

Straight faculty members in both 2002 and 2009 indicated they were prepared to respond to student homophobia. These heterosexual allies played an integral role, especially in regard to student safety:

> I was appalled at a heterosexual student's verbal abuse of a gay student … I helped the student to write a letter of complaint. Much to my chagrin the heterosexual student graduated and started teaching in a religious school. I would have loved to have been able to stop bigots and religious zealots like her from graduating. (straight, survey, 2009)

Participants in both studies were asked if they felt their institution was 'generally supportive of sexual diversity'. This rather broad question had its underlying focus on whether or not respondents felt the conditions were safe and empowering for all faculty and students.

Table 12.1: Sexual diversity support

| My institution is supportive of sexual diversity | 2002 ($n$ =71) | 2009 ($n$ =35) |
| --- | --- | --- |
| Agree or strongly agree | 57% | 50% |
| Neutral or unsure | 23% | 44% |
| Disagree | 20% | 6% |

The proportion of respondents indicating that the institution was supportive remained relatively stable across the two surveys (see Table 12.1). By 2009, however, a much larger percentage reported they were neutral/unsure about the degree of supportiveness for sexual diversity in their workplace. This was a shift from the 2002 survey in which 20 per cent of respondents reported they considered their workplace was not supportive. The movement in perception of attitudinal change within the institution over the seven years was generally positive, but the shifts were small. Despite the introduction of national legislation that could have supported institutional action, support for queers and their lifestyles remained largely static between 2002 and 2009. In our view, heteronormativity pervaded

ITE: most queer faculty did not feel safe to 'come out', let alone address visibility and inclusion issues, and those with power in ITE felt little or no pressure from colleagues to initiate change. Such slow institutional progress is perhaps reflective of wider public attitudes to LGBTQ equity and rights.

Taking action against heteronormativity and homophobia requires educators to be conscious of the myriad ways these forms of bias are manifest. Comments in both studies showed that the degree to which LGBTQ students and staff were supported at the faculty, and prejudices challenged, depended to some extent on the consciousness and comparative authority of individual faculty members. Ferfolja and Robinson (2004) write of the 'liberal tolerance' that is common in education and leads to presumptions of sameness. Such an attitude does not assist the inclusion of non-heterosexual identities. Liberal tolerance was evident in the 2002 and 2009 responses.

In 2002 a bisexual faculty member commented that people who do not acknowledge the existence of diverse sexualities would be unlikely to notice or confront issues:

> *You don't have to acknowledge what you don't really recognise. [Our ITE institution] isn't that anti – it's just very passive. (LGBTQ, survey, 2002)*

Some 2009 responses pointed to a mellowing of attitudes to sexual diversity, and a deepening understanding of the complexities involved. Also evident were strong allies among straight staff:

> *One of the dangers is to assume that, because there are sanctions around discriminatory behaviours, there will be no problem. I would suggest that sexual orientation remains one of the most pervasive sources of discriminatory behaviour and that this is why there may be some reluctance to openly acknowledge one's sexual orientation. (straight, survey, 2009)*

> *The Faculty of Education doesn't address [discrimination] unless someone makes them. I guess they cross their fingers and hope it doesn't come up. When it does – they act equitably. Just like members of other stigmatised groups [LGBTQs] are supposed to act as if they are sexless, race-less, neutral beings. (straight, survey, 2009)*

> *We have an openly gay lecturer in our [department] and we celebrated as a group when he had a civil union.[7] (straight, survey, 2009)*

---

7   See NZ policy context section regarding changes in the Marriage Act, 2013.

In summary, while there was evidence of positive shifts in heteronormative and homophobic attitudes over the seven years, heteronormativity in particular remained ubiquitous. The following section addresses ITE curriculum and teaching matters – what happened or did not happen in classrooms in relation to sexual orientation.

### 3. Teaching and curriculum

In both research projects, teacher educators were asked if they were inclusive (supporting, acknowledging) of sexual orientation in their day-to-day teaching. They were asked about their classroom dialogue, the references students were guided to, and who they invited into their classrooms or lectures as guest speakers or 'experts'. In 2002 the majority of heterosexual faculty considered diverse sexualities irrelevant. Such a position is exemplified by the statement of a straight faculty member who felt pressured just covering course content, and another who saw his/her work as asexual:

> *I do not cover sex, religion or politics in the classroom, it is enough just covering the subject area. (straight, survey, 2002)*

> *My work is asexual, requiring neither acknowledgement nor reference to sexual orientation. (straight, survey, 2002)*

While there was a shift by 2009, it is noticeable that most heterosexual faculty still did not see inclusivity of sexual orientation as work-relevant. Some continued to consider the topic of diverse sexualities as additional and unimportant:

> *In the courses I teach, sexual orientation is superfluous. (straight, survey, 2009)*

In Ferfolja and Robinson's (2004) study, mentioned previously, many faculty members believed the inclusion of sexual orientation curriculum content was relevant only in secondary ITE; they too were concerned about an already crowded curriculum. One respondent in their study asked, 'How much more will teachers be expected to do?' (18).

It appears, however, that there were changes in teaching and curriculum over the seven years. Bearing in mind that respondents were self-reporting, and the 2009 survey did include fewer people, in 2009 a greater percentage of heterosexual and LGBTQ staff stated they were likely to be inclusive of sexual orientation in their pedagogies. The results are especially heartening

Table 12.2: Inclusivity and the faculty

| Faculty members and inclusivity | 2002 survey (*n* = 71) | 2009 survey (*n* = 35) |
| --- | --- | --- |
| Heterosexual staff inclusive of sexual orientation in their teaching (self-reported) | 26% | 42% |
| LGBTQ staff inclusive of sexual orientation in their teaching (self-reported) | 45% | 59% |

in the case of heterosexual faculty members: almost half indicated they were more inclusive, as shown in Table 12.2.

Most respondents reported inclusion through the use of particular readings, resources and class discussions. Although our research findings showed that some faculty members questioned the validity of learning about sexual orientation, others used their agency and worked hard to provide a supportive and inclusive learning environment. For example, one heterosexual faculty member in 2009 advocated an integrated approach. He felt it was his responsibility to show a welcoming attitude towards all student teachers in every course he taught:

*If sexual orientation comes up I like to create some ambivalence around [it] to highlight to students that straight is often assumed by default ... I want to make sure [there isn't] a silent message that says: 'Teaching, or teacher education, isn't for you. You shouldn't be here.' (straight, FG, 2009)*

One faculty member expressed surprise at a narrow view of diversity portrayed for students:

*I was at a lecture last night and the topic was diversity, but not once did sexual diversity get a mention. (LGBTQ, FG, 2009)*

Ferfolja and Robinson (2004) noted similar issues in their study of ITE in Australia. As previously indicated, the authors believed that there is a diversity hierarchy, with sexualities the least recognised and acknowledged.[8]

Ironically, contradictions are demonstrated among pre-service teachers when inequality and discrimination are placed within contexts other than

---

8   For further discussion on the hidden curriculum of heteronormativity evident in the 2009 findings see Carpenter & Lee (2010).

sexuality. When it comes to issues such as racism and/or sexism, some are willing to assume a social justice position in their future teaching practice, even if it means challenging the beliefs and moral values of parents. For others, however, lesbian and gay concerns transcend the definition of what constitutes an 'appropriate' social justice issue (Robinson & Ferfolja 2002, 60).

The challenge of including sexualities content in ITE is mirrored in other education contexts. For instance, ECEC environments tend to be heteronormative; it is rare for teachers to include curriculum content relevant to children from LGBTQ families, even when such children attend the centre (Lee 2010). Quinlivan (2002) argues that in New Zealand, when sexualities are addressed with school students, the topic tends to be addressed from a deficit perspective. There is little research pointing to New Zealand tertiary environments that provide safe, open and welcoming environments for queer students and staff.

In summary, over the seven years there were positive moves in terms of the inclusivity of ITE curriculum and teaching where sexualities were concerned. Faculty members became more proactive, whether they were straight or queer. Yet while the institution became slightly more supportive of sexual diversities, the topic remained low on the hierarchy of diversity. A high percentage of queer faculty members remained reticent about sharing their sexual orientations.

All of this transpired during years in which national laws changed: homophobia was made illegal in the workplace (2002), and civil unions legislated (2004). We now turn our attention to an evaluation of the 2014 FoEd context.

## The contemporary context – 2014

We are of the view that progress with the visibility and inclusion of non-heterosexual students and faculty members has been more evident in recent years (since 2009). While new research will be necessary to provide evidence of this in teaching and curriculum, there is now 'hard to be ignored' queer visibility and inclusion on campus. For instance, queer representation on the FoEd equity committee was mandated in 2011. That same year, the Rainbow Education Staff (RSG) group requested that their contact details and meetings be advertised under a rainbow banner in the weekly faculty electronic notice to students, and on a large public screen in a main campus building.

With faculty equity committee support, the RSG organised well-attended workshops on queer issues in 2011. In 2012 the committee awarded the RSG a generous grant to run the inaugural Queers in Tertiary Education hui, which received strong support and positive feedback. This, and subsequent hui led by other institutions, have led to greater visibility of queers in Auckland's tertiary environments and the development of stronger inter-institutional networks.

As a result of these initiatives, the RSG project Queer/trans Visibility and Action was awarded a UofA Excellence in Equity award in 2012. In 2013 the faculty equity committee funded the design and printing of Rainbow Group bookmarks to be handed out during student orientation, and the RSG also received funding in 2013 to run workshops at both the city campus and the FoEd, such as the 'Affirming diversity workshops for staff and students: A forum on sexual/gender identity and same-sex attractions', run by Jamie Burford. Queer visibility on campus has increased, largely through RSG and equity committee initiatives, and also because a larger group of faculty members are now prepared to be out and visible to both colleagues and students.

FoEd initiatives have filtered throughout the university. The 2012 hui brought queer matters to the attention of the UofA equity committee and a university-wide LGBTQ group was established for both faculty and students (in addition to UniQ, the student-only group). A university queer rights officer was appointed and a queer space provided at another campus. These are significant changes, and future research will determine their effectiveness.

While the steps taken in the FoEd were all initiated by queer faculty, straight support was willingly given, and invaluable. Straight allies who challenge heteronormativity in ITE make a very important contribution and help precipitate positive change (Clark 2010). Heteronormativity impacts on everyone; it expects straights to be straight and queers to be queer and expectations exist on both sides of the 'binary'.

## Discussion and conclusion

As a result of proactive measures undertaken by staff, as well as insitutional policy changes, queer issues are now more public and present in the FoEd and the Auckland campus environment. Heteronormativity pervaded ACE in 2002; while some positive changes were apparent by 2009, the FoEd climate had, however, changed little. In 2011 strategies instigated by the

RSG and implemented by the institution better addressed queer visibility across campus; we believe these and subsequent actions were precursors to the recent emergence of more positive and inclusive practices.

Now, as we are write this in 2014, there are positive signs concerning visibility and inclusion. However, we suspect that there are still some (perhaps covert) heteronormative attitudes and practices perpetuated in pedagogy, curriculum design and implementation. We need evidence to support or refute this claim and therefore more research is necessary.

It is hard to draw a direct link between the effects of legislative changes on social justice-related agency or change on campus, but our feeling is that, in this case, with respect to the visibility and inclusion of sexual diversity at the university, that structure is preceding agency. ITE, conservative in nature, follows the rules; however, the country's laws have changed and so too, we think, will some ITE faculties.

Our data about heteronormativity and ITE adds to and mirrors an international picture of ITE with respect to sexual diversity and inclusivity (see DePalma & Atkinson 2006; Ferfolja & Robinson 2004). If we are serious about addressing this in the interests of social justice and human rights, however, educators and ITE faculty members must engender critical social justice-based dispositions in emerging teachers and make ITE curriculum and environments more inclusive (Hatton 1996; Rankin et al. 2010). Through our queer lens we can see that positive change is possible and has been occurring, albeit slowly, at our own FoEd. Heteronormativity, it seems, is waning.

ITE is powerful and can lead change in education. Our research has uncovered part of a story of change in one Auckland ITE institution, but little is known about what is happening elsewhere. We argue that a queer lens on practices in other New Zealand ITE institutions is necessary and long overdue. Given our findings about ITE accommodating policy rather than using it as a vehicle to drive positive change, the conditions are ripe. Our education system would benefit from pro-active leadership and ITE faculty members having a strongly motivated social justice stance concerning sexualities and gender diversities.

## Acknowledgements

Thanks to students and faculty participants. Special thanks to our colleagues in the RSG. Constanza Tolosa ably assisted us with data analysis. Sue Osborne provided valuable feedback. We are grateful for funding and other support from ACE and our schools in the FoEd. Special thanks to the late Dr Ruth Williams, our champion and ally in her role as Chair of the Faculty Equity Committee.

## References

Alcorn, N. (1999), 'Initial teacher education since 1990: Funding and supply as determinants of policy and practice', *New Zealand Journal of Educational Studies*, 34(1), 110–20.

Allen, L. (2011), '"Undoing" the self: Should heterosexual teachers "come out" in the university classroom?', *Pedagogy, Culture & Society*, 19(1), 79–95.

Butler, J. (1991), 'Imitation and gender insubordination', in D. Fuss (ed.), *Inside/Out: Lesbian theories, gay theories* (13–31), New York: Routledge.

Carpenter, V.M. & Lee, D. (2010), 'Teacher education and the hidden curriculum of heteronormativity', *Curriculum Matters*, 6, 99–119.

Clark, C.T. (2010), 'Preparing LBGTQ-allies and combating homophobia in a US teacher education program', *Teaching and Teacher Education*, 26, 704–13.

DePalma, R. & Atkinson, E. (2006), 'The sound of silence: Talking about sexual orientation and schooling', *Sex Education*, 6(4), 333–49.

Ferfolja, T. & Robinson, K.H. (2004), 'Why anti-homophobia in teacher education? Perspectives from Australian teacher educators', *Teaching Education*, 15(1), 9–25.

Fisher, D., Carpenter, V.M. & Tetley, P. (2003), *'Is This Really an Issue?': Institutional heterosexism in a college of education*, Auckland: Auckland College of Education.

Hatton, E. (1996), 'Dealing with diversity: The failure of teacher education', *Discourse: Studies in the cultural politics of education*, 17(1), 25–42.

Jones, M.K. & Sullivan, G. (2002), 'Psychiatric disorder or straight prejudice? The role of education in overcoming homophobia', in K.H. Robinson, J. Irwin & T. Ferfolja (eds), *From Here to Diversity: The social impact of lesbian and gay issues in education in Australia and New Zealand* (95–105), Binghamton, NY: Harrington Park.

Kane, R.G. (2005), *Initial Teacher Education: Policy and practice*, Wellington: Ministry of Education.

Kenney, L.M. (2010), 'Being out and reading queer-inclusive texts in a high school English classroom', in M.V. Blackburn, C.T. Clark, L.M. Kenney & J.M. Smith (eds), *Acting Out! Combating homophobia through teacher activism* (56–73), New York: Teachers College Press.

Kumashiro, K. (2000), 'Toward a theory of anti-oppressive education', *Review of Educational Research*, 70(1), 25–53.

Lee, D. (2010), 'Gay mothers and early childhood education: Standing tall', *Australasian Journal of Early Childhood*, 35(1), 16–23.

Lee, D. & Carpenter, V.M. (July, 2014), '"What would you like me to do? Lie to you?" Teacher education responsibilities to LGBTI students', *Asia-Pacific Journal of Teacher Education*, 43(2), 169–80.

McConaghy, C. (2004), 'On cartographies of anti-homophobia in teacher education (and the crisis of witnessing rural student teacher refusals)'. *Teaching Education*, 15(1), 63–79.

McNaughton, T. (2009), *Equity Policy*, Auckland: University of Auckland.

Morris, J.F. & Rothblum, E.D. (1999), 'Who fills out a "lesbian" questionnaire?', *Women Quarterly*, 23, 537-57.

New Zealand Teachers Council (2007), *Graduating Teacher Standards: Aotearoa New Zealand*, Wellington: www.teacherscouncil.govt.nz/sites/default/files/gts-poster.pdf

Quinlivan, K. (2002), 'Whose problem is this? Queerying the framing of lesbian and gay secondary school students within "at risk" discourses', in K.H. Robinson, J. Irwin & T. Ferfolja (eds), *From Here to Diversity: The social impact of lesbian and gay issues in education in Australia and New Zealand* (17-32), Binghamton, NY: Harrington Park.

Rankin, S., Weber, G., Blumenfeld, W. & Frazer, S. (2010), *2010 State of Higher Education for Lesbian, Gay, Bisexual & Transgender People*, Charlotte, NC: Campus Pride.

Robinson, K.H. & Ferfolja, T. (2001), '"What are we doing this for?" Dealing with lesbian and gay issues in teacher education', *British Journal of Sociology of Education*, 22(1), 121-33.

Robinson, K.H. & Ferfolja, T. (2002), 'A reflection of resistance. Discourses of heterosexism and homophobia in teacher training classrooms', in K.H. Robinson, J. Irwin & T. Ferfolja (eds), *From Here to Diversity: The social impact of lesbian and gay issues in education in Australia and New Zealand* (55-64), New York: Haworth.

Sears, J.T. (ed.), (2005), *Youth, Education and Sexualities: An international encyclopedia*, Westport, CT: Greenwood.

Sherwin, G. & Jennings, T. (2006), 'Feared, forgotten, or forbidden: Sexual orientation topics in secondary teacher preparation programs in the USA', *Teaching Education*, 17(3), 207-23.

Surtees, N. (2006), 'Queering the hetero(norm) in research: Unsettling notions of the sexual other', in C. Mutch (ed.), *Challenging the Notion of 'Other'* (63-81), Wellington: New Zealand Council for Educational Research.

Terreni, L., Gunn, A., Kelly, J. & Surtees, N. (2010), 'In and out of the closet: Successes and challenges experienced by gay and lesbian headed families in their interactions with the education system in New Zealand', in V. Green & S. Cherrington (eds), *Delving into Diversity* (151-61), New York: Nova Science.

Vincent, K. & Ballard, K. (1997), 'Living on the margins: Lesbian experience in secondary schools', *New Zealand Journal of Educational Studies*, 32(2), 147-61.

Warner, M. (1993), 'Introduction', in M. Warner (ed.), *Fear of a Queer Planet: Queer politics and social theory* (vii-xxxi), Minneapolis, MN: University of Minnesota Press.

# 13.
# Pulling the monstrosity of (hetero) normativity out of the closet

Teacher education as a problem and an answer

lisahunter, Debi Futter-Puati & Janette Kelly

## Background to the monstrous spectre of (hetero)normativity

For the purposes of this chapter we suggest that (hetero)normativity[1] is a 'malaise' and a 'monstrous spectre', a menacing form of 'symbolic violence' in classrooms within universities, schools and early childhood centres. It is time to bring it out of the closet, not because it is hidden from view but because it is ubiquitous as a naturalised or taken-for-granted practice in the closets of our perceptions. As authors and activist teacher educators/academics/researchers working in a range of education settings, we are committed to changing the status quo by challenging this malaise and monstrosity. The question we face is: *How might (hetero)normativity be exposed, challenged and addressed within initial teacher education (ITE) programmes?*

In this chapter we introduce and contextualise the issue of (hetero)normativity within our own ITE programmes, and identify some useful concepts. We provide a narrative that illustrates (hetero)normativity in education within Aotearoa/New Zealand. Writing in a manner so you, the reader, can 'perch on the periphery' and 'listen in' to the issues and dilemmas we are contending with in our work, we apply Bourdieu's theoretical framework to aid reflection. Our chapter concludes by offering some questions to consider how we, and you, might negotiate our situated practices to accost the spectre – that is, how we might expose and challenge heterosexuality and educate for positive change in relation to sexual diversity in schooling and teacher education.

---

[1] While sex/gender/sexuality is our focus we see normativity as a bigger issue in which heteronormavity is manifested, hence our use of (hetero)normativity. We use heteronormativity when referring to others' work.

Over 15 years ago, Eyre (1997) noted that the term homophobia 'diverts attention away from larger social forces that support and maintain the normalisation of heterosexuality as well as away from the growing collective political activism of gay and lesbian groups' (199). At that time, heterosexism and heteronormativity were fairly new concepts in popular and academic discourse. According to Rubin (1993) the 'charmed circle' of normative heterosexuality, referred to in this chapter as (hetero)normativity, was characterised by a married, monogamous, procreative male–female heterosexual couple, who had a private sex life and did not use sex toys or pornography. The malaise – the durable social signs that seem so obvious that they avoid recognition, critique, challenge or change – has meant that normativity, in the form of heteronormative discourses that include heterosexism and homophobia identified in the charmed circle, still operates in contemporary times. Normativity – a set of ideas, attitudes, biases and discriminations – can shape the way people think, speak and act, and serves to 'other' those marginalised or alienated by the normalised or dominant identities, positionings and practices. The socially constructed 'normal' becomes naturalised and assumed.

Sedgwick (1990), among others, argues that normative understandings of gender and sexuality preserve heteronormativity. These understandings permeate our educational institutions such as schools, early childhood centres and sites of teacher education (Carpenter & Lee 2010; Ferfolja 2007; Meyer 2007; Prettyman 2007; Wickens & Sandlin 2010). Despite the development of critical theory, queer theory, seminal texts[2], and research showing how teachers have been able to counter heterosexism and improve conditions for young people in relation to sex, gender and sexualities[3], issues associated with (hetero)normativity are enduring and pervasive. While some positive changes are documented, educational institutions remain guilty of exacerbating heterosexism and homophobia through heteronormative discourses (Clark 2010; DeJean 2010; Hermann-Wilmarth & Bills 2010; Stiegler 2008; Wickens & Sandlin 2010). Many scholars argue that ITE programmes should incorporate into their curricula topics ranging from sexual orientation to heteronormativity (Bower & Klecka 2009; Clark 2010; Rofes 2005; Talburt 2004). The North American activist research project between teachers and teacher educators, *Acting Out* (Blackburn, Clark,

---

2   Such as Sears & Williams' 1997 *Overcoming Heterosexism and Homophobia: Strategies that work.*
3   For example see Athanases & Larrabee 2003; Robinson & Ferfolja 2008; Russell, Seif & Truong 2001; Wyatt et al. 2008.

Kenney & Smith 2010), captures some practices and reflections on anti-homophobic work. In a New Zealand context, Carpenter and Lee (2010, 115) noted that:

> The problem [in our teacher education institution] appears to be how to build the bridge from where we are now – a situation where the hidden curriculum is heteronormativity – to an ideal faculty world where all groups and individuals are included and affirmed – where diversity truly means diversity – and which meets basic human rights obligations.

Like others before them, Carpenter and Lee argued for change and proposed actions to disrupt the hidden curriculum of heteronormativity. While they were referring specifically to their institution, their problem resonates with ours.

## Setting the scene

We, the authors of this chapter, work with pre-service 'emerging teachers'[4] in a contemporary Aotearoa/New Zealand education setting. We have tried many suggestions from authors mentioned above, and more, as we assist educators to affirm sexual diversity and enhance learning possibilities for all. Our objectives are first, to aid emerging teachers to expose and destabilise normativity. Second, we aim to promote social inclusion through the understanding that diversity is often hidden and powerfully used. Third, we want others to recognise that they may be influenced by conscious and unconscious choices in their own embodiment of education. Finally, we want to encourage a critical education that generates positive outcomes for everybody. In these tasks we have experienced mixed results and associated complexities, as will be conveyed in our fictional narrative below.

We start by introducing a framework rooted in Bourdieu's (1991; 1998) concepts of *field*, *habitus*, *capital*, *symbolic violence* and *doxa*. Next we draw on field texts (Clandinin & Connelly 2000) – including emerging teacher surveys, anecdotal memories associated with our teaching, personal academic journal entries, and emerging teacher correspondence, which record and reflect on recently encountered situations related to sex/gender/sexuality. From these texts we create an interim research text (Clandinin

---

4   We are using the term 'emerging teacher' to refer to the student teachers in our pre-service programmes. This includes those in early childhood, primary and secondary education cohorts.

& Connelly 2000) in the form of a co-constructed fictional narrative. The narrative involves several characters: emerging teachers, teacher educators, and our imagined colleague Pierre. In it we dialogue with Bourdieu's concepts, and explore the logic of our teaching practices relative to notions of sex, gender and sexualities. In this way we hope to show how Bourdieu's concepts might translate in a conversation about (hetero)normativity, in order to help us understand our practices and devise ways to counter (hetero)normativity. Finally, we offer a series of reflexive questions to guide the next iteration of our practice, and perhaps yours. We seek to keep the 'idealistic' agenda alive, accepting that modest and reflexive attempts at practices that address our central question – how (hetero)normativity might be exposed and addressed within ITE programmes – are still valid. Positive transformation in the form of changing socialised norms may occur slowly, perhaps even only as intergenerational change (Bourdieu 1999). As the narrative shows, it is complex; there is no easy answer or clear 'one size fits all' path. As educators, therefore, we must continue to be diligent in our ITE pedagogical practices.

We are consciously telling a story embedded in contemporary New Zealand at the micro-level of the education *field* in which there are multiple players: emerging teachers in ITE programmes, the policy and institutional *doxa* of education/teacher education, and the schools and centres where emerging teachers experience teaching practice. At the same time our story is embedded in the macro-level *field* where (hetero)normativity is so taken-for-granted and unrecognised that we suggest it is a relatively unfamiliar concept to most people. This certainly holds true in our experiences with emerging teachers. We take the view that all of us need to 'do better' if the oppressive outcomes of (hetero)normativity are to be recognised and reduced.

## Operationalising Bourdieu's concepts

Pierre Bourdieu was a well-known teacher, scholar, academic and activist in France in the latter half of the twentieth century. He was curious about how societies worked to (re)produce themselves. His desire for social justice meant he worked to expose violence in human practices at macro (society) and micro (individual) levels. What follows are brief plain-language explanations of concepts he developed in dialogue with his observations of the world – ones that challenge us to work in ways that bind theory and practice together.

## Doxa

*Doxa* acts as an explanation of how (hetero)normativity can be so powerful that it is hidden. *Doxa* is 'an orthodoxy, a right, correct, dominant vision which has more often than not been imposed through struggles against competing visions' (Bourdieu 1998, 56). 'Straight' and 'gay' are not new terms for sexuality, yet the first is constructed as dominant, representing the norm, and the second as 'other', representing the marginalised and demonised. (Hetero)normativity then is understandable as a form of *doxa* – (hetero)*doxa* – a particular point of view, privileging that of the dominant. That these two constructs for sexuality are taken for granted as a catch-all for all forms of sexuality is an effect of (hetero)normativity.

> *[Doxa] presents and imposes itself as a universal point of view – the point of view of those who dominate by dominating the state and who have constituted their point of view as universal by constituting the state ... The major effect of historical evolution is to abolish history by relegating to the past, that is, to the unconscious, the lateral possibles that it eliminated (Bourdieu 1998, 7).*

In this case the diminished 'lateral possibles' include intersex, transgender, transsexual, pansexual, queer, lesbian, bisexual, gay, questioning and more. Having no perception or knowledge of what these laterals are, is an illustration of *doxa*. People who occupy the dominant space may not even perceive the common sense of a heterosexual world, as perception is the key to recognising difference and then embracing diversity. 'The primary experience of the world of common sense is a politically produced relation, as are the categories of perception that sustain it' (Bourdieu 1998, 56). We may use this concept in our consideration of sexualities, therefore, to ask:

- What *doxa* exist in teacher education and in the *field* of education?
- How do we sensitise both ourselves and emerging teachers to the orthodoxies?
- Who gains and who loses from the *doxa* that dominate?
- Which of the lateral identities are we familiar with?
- What processes operate to legitimate some while erasing others? How?

## Field, habitus, capital and practice

Bourdieu used the term *field* to reflect relatively autonomous sets of social practices, such as education, medicine or media, often embodied in the practices of institutions such as schools, hospitals or television. While integrated in policies, rules, regulations and historical ways of doing things, including taken-for-granted assumptions (*doxa*), these practices only come to life through humans embodying them in actions. Actual *practice* becomes pivotal to Bourdieu's explanation of what is going on. He used *habitus* to refer to our dispositions, attitudes and beliefs; our histories that work through our bodily practices; and our habits, often not at the conscious level and to some extent determined by the structures that socialise us to perceive and understand our world in a particular way. Where our *habitus* is valued within a *field*, we gain forms of *capital*, whether economic, social or cultural. To illustrate, a student announcing they are transgender who then loses friends, loses social capital and is valued less; an 'out' queer parent who is overlooked for the school board misses out on the prestige that might come from that position. Bourdieu believed, however, that we are able to reflect on what we do, and to change our dispositions, beliefs and attitudes, at the same time changing the social structures or *fields* to which we belong. With these concepts in mind, we might ask:

- How does our *habitus* challenge or reproduce (hetero)normativity?
- Which forms of *habitus* are strongly or poorly positioned within the *field*?
- What is valued and devalued in people and practices in relation to sex/gender/sexualities in education? Why and how?

*Field* and *habitus* are two sides of the same coin: they constitute each other. For example, in a teacher education class in which queer parents are never mentioned, (hetero)normativity plays out twice at the same time. It plays out in the *habitus* of the individuals who refer explicitly or implicitly to parents being a male–female couple, as well as in the *field* of education via supported structures, for example by a lack of acknowledgment of any parents who are not heterosexual. In educational settings, examples might include discouraging a boy from using a pink handbag; referring to parents without being explicit that alternatives to dominant heterosexual parenting exist; presenting only traditional parent/family representations in children's picture books; insisting on male–female partnerships for school balls; and the presence or lack of allied associations at the university campus.

(Hetero)normativity also plays out in the hidden curriculum. For example, diversity targets for teacher education are regularly associated with ethnicity and gender but not sexualities; teachers may refuse to acknowledge children's/students' sexuality; schools have 'boys' and 'girls' toilets; there are difficulties in talking about sexuality across teacher education programmes other than in courses about 'diversity' or 'health'; and 'being out' in education settings is censored, especially for emerging teachers who are regularly counselled by peers, teachers and others to remain closeted while on practicum.

These are all illustrations of *symbolic power* and violence, forces that may not seem as important or recognisable as physical power and violence and are therefore perhaps even more powerful. With these things in mind, we ask:

- How do we recognise and critique *field* and *habitus* to understand what part teachers/teacher educators play in perpetuating (hetero) normativity?
- What forms of power, *capital* and violence are circulating?

*Symbolic power, capital and violence*

*Symbolic power* is 'invisible power which can be exercised only with the complicity of those who do not want to know that they are subject to it or even that they themselves exercise it' (Bourdieu 1991, 164). Those who have *capital*, or value, have this power. With this authority they have more opportunity to frame those practices and dispositions that are most valued – and which they are already more likely to have. It is a bit like the rich getting richer because they possess *economic capital* to hire lawyers to find loopholes in tax laws, which enable them to profit. Heterosexuals value and reinforce heterosexuality as dominant and as the 'normal' way of being. Historically, there were advantages to being considered heterosexual; those who were not were encouraged to hide under the cover of that which had value: assumed heterosexuality (sometimes referred to as 'not coming out', 'passing' or being 'in the closet'). *Symbolic violence* occurs where the 'dominated lifestyles [e.g. queer] are almost always perceived, even by those who live them, from the destructive and reductive point of view of the dominant aesthetic' (Bourdieu 1998, 9).

*Symbolic violence* plays out when practices, embodied as the (individual or group) *habitus*, are complicit in one's own oppression. When this occurs it supports the illusion of the naturalness of the practice that counteracts one's own interest. Embedded in institutional structures, symbolic violence may become difficult to recognise, let alone to speak about and heal. This is because such structures become second nature and are 'common sense' practices within that *field*'s operation. For example, a negative and homophobic response towards a transgendered peer from a 'closeted gay' pre-service teacher could be considered an act of symbolic violence, because the gay teacher is adding to his own oppression by devaluing his non-normative peer. Further examples of symbolic violence include lining children up as 'girls and boys'; assigning roles to students in school productions in ways that fit heteronormative stereotypes; only talking about diversity/inclusion in terms of disability; assuming heterosexual families are safe for children; imposing a religious belief system on classroom interactions; teaching sexuality as only biological reproductive sex; allowing students to opt out of sexuality education; avoiding discussions of cisnormativity for fear of being outed; or introducing a lecturer's same-sex partner to students as a 'colleague' rather than partner. These practices can trap already marginalised people into no-win situations, adding more *symbolic violence* to the taken-for-granted state of (hetero)normativity. With these ideas in mind we ask:

- How might we value all forms of sexuality using different forms of *capital*? What do teachers/teacher educators do to contribute to or counteract *symbolic violence* in relation to sex/gender/sexualities?

As we reflect on our practices with emerging teachers, in the narrative that follows, we use Bourdieu's concepts of *doxa, field, habitus, capital* and *symbolic violence* as a framework for understanding 'what is going on'. We illustrate the complexity of 'where we are now' (Carpenter & Lee 2010, 115) as we ask ourselves, our readers, our future students and our colleagues, 'Where to next?' This questioning is vital if we are to resist the malaise of the status quo and honour basic human rights as we challenge (hetero) normativity.

### (Hetero)*doxa* of practices in relation to sex, gender and sexualities in our courses: An interim research text

'Well THAT was interesting,' says James, an emerging teacher in the PGDip primary programme, sitting down in his usual chair in the student cafeteria for morning break, '– NOT,' he followed up quickly. 'There's just too much to know and figure out. There's the policy on sex ed that the school has to follow, and the health and physical education [HPE] curriculum document the lecturer said there are two of, but I still don't know what I've gotta teach.'

'Yeah, there's a lot to cover,' says Matt, sitting in his usual place. 'When you asked that question about the two curriculum documents I think Debi was trying to explain that the 1995 curriculum document was like a previous version of this 2007 one. It has more detail but still doesn't spell out the key area of learning [KAL] for sex ed. I think the school will sort it all out before it gets to us. I only want to teach the little kids so I won't have to teach any of that stuff anyway.' Overhearing this conversation while waiting for his colleagues lisahunter, Debi and Janette to arrive, Pierre recognises these ideas as *doxa*. From Matt and James's conversations he identifies their dominant views: that young people should not/cannot be sexual, and therefore sexuality education should not be taught in lower primary, let alone early childhood education.

'Yeah you will, and its sexuality education, not sex ed,' pipes up Sarah from the next table, where she is nursing a coffee after having left the lecture early for a phone call from her daughter's crèche. 'It's supposed to be taught across the levels but it includes stuff like belonging and relationships – and that *Curriculum in Action* resource *Positive Puberty* looks helpful. All *we* ever got at school was birds and bees stuff in Year 7, boys in one class and girls in the other, at least until we got into biology in Year 11. My parents never told me anything, but I talk to my eight-year-old about people being different, about his gay uncle, about reproduction and about treating people how you'd like to be treated. It's all of that stuff too.'

Matt and James look at each other, raising eyebrows at the word 'gay'. 'How do you know what's "age appropriate" stuff, like it says in that Family Planning resource?' Matt asks Sarah. 'I haven't got any kids, so why don't they just tell us do this in Year 1, that in Year 2, and all that?'

Pierre listens intently to Matt and James as they reflect on what they are learning. He knows their ideas, values and beliefs about education are being challenged, their *habitus* reviewed, and that they are possibly reformulating their ideas about sexuality education. James continues, 'I didn't need to know anything until I was, well, you know … a bit older, and it all came pretty natural. All you need is a good-looking chick.' He laughs, doing a high-five with Tony who catches the 'I didn't need to know' throwaway line. 'But I don't want to be accused of anything! Remember what they said about male teachers being really careful because of that paedophilia suspicion stuff.'

James sits forward and speaks in a lowered voice, 'If we follow the Bible and go with abstinence and love, there's nothing they need to know except maybe wet dreams and periods.' Pierre notices *symbolic violence* as James uses religion to suggest his peers avoid teaching sexuality education in a critical way. James continues, 'There's too much else to worry about, like passing the maths assessment. If we ever have to teach anything, they'll tell us. I know you can get away with saying very little, according to a couple of church friends who are already teaching.'

'I guess you're right,' Matt replies, standing up. Joining the queue behind Leanne and other secondary undergrads, his ears prick up on hearing the word 'sex'. Pierre follows and overhears Leanne mention how she likes the idea of telling the kids about making their 'sexual debut' as opposed to the deficit perspective of 'losing your virginity'. 'A sexual debut,' she says, 'to me brings a positive perspective to a normal and healthy life experience – rather than "losing" something, we are gaining something; rather than becoming "less than" we become "more than" we were before.' Pierre notes that he is observing a change in *habitus* as these students reflect on their classes, where possibilities for alternative world views are explicitly facilitated; and how the teaching has disrupted their prior thinking, producing a cognitive conflict for new possibilities.

Leanne looks to Connie, her classmate, who responds, 'The biggest strategies I had for teaching sexuality this year were creating clear boundaries and making sure all my students were clear on them to ensure their safety. Once these were established, I saw that students were comfortable with each other and with talking about this topic. Then we could start covering the big stuff about sexuality. I think that because my associate teacher is lesbian herself, students felt like they could open up to her. Especially one student who was transgender – she became a lot more confident in the class.' Pierre notes an example of the positive uses of *symbolic power* as he listens. A teacher, someone with authority in the classroom, has openly shared her sexuality with the class and given sexuality *capital*. This has opened the door, sanctioned the exploration of difference, and challenged (hetero) normativity.

'What? The kids actually knew she was a leso?' Matt asks. 'A transgender in the class? Glad I'm not teaching in secondary school. I like it clean cut, boys here, girls there. I don't know what the lecturer was going on about, that we should "avoid saying boys and girls". That's so gay! Wait until I tell the boys about this story.' Pierre shakes his head at the (hetero)*doxa* and sighs, recognising that such attitudes are common in his experience of emerging teacher *habitus*. This did not bode well for emerging teachers challenging (hetero)normativity in the schooling *field*.

Rose, also in the secondary group, adds, 'On both my teaching practicums it was really interesting to discover that all students, both males and females and mainly in Year 9, were absolutely fascinated by sexuality education. They were really interested and eager to learn about it. Until high school they had been left in the dark about the topic. Yet it was obvious some students in the class had already had experiences with sex and sexuality. To me this reinforced that maybe their parents or previous teachers had not been teaching sexuality education at all. Whereas I believe what was taught in our health course – that "sexuality happens throughout our life" – so shouldn't students have some knowledge of the broad topic before they enter high school? Students were a bit embarrassed to engage at times, but once I showed them there was nothing to be embarrassed about, they were all go! It's really important to create a safe environment where everyone can participate, no matter what their experiences with sexuality have been.'

Debi, Janette and lisahunter, their arms full of laptops and books, walk through the doors and head for Pierre, who is now sitting in the corner. They exchange smiles and Debi offers to get coffees. The others sink into their chairs, each having just completed a two-hour lecture. Janette had emailed the previous day, wanting to debrief about a scenario she had just marked from her Year 3 early childhood education class. Her student responses to the assessment were strongly heteronormative, despite Janette's purposeful teaching for social justice, equity and inclusion.

lisahunter nods. 'It's similar in primary. In the official documents I can read "social justice", "learning for all", "inclusivity", and "teaching for difference", but trying to paint a picture for the emerging teachers brings mixed reactions. They imagine the *field* of education from their experience as school students. Today I was telling them how the old curriculum had more detail, painting a fuller picture about what constituted HPE curriculum. They struggled to interpret the current document, even though I'd already shown them examples to illustrate the seven key areas of learning, one being sexuality education. Their HPE world was really opened up from the norm of their experience. You should have seen some of their faces when I explained what they could teach in sexuality ed. Many didn't even realise sexuality ed was part of HPE, according to the survey of their background knowledge I did with them before the course.' lisahunter flicks through the papers tucked in the picture books *Best Best Colors* and *My Princess Boy* that were shown in the lecture. 'There are some who keep calling the subject 'PE' and ignoring the health aspect of it, but the majority are onside and accept that health is important, so they've been open to understanding that there's scope for topics through HPE. It's just having enough time to really unpack their *habitus*, their taken-for-granteds, and to broaden their minds, that's hard! It's been a long road trying to expand their imagination beyond sport, games and food and nutrition. See,' she says, pointing to the page with the graphs from the survey, 'I asked them about their confidence in addressing sexualities education with their students. I know Debi also asked those questions at the start of last year – she told me that 100 per cent in the secondary programme were not confident about teaching sexuality education.'

'In my group about half were very confident or confident,' continues lisahunter. 'The really confident ones were positive and said things like, "I feel very comfortable in teaching sexualities education – an important topic for students to know about." The next group seemed pretty open: "I will be confident once I have learned the material! Not phased by any content; I'm comfortable talking openly with young people and looking forward to learning what the professional guidelines for teachers are." Quite a few didn't answer the question though so I'm wondering why. Some aren't comfortable but raise some important points, like these ones.' She points to the last three responses, reading them aloud: '"My concern is teaching this in a class where there is a diverse range of ethnic backgrounds, teaching this area to year 5/6 boys who are Somalian and Muslim"; "Doesn't concern me as long as I am well prepared"; "A very important topic, even more so in our over-sexualised culture".'

Debi returns with coffees. 'I just ran into some of my students in the line, the ones I have for secondary health. Rory was telling me about his prac. There's good stuff happening in some schools, but it's pretty rare. He had limited time teaching and few opportunities to observe planned teaching of sexuality content. His school's approach was based around students learning to form their own ideas around issues. Far less time was spent saying things like "don't have sex because you will get pregnant". Students were asked what they thought instead of the teacher telling them what they should think. I asked him if he feels prepared to teach sexuality education and challenge heteronormativity. He thinks so. He mentioned the tools that he had seen me use would be of great help when dealing with heteronormativity, yet he reflected that on his first placement he had reverted to a form of fear-based sexual reproductive health/sex education as opposed to healthy relationships education. It just shows how difficult it can be to change *habitus*, but at least he's now conscious of it and looking out for heteronormativity raising its ugly head. I should have asked him how he might use what I taught him!

I also asked if I'd encouraged him to think about discussing diversity like inclusion and LGBT, and if so, how? He said I'd made him think a lot more about diversity. He said he now considered others who he may normally have forgotten, when talking in other classes. For example, when they were discussing forming relationships with students, the question was raised: "What if a student is gay?" People had different views, but on a personal level Rory felt he had learnt the necessary skills to approach the situation in a positive way.'

As time is running out, Janette passes a page to Debi, Pierre and lisahunter, saying, 'I had this scenario for students to respond to.' They all read:

> *Caleb, a boy in your centre, has two mothers. One brings him to the centre and the other collects him. A staff member who always opens the centre in the mornings did not realise his mothers were in a lesbian relationship and is now ignoring the mother that drops Caleb off in the mornings. You have also observed her behaving negatively towards Caleb when she speaks and interacts with him. What will you do?*

'I use a "heterosexual contextual twist"[5] scenario that really gets them thinking about how ridiculous these sorts of behaviours are,' says Debi. 'So you turn these sorts of scenarios on their heads. As an example, in this case you might present the scenario as if the parents were heterosexual and the lesbian teacher behaves negatively towards the parents when she realises they are straight. Then ask students to respond and see what their responses are!'

'When students were reflecting on this clearly homophobic behaviour towards a same-sex-parented family, several students responded by stating, "It's not the child's fault her/his parents are gay." Others suggested that regardless of the teacher's personal feelings about homosexuality, they have a professional responsibility to welcome and respect this family and others. Other students referred to work by Burt and Klinger Lesser (2008) suggesting that our religious beliefs or ethnic values shouldn't get in the way of the education/care we give to children. What do you think?' Janette asks.

Pierre comments that this scenario exemplifies how the orthodoxy

---

5   A contextual twist is taking normalised experiences and twisting the context to allow for understanding of marginalised groups. As an example see: www.youtube.com/watch?feature=player_embedded&v=XM2J7nOp3nU#action=share

of heternormativity is entrenched, but since the students were critically discussing the scenario there was space for the *field* and *habitus* of early childhood education and its teachers to rethink their practices in the future. His view is that the scenario facilitates students, in a straight world, to be agents of change – but there is a long way to go. 'Remember that article by Alex and Nic[6] though, there are real dilemmas for queers doing anti-homophobic work in ITE and schools. It can be a double bind, an unsafe space that devalues those already devalued. Straight teachers with the capital need to know about queer theory.'

'What are you working with? What's the habitus and consensus among students? Not that I want to encourage normative consensus!' laughs lisahunter.

Janette responds, 'While most identified shifts in their thinking through researching and responding to the vignette, and most acknowledged the overt homophobic behaviour described in the vignette was unacceptable, very few responded to the broader contextual issues like heteronormativity. This was despite having several relevant extracts in their course readings.'

lisahunter nods and crunches her paper cup in frustration, saying, 'We've got so far to go.' The others lament that there is much work to do at the class, department and institutional level. 'I wonder what it will take to get heteronormativity out of the closet? What would we need to create an environment where doing stuff like this wouldn't even be seen as risky?' asks lisahunter. Debi rolls her eyes, 'Well, we've got to keep trying to break through this heteronormative malaise.'

## Ten triggers to (continue to) break the (hetero)normative malaise

Bourdieu noted that social sciences are 'concerned with figuring out and understanding the true causes of the malaise that is expressed only through social signs that are difficult to interpret precisely because they seem so obvious' (1999, 628). His theoretical contribution asks us to go beyond appearances and to understand how we, as agents, (re)produce society through the politics of cultural authorisation (Adkins 2004). Bourdieu offers

---

6   Gunn, A. & Surtees, N. (2004), 'Engaging with dominance and knowing our desires: New possibilities for addressing sexualities matters in early childhood education', *Journal of the New Zealand Educational Administration and Leadership Society, Special Issue: Social Justice* 19, 79–91.

an 'explanatory power' (Skeggs 2004, 19) and methodological framework that can assist educators in affirming sexual diversity and enhance learning possibilities for all.

To conclude, we offer suggestions about how one might go beyond appearances, using the questions we list below. You could reflect upon the narrative to check how you might 'recognise' Bourdieu's concepts at play. You might apply these questions to your own social spaces including those related to education. You might also use them as a way to analyse your teacher education curriculum, whether as teacher educators or as emerging teachers. Let's talk ...

1. Why pay attention to (hetero)normativity in the *field* of education?
2. What are the social origins of normativity, heteronormativity, heterosexism, homophobia, transphobia, intersexism, queering, etc?
3. Where are we (*habitus* and *field*) now in terms of embodying or challenging (hetero)normativity?
4. What are the sex, gender and sexuality orthodoxies of our everyday lived experiences in teacher education faculties, early childhood centres and schools?
5. How can we sensitise ourselves to these *doxa*?
6. Who gains, loses, is visible or absent, and who gets to (re)legitimise or challenge such *doxa*?
7. What are the violences of (hetero)normativity in classroom practices and education?
8. What practices (de)stabilise (hetero)normativity?
9. What practices can we trial to expose (hetero)normativity and now also homonormativity[7], instead embodying diversity?
10. How can we be more powerfully positioned to work towards inclusivity and diversity, challenging (hetero)normativity?

The situation for the *field* of teacher education is clearly complex with multiple agents either resisting or facilitating an awareness of, and changes to, (hetero)normativity. The malaise towards (hetero)normativity suits those with heterosexual capital, to the point where it is often not even a

---

7   Homonormativity is described as the normalisation of ways of being according to homosexual categories, for instance, a 'lesbian'. Stereotypes frame the normalisation which perpetuates stereotypes and generalisations, e.g. 'flamboyant gay', 'butch lesbian', etc. It also points to the adoption of heternormative practices in queer encounters, e.g. masculine and feminine parent roles played out by same-sex couples.

perceivable problem. Worse still, the *symbolic violence* towards those already disadvantaged by (hetero)normativity means they may be complicit in maintaining a system that marginalises or alienates them. This chapter illustrates the monstrous spectre of (hetero)normativity that, for most of us, is still in the closet. The door continues to be forced open, however. Working with concepts such as Bourdieu's helps illustrate how we might practise differently in teacher education.

## Acknowledgement
Thanks to editors for their valuable feedback on chapter drafts.

## References
Adkins, L. (2004) 'Reflexivity: Freedom or habit of gender?', in L. Adkins and B. Skeggs (eds), *Feminism after Bourdieu* (191–209), London: Blackwell.

Athanases, S.Z. & Larrabee, T.G. (2003), 'Toward a consistent stance in teaching for equity: Learning to advocate for lesbian- and gay-identified youth', *Teaching and Teacher Education, 19*, 237–61.

Australian Government Department of Education, Employment and Workplace Relations (2009), *Belonging, Being and Becoming: The early years learning framework for Australia*, National Circuit, Barton, ACT: Author.

Blackburn, M., Clark, C., Kenney, L. & Smith, J. (eds), (2010), *Acting Out: Combating homophobia through teacher activism*, New York: Teachers College Press.

Bourdieu, P. (1991), *Language and Symbolic Power*, Cambridge, MA: Harvard University Press.

Bourdieu, P. (1998), *Practical Reason: On the theory of action*, Cambridge: Polity.

Bourdieu, P. (1999), *The Weight of the World: Social suffering in contemporary society*, Oxford: Polity.

Bower, L. & Klecka, C. (2009), '(Re)considering normal: Queering social norms for parents and teachers', *Teaching Education, 20*(4), 357–73.

Burt, T. & Klinger Lesser, L. (2008), 'Lesbian, gay, bisexual and transgender (LGBT) families', *Exchange*, 62–65.

Carpenter, V. & Lee, D. (2010), 'Teacher education and the hidden curriculum of heteronormativity', *Curriculum Matters, 6*.

Clandinin, D. & Connelly, F. (2000), *Narrative Inquiry: Experience and story in qualitative research*, San Francisco: Jossey-Bass.

Clark, C. (2010), 'Preparing LGBTQ-allies and combating homophobia in a US teacher education program', *Teaching and Teacher Education, 26*, 704–13.

DeJean, W. (2010), 'Courageous conversations: Reflections on a queer life narrative model', *The Teacher Educator, 45*, 233–43.

Eyre, L. (1997), 'Re-forming (hetero)sexuality education', in L. Roman & L. Eyre (eds), *Dangerous Territories: Struggles for difference and equality in education* (191–204), New York: Routledge.

Family Planning New Zealand, 'The Sexuality Road': http://education.familyplanning.org.nz/courses/14-hp-the-sexuality-road

Ferfolja, T. (2007), 'Schooling cultures: Institutionalizing heteronormativity and heterosexism', *International Journal of Inclusive Education, 11*(2), 147–62.

Herman-Wilmarth, J. & Bills, P. (2010), 'Identity shifts: Queering teacher education research', *The Teacher Educator, 45,* 257–72.

Hoffman, E. (2002), *Best Best Colors. Los mejores colores,* St Paul, MN: Redleaf.

Kilodavis, C. (2010), *My Princess Boy,* New York: Aladdin.

Meyer, E. (2007), '"But I'm not gay": What straight teachers need to know about queer theory', in N. Rodriguez and W. Pinar (eds), *Queering Straight Teachers* (1–17), New York: Peter Lang.

Ministry of Education (1996), *Te Whāriki: He whāriki mātauranga o ngā mokopuna o Aotearoa: Early childhood curriculum,* Wellington: Learning Media.

Ministry of Education (2007), *The New Zealand Curriculum for English-medium teaching and learning in years 1–13,* Wellington: Learning Media.

New Zealand Teachers Council (2010), 'Registered teacher criteria handbook': www.teacherscouncil.govt.nz/content/registered-teacher-criteria-handbook-english-2010pdf

Prettyman, S. (2007), 'Pressure points: Intersections of homophobia, heterosexism, and schooling', *Educational Studies, 41*(1), 3–6.

Robinson, K. & Ferfolja, T. (2008), 'Playing it up, playing it down, playing it safe: Queering teacher education', *Teaching and Teacher Education, 24,* 846–58.

Rofes, E. (2005), *A Radical Rethinking of Sexuality and Schooling: Status quo or status queer?* Lanham, MD: Rowman & Littlefield.

Rubin, G. (1993), 'Thinking sex: Notes for a radical theory of the politics of sexuality', in H. Abelove, M. Barale & D. Halperin (eds), *The Lesbian and Gay Studies Reader,* (3–44), New York: Routledge.

Russell, S., Seif, H. & Truong, N. (2001), 'School outcomes of sexual minority youth in the United States: Evidence from a national study', *Journal of Adolescence, 24,* 111–27.

Sears, J. & Williams, W. (eds), (1997), *Overcoming Heterosexism and Homophobia: Strategies that work,* New York: Columbia University Press.

Sedgwick, E. (1990), *Epistemology of the Closet,* Berkeley, CA: University of California Press.

Skeggs, B. (2004), 'Context and background: Pierre Bourdieu's analysis of class, gender and sexuality', in L. Adkins and B. Skeggs (eds), *Feminism After Bourdieu,* (19–33), Oxford: Blackwell.

Stiegler, S. (2008), 'Queer youth as teachers: Dismantling silence of queer issues in a teacher preparation program committed to social justice', *Journal of LGBT Youth, 5*(4), 116–23.

Talburt, S. (2004), 'Constructions of LGBT youth: Opening up subject possibilities', *Theory Into Practice, 43*(2), 116–21.

Wickens, C. & Sandlin, J. (2010), 'Homophobia and heterosexism in a college of education: A culture of fear, a culture of silence', *International Journal of Qualitative Studies, 23*(6), 651–70.

Wyatt, T., Oswalt, S., White, C. & Peterson, F.L. (2008), 'Are tomorrow's teachers ready to deal with diverse students? Teacher candidates' attitudes toward gay men and lesbians', *Teacher Education Quarterly, 35*(2), 171–85.

## 14.
# Challenging the pervasiveness of heteronormativity

Lee A. Smith & Alexandra C. Gunn

Numerous recent national and international studies show that heteronormativity remains a ubiquitous force in all sectors of education, from early childhood to tertiary. In New Zealand, research has documented how queer and trans* students experience educational environments as more hostile and alienating spaces than their heterosexual counterparts. Yet we operate education institutions within frameworks of policy and law that demand the exact opposite. Chapters in this collection have expanded our understanding of how heteronormativity is playing out in early childhood, school and tertiary education. While they report continued evidence of heteronormativity, they also show that many queers and heterosexual allies are challenging this.

Our final chapter highlights the themes that run through this collection, in order to support the work of students, educators and researchers who would practise further towards disrupting the (hetero)normative status quo. To begin, we discuss limitations of this edited collection and point towards areas for further research on heteronormativity in New Zealand educational settings. We then offer some possible reasons for the continued silencing of social diversity in terms of sexualities, families and genders, which remains a persistent problem. Following this we examine some of the challenges for teachers in the contemporary education system, and conclude with a number of strategies for change.

### Areas for future research

There are numerous studies on how heteronormativity is promoted and/or resisted in New Zealand's early childhood centres,[1] secondary schools and

---

[1] See for example, Gunn 2008, 2009, 2011; Gunn & Surtees 2011; Jarvis 2009; Jarvis & Sandretto 2010; Lee 2010a, 2010b, 2012; Lee & Duncan 2008; Surtees 2008, 2012; Surtees & Gunn 2010; Terreni et al. 2010.

tertiary education settings.[2] We argue, however, that there is plenty of scope for more research on how heteronormativity shapes teaching, learning and social spaces in primary schools in New Zealand. Work in this domain would help us better understand how children in middle childhood and the context of increasingly independent peer groups are able to police and disrupt gender norms and standards for what constitute 'normal' families and 'proper' sexualities. As Sandretto (Chapter 4) and Hardie (Chapter 3) demonstrate, social justice-minded teachers can and sometimes do work to develop children's critical awareness and agency in this regard. Studying the effects of such teaching practices would enable better understanding of the full implementation of current curriculum policy as well as the impacts, in education, of progressive public law.

This collection touches lightly on the educational experiences of Māori and Pasifika queer, takatāpui and fa`afafine students and parents. Research on heteronormativity in New Zealand educational settings needs to provide information on how these students navigate their home and school cultures. Further, as New Zealand is an increasingly multicultural country where people practise a number of religions, research is needed on how heteronormativity impacts on cultural- and religious-diverse students as they live across their varying worlds.

Research on trans* students' and parents' experiences in New Zealand educational settings is also rare, although some work in this domain is beginning to emerge (Burford, Lucassen, Penniket & Hamilton 2012; Clark et al. 2014). We need to know more about how heteronormativity and cisnormativity intersect to oppress trans* students in New Zealand generally, as well as in our education system.

We also consider the experiences of queer teachers an under-researched domain in Aotearoa. Issues with disentangling conflations of childhood, safety, risk and innocence, and notions of normal/abnormal genders and sexualities, have long been reasons for why queer teachers remain closeted within the landscape of education and schooling (King 2004; Silin 1997). These, coupled with lingering social anxiety about teachers, children and sexualities which emerged with fervour in New Zealand in the aftermath of Christchurch's Civic Childcare Case in 1991 (Farquhar 1997; Jones 2001, 2003, 2004), provide some rationale for the omission; however, the

---

2   See for example, Lee & Carpenter 2014; Fe 2005; Giddings & Pringle 2011; Henrickson 2007; Painter 2009; Quinlivan 1996, 1999, 2002a, 2002b; Smith 2006; Stapp 1991; Town 1999, 2002.

impossibility of sexually diverse and gender-diverse teachers to be 'out' at work, without fear of recrimination or abuse, must continue to be challenged. With increasing emphasis on workplace safety for queers in New Zealand (New Zealand Council of Trade Unions 2014; New Zealand Post Primary Teachers' Association 2012) and strong leadership and policy at the local level (by boards of trustees, management committees, principals and other education organisations such as teacher unions), it should be increasingly possible to both teach and be 'out'. We need to understand more about how and when this happens, and why, in many instances, it cannot.

## Weaving the threads

Research on the experiences of queer students in New Zealand educational settings reports a pervasive silence in the curriculum regarding same/both sex attraction.[3] Many of these studies were conducted before the promulgation of New Zealand laws such as the Civil Union and Care of Children Acts 2004 and the Marriage (Definition of Marriage) Act 2013, which, it can be argued, are representative of societal change and the overhaul of traditional heteronormative policy and law. Despite the altered legal and social climate, however, it appears that little has shifted in the primary school curriculum to reflect changing attitudes and beliefs, at least in the 15 or so years since some of the initial studies were carried out. Both Hardie (Chapter 3) and Sandretto (Chapter 4) report there were no mentions of same-sex attractions and queer families in school library or literacy resources such as storybooks and the *School Journal*. Furthermore, Carpenter and Lee (Chapter 12) and lisahunter, Futter-Puati and Kelly (Chapter 13) describe how, in their experiences of initial teacher education (ITE) curriculum, queer desires are largely silenced and any change to this is very slow. It seems the continued silencing of social diversity in terms of sexualities, families and genders remains a persistent problem. Later in this chapter we offer some possible reasons for this.

As Gunn (Chapter 2) and Sandretto (Chapter 4) explain, the content of the early childhood and school curriculum policies is inclusive; it provides a great deal of support for teachers and policy-makers to work actively in the interests of social justice and against the oppressions of the (hetero)norm. Any systematic reluctance on the part of education settings and teachers

---

[3] See for example McAllum 2014; Painter 2009; Quinlivan 1994, 1996, 1999; Stapp 1991; Town 1999, 2002; Vincent & Ballard 1997.

to reflect gender and sexual diversities in the curriculum – through, for instance, lack of resourcing, non-inclusive policy and language, omission or direct oppression – is a failure to engage fully with the curriculum and with social diversity: a stated expectation of the profession. Within teaching, and in relation to the standards of practice expected of beginning and experienced teachers, diversity is understood as a valuable and valued dimension of all learning environments. Teachers are expected to respond positively to the diversity of language and cultural experiences of students and their families. Newly qualified teachers may find it difficult to reflect family, gender and sexual diversity, however, if they have limited opportunity to think about and practise how to do this in the context of their ITE (Pascoe 2007). Without school-wide or early childhood centre-wide support, practising teachers may struggle to achieve the same.

Heteronormativity – and we extend this to include cisnormativity – is a spatial practice.[4] As a consequence, heterosexuals and cisnormative people have greater access to public space than queer and trans* subjects. Burford, MacDonald, Orchard and Wills (Chapter 10) explain that cisnormativity is so pervasive in educational settings it shapes school architecture itself, for instance through the provision of male and female changing rooms. This gendered distinction in school amenities can be traumatic for trans* students, who may be forced to use a bathroom inconsistent with their gender identity or harassed if they use one consistent with their gender identity. Furthermore, there is some evidence that trans* students may be prevented from engaging with the full spectrum of curriculum if education settings fail to account suitably for student privacy needs (Sykes 2011), for example in physical education, where students may struggle to participate easily if they are engaging in body practices such as breast-binding.

Heterosexuals also have greater freedom to express affection in public spaces than their queer counterparts (Hubbard 2008; 2013). Allen (Chapter 7) explains how the students in her study photographed heterosexual students freely expressing their sexuality in public spaces, while a student who photographed a lesbian couple embracing commented that the two young women had been harassed because of their relationship. Sexton's (Chapter 5) study describes young men's experiences of homophobic bullying in New Zealand schools, and Smith (Chapter 6) describes how one school deliberately discouraged students from attending the formal with same-sex

---

4   Hubbard 2008, 2013; Johnston & Longhurst 2010; Smith, Nairn & Sandretto 2015.

partners to 'protect' them from the harassment they would likely receive if they chose to do so. Such findings support the New Zealand Post Primary Teachers' Association's (NZPPTA) (2012) assertion that homophobia, or heteronormative abuse, remains one of the largest forms of abuse that goes unaddressed in many secondary schools.

Although heteronormativity is ubiquitous in the public spaces of educational settings, it is not entirely dominant (Baydar 2012; Kjaran & Kristinsdóttir 2014). Incidences of young women transgressing the sexual order, in both Smith's (Chapter 6) and Allen's (Chapter 7) studies, challenged this dominance. Such displays highlight that there is always the possibility of resistance and transgression even in the most heteronormative of spaces (Rasmussen 2004a; Smith, Nairn & Sandretto 2015).

Some institutions and staff are more inclusive of sexual diversity than others. For instance, some queer students in Sexton's (Chapter 5) study explained that their teachers ignored homophobic remarks, while another stated that his school was 'gay-friendly'. Quinlivan (Chapter 9) describes a school principal who supported the establishment of a Queer–Straight Alliance in his school and stated he would challenge anyone who made negative comments about the group. Smith (Chapter 6) mentions one school with a school-wide policy of protection and celebration of diversity. These school and teacher practices are worth highlighting because they sit in counterpoint to others that fail to even acknowledge that they have queer and trans* students attending (see Epstein, O'Flynn & Telford 2001). Understanding why and how it is possible for some educational institutions to work for positive change is an area for further research, as we argued earlier in the chapter.

Many heterosexual students are inclusive of their queer and trans* classmates (Nairn & Smith 2003; Smith 2012). But due to their privileged positioning in the sexual order, some heterosexual students fail to see how queer students are denied the opportunities they themselves take for granted. For instance, although many students in Smith's study (Chapter 6) reported that queer students would be accepted if they chose to attend the school formal with a same-sex partner, a queer participant explained he chose to attend with a female friend in order to avoid negative comments. Heterosexual students in Sexton's (Chapter 5), Smith's (Chapter 6) and Fitzpatrick's (Chapter 8) studies used terms and phrases such as 'that way inclined', 'gay' or 'that's so gay', targeting these at one another. Although these terms and actions may not have been used to cause harm (as Sexton's chapter implies), we argue that they do reinscribe the normal/abnormal status of queer students in the heterosexual/homosexual binary and, as such, should be open to scrutiny.

Young people's changing uses of labels and identity categories was also a feature of Quinlivan's Queer–Straight Alliance work (Chapter 9). In that, students rejected traditional sexual identity categories and instead chose signifiers such as 'arty' and 'passionate' to describe themselves and others. The use of such terms blurs understanding of what is meant by heterosexual and homosexual and therefore challenges the heterosexual/homosexual binary (see Sedgwick 1990; Smith 2006). Such labels also highlight how adult understandings of sexuality may not be consistent with students' sexual cultures.

In contemporary times normative constructions of femininity, produced and regulated by heteronormativity, are also shaped by neo-liberal ideology. Under a neo-liberal framework, the ideal feminine subject is constituted as a young woman who finishes school, develops a career and then starts a family (Harris 2004). As a consequence, pregnant teens – such as those described by Hindin-Miller and Hibbert (Chapter 11) – are pathologised for failing to perform an appropriate version of femininity (Harris 2004; McRobbie 2007). Neo-liberal discourse suggests they are neglecting their responsibilities to be (and even become) proper female citizens and considers them burdens on the state (Harris 2004). A number of pregnant teens in Hindin-Miller and Hibbert's study reported that they had been encouraged to leave school, perhaps because the schools did not want to tarnish their own reputations in the educational marketplace. The inequity for young female students revealed by these studies provides a further example of heteronormativity at work.

## Queering New Zealand's education system: Challenges for the teaching profession

New Zealand schools receive government funding on the basis of student numbers and other contextual factors, and as a result often compete with each other for students. Schools therefore wish to protect their reputation in order to attract parents and students (Nairn, Higgins & Sligo 2012). In Quinlivan's (2002b) research on how schools provide for their queer students, one queer teacher participant argues that any school that is seen to be doing more than simply providing queer students with support through the guidance network runs the risk of being labelled as 'promoting and recruiting for queer sexualities' (25). In the competitive educational marketplace, however, Quinlivan (2002b) questions whether the only option available to schools is to frame queer students as 'at risk' and in need of support.

New Zealand's right-leaning coalition government, in power for a third consecutive term, has implemented a number of changes in education that have boosted competition between institutions and challenged the credibility of the teaching profession. For example, changes in the early childhood sector saw the former target of 100 per cent of teaching positions in teacher-led ECE services to be filled by qualified and registered staff, replaced with a requirement of only 50 per cent. There has also been a narrowing of priorities and, within ECE, of teaching accountabilities, towards so-called priority learners and underserviced communities: those of low socioeconomic status, Māori, Pasifika and disabled learners. To expect teachers to meet the full demands of inclusive curriculum policy when all real measures of teachers' work are currently targeting such a specific remit is a challenge. While we fear that the demands for a greater recognition of social diversity within teachers' practices in early childhood curriculum are likely to remain for the moment aspirational (for the system) or ad hoc and localised to particular services responding to community realities and needs, we hope the kinds of arguments and practices showcased within this volume will support ongoing and positive change.

In 2009 National Standards were introduced to primary schools and students' learning progression became subject to measurement against a set of standards for achievement at year-level bands in literacy, writing and maths (Thrupp & White 2013). The subsequent publishing of schools' aggregated achievement data has lead to an intensified interest in the core subjects of a primary school education: the so-called 'STEM' subjects of science, technology, English and maths (of which elements of the latter two are now subject to scrutiny via the national standards). The primary curriculum is at risk of narrowing (Thrupp & White 2013) as the worth of a teacher's work in this sector becomes subject to interpretation through such assessment data. Teachers are now spending more time on assessment tasks than on teaching, and aspects of their role – such as pastoral care and non-assessed subjects like health – are likely to suffer (Sinkinson & Burrows 2011; Thrupp & White 2013).

In 2012 the government began trialling a partnership school model of education (charter schools). In this approach, special interest groups, businesses, religious or cultural groups partner with the school to deliver education services to a particular student group, community or population. Part of the accountability for partnership schools is expected to be a demonstrated raising of achievement standards of their students. Teachers within partnership schools do not need a teaching qualification or practising certificate, and schools have more flexibility in how they deliver curriculum. The introduction of such schools to the mix of educational provision serves to diminish the importance of subjects such as health education, in which sexuality education is compulsory and discussions around sexual diversity are more likely to occur (Smith 2006). It is possible that queer identities and practices will remain invisible in those charter schools that are formed by religious groups.

Change in ITE is also ongoing. The government is currently trialling the introduction of post-graduate qualifications for teachers in primary and secondary education (with early childhood slated to follow). The initiative couples a higher entry standard for places within ITE with study at the post-graduate level (a change from the current graduate-level qualifications for teaching that currently exist). Programmes comprise more intensive and ongoing school-based experiences with increased emphasis on research and inquiry teaching. An emphasis on meeting the needs of priority learners (as described earlier) is also expected. The extent to which graduates of these higher-level ITE programmes will be able to address social diversity, in terms of genders and sexualities, remains to be seen.

Given these challenges to the teaching profession, how are teachers who wish to challenge heteronormativity and create a more socially just classroom environment to do so? In the following section we provide a number of practical suggestions for how educational institutions, teachers and students can challenge heteronormativity, cisnormativity and the gender codes they hold in place, which oppress all student regardless of their sexuality or gender.

## Strategies for change

As Allen (Chapter 7) and Burford et al. (Chapter 10) explain, hetero-normativity and cisnormativity are evident in the gamut of school practices, from official policy and architecture through to student peer-group cultures. Although Smith (Chapter 6) reports a policy of protection of diversity in one school, and Quinlivan (Chapter 9) describes how staff in another backed their Queer–Straight Alliance, research conducted on queer and trans* students' experiences in New Zealand shows that these schools are exceptions rather than the rule (Nairn & Smith 2003; Painter 2009; Smith 2006; 2012).

When it comes to the affirmation of sexual and gender diversities, management in early childhood centres, schools and tertiary institutions play an important role. They must:

- Develop institution-wide policies that: address heteronormativity, homophobia and cisnormativity in the learning environment; affirm sexual and gender diversity; and protect students from homophobic as well as cisnormative bullying.
- Provide resources and curriculum materials that enable staff to make visible gender, sexual and family diversities, such as books with queer themes or representations of diverse family forms.
- Support and encourage queer students to attend school functions, such as the senior formal, with their same-sex partners.
- Encourage staff to undergo professional learning and development on sexuality and gender diversities.
- Seek and make use of resources that provide practical strategies to help make schools safer and more equitable spaces for trans* and queer students.
- Provide gender-neutral facilities such as locker rooms and bathrooms, and private spaces where trans* students can change their clothing without fear of harassment or disclosure.
- Encourage the formation of Queer–Straight Alliances and groups for queer students.
- Publicise queer support contacts to all staff and display posters that show the institution is a queer-friendly space.

Teachers in all sectors of education need to reflect on their own practices and examine how their attitudes towards gender, sexuality and family diversities play out in their work with learners, families and colleagues. They must:

- Challenge their binary thinking and develop a commitment to inclusivity that underlies their practice.
- Include family and whānau in the daily running and rituals of the

centre/school. If people feel they belong, the curriculum will follow.
- Use gender-neutral terms such as 'partner' and note which personal pronouns trans* students and parents use – and address them accordingly.
- Include sexual and gender diversities and variation in family forms in all areas of the curriculum, and do not assume that a learner has two opposite-sex parents.
- Unpack and explore concepts such as homophobia, heterosexism, transphobia, cisnormativity and heteronormativity with students and colleagues.
- Utilise critical literacy to deconstruct popular cultural or school texts that promote heteronormativity and normative gender codes.
- In sexuality education, include information about gender and sexual diversities and the fluid nature of sexuality and gender, in safe and informative ways.
- Invite trained peer educators from groups such as Rainbow Youth or Queer Support to discuss issues of gender and sexual diversities in the classroom.
- Introduce and analyse with students discourses of neo-liberal ideology, such as those that depict teenage pregnancy as abhorrent.

This book is intended to make a difference in the lives of all, especially queer and trans* students, families and colleagues. After all, even the most recent research reports that queer and trans* students and staff are experiencing their educational settings as hostile spaces (Clark et al. 2014; McAllum 2014). Clearly this situation must change if we are to provide a safe and inclusive space in which all learners enjoy the same opportunities for success. We invite you to take up these suggestions and discuss the material included in this book with your friends, family, colleagues, support staff, managers and students. It is 2015; in Aotearoa New Zealand same-sex marriage and adoption (for single queers or married/civil union same-sex couples) is legal. We have an ethical and moral responsibility to ensure our progressive societal attitudes are also evident in our education spaces, so that queer and trans* parents and colleagues feel welcomed and affirmed, and queer students develop a healthy sense of self.

## References

Baydar, G. (2012), 'Sexualised productions of space', *Gender, Place & Culture*, 19(6), 699-706. DOI: 10.1080/0966369X.2012.675472

Burford, J., Lucassen, M.F.G., Penniket, P. & Hamilton, T. (2013), *Educating for Diversity: An informative evaluation of the Rainbow Youth sexuality and gender diversity workshops*, Auckland: Rainbow Youth Inc.

Carpenter, V.M. & Lee, D. (2010), 'Teacher education and the hidden curriculum of heteronormativity', *Curriculum Matters*, 6, 99-119.

Clark, T.C., Lucassen, M.F.G., Bullen, P., Denny, S.J., Fleming, T.M., Robinson, E.M. & Rossen, F.V. (2014), 'The health and wellbeing of transgender high schools students: Results from the New Zealand Adolescent Health Survey (Youth'12), *Journal of Adolescent Health*, 55, 93-99.

Epstein, D., O'Flynn, S. & Telford, D. (2000), '"Othering education": Sexualities, silences and schooling', *Review of Research in Education*, 25, 127-79.

Farquhar, S. (1997), *A Few Good Men or a Few Too Many? A study of male teachers*, Palmerston North: Massey University.

Fe, D. (2005), 'Of rainbows and reassurance: Why it is important to support LGBTQ students as they enter tertiary education', *Journal of the Australian and New Zealand Student Services*, 26, 3-26.

Giddings, L.S. & Pringle, J.K. (2011), 'Heteronormativity at work: Stories from two lesbian academics', *Women's Studies Journal*, 25(2), 91-100.

Gunn, A.C. (2008), 'Heteronormativity and early childhood education: Social justice and some puzzling queries', Doctoral dissertation, University of Waikato, Hamilton.

Gunn, A.C. (2009), '"But who are the parents?": Examining heteronormative discourses in New Zealand government early childhood reports and policy', *Early Childhood Folio*, 13, 27-31.

Gunn, A.C. (2011), 'Even if you say it three ways, it still doesn't mean it's true. The pervasiveness of heteronormativity in early childhood education', *Journal of Early Childhood Research*, 9(3), 280-90.

Gunn, A.C. & Surtees, N. (2011), 'Matching parents' efforts: How teachers can resist heteronormativity in early education settings', *Early Childhood Folio*, 15(1), 27-31.

Harris, A. (2004), *Future Girl: Young women in the twenty-first century*, London: Routledge.

Henrickson, M. (2007), '"You have to be strong to be gay": Bullying and educational attainment in LGB New Zealanders', *Journal of Gay and Lesbian Social Services*, 19(3-4), 67-85.

Hubbard, P. (2008), 'Here, there, everywhere: The ubiquitous geographies of heteronormativity', *Geography Compass*, 2(3), 640-58.

Hubbard, P. (2013), 'Kissing is not a universal right: Sexuality, laws and the scale of citizenship', *Geoforum*, 49, 224-32.

Jarvis, K. (2009), 'Exploring heteronormativity: Small acts towards queer(y)ing early childhood education', Master's dissertation, University of Otago, Dunedin.

Jarvis, K. & Sandretto, S. (2010), 'The power of discursive practices: Queering or heteronormalising?', *New Zealand Research in Early Childhood Education*, 13, 43-56.

Johnston, L. & Longhurst, R. (2010), *Space, Place and Sex: Geographies of sexualities*, Plymouth: Rowman and Littlefield.

Jones, A. (ed.), (2001), *Touchy Subject: Teachers touching children*, Dunedin: University of Otago Press.

Jones, A. (2003), 'The monster in the room: Safety, pleasure and early childhood education', *Contemporary Issues in Early Childhood*, 4(3), 235-50.

Jones, A. (2004), 'Social anxiety, sex, surveillance, and the "safe" teacher', *British Journal of Sociology of Education*, 25(1), 53-66.

Kjaran, J. & Kristinsdóttir, G. (2014), 'Queering the environment and caring for self: Icelandic LGBT students' experience of the upper secondary school', *Pedagogy, Culture and Society*. DOI: 10.1080/14681366.2014.910250

King, J. (2004), 'The (im)possibility of gay teachers for young children', *Theory into Practice*, 43(2), 122–27.

Lee, D. (2010a), 'Gay mothers and early childhood education: Standing tall', *Australasian Journal of Early Childhood*, 35(1), 16–23: http://hdl.handle.net/2292/17733

Lee, D. (2010b), 'The right to belong? Gay mothers and their families in infant and toddler education', *The First Years: Ngā Tau Tuatahi: NZ Journal of Infant and Toddler Education*, 12(1), 23–26.

Lee, D.J. (2012), 'Beyond heteronormativity: Hospitality as curriculum', in J. Duncan, & S. Te One (eds), *Comparative Early Childhood Education Services: International perspectives*, (125–45), New York: Palgrave Macmillan.

Lee, D. & Carpenter, V.M. (2014), '"What would you like me to do? Lie to you?" Teacher education responsibilities to LGBTI students', *Asia-Pacific Journal of Teacher Education*. DOI: 10.1080/1359866X.2014.932331

Lee, D.J. & Duncan, J. (2008), 'On our best behaviour: Lesbian-parented families in early childhood education', *Early Childhood Folio*, 12, 22–26.

McAllum, M-A. (2014), '"Bisexuality is just semantics ...": Young bisexual women's experiences in New Zealand secondary schools', *Journal of Bisexuality*, 14, 75–93.

McRobbie, A. (2007), 'Top girls?: Young women and the post feminist contract', *Cultural Studies*, 21(4–5), 718–37.

Nairn, K., Higgins, J. & Sligo, J. (2012), *Children of Rogernomics: A neoliberal generation leaves school*, Dunedin: Otago University Press.

Nairn, K. & Smith, A.B. (2003), 'Taking students seriously: Their rights to be safe at school', *Gender and Education*, 15(2), 133–49.

New Zealand Council of Trade Unions (2014), 'CTU Out@Work Network': http://union.org.nz/outatwork

New Zealand Post Primary Teachers' Association (2012), *Affirming Diversity of Sexualities and Gender Identities in the School Community: Guidelines for boards of trustees and principals*, Wellington: Author.

Painter, H. (2009), 'How safe?: How safe and inclusive are Otago secondary schools? Ae ranei he haumaru, he wahi whāi kit e katoa ngā kura tuarua o Otago?' A report on the implementations from the 'Safety in our schools – Ko te harumaru i o tatuu kura' action kit: He purongo ūruhi i ngā tuanaki a te kete mahi 'Safety in our schools – Ko te harumaru i o tatu kura', Dunedin, NZ: OUSA Queer Support.

Pascoe, C.J. (2007), *Dude, You're a Fag: Masculinity and sexuality in high school*, Berkeley: University of California Press.

Quinlivan, K. (1994), 'Ten lesbian students reflect on their secondary school experiences', Master's thesis, University of Canterbury, Christchurch.

Quinlivan, K.A. (1996), 'Claiming an identity they taught me to despise: Lesbian students respond to regulations of same-sex desire', *New Zealand Women's Studies Journal (Special Issue: Girl Trouble? Feminist inquiry into the lives of young women)*, 15(2), 51–69.

Quinlivan, K.A. (1999), '"You have to be pretty, you have to be heterosexual I think": The operation and disruption of heteronormative processes within peer cultures of two single sex girls' schools in New Zealand', *New Zealand Women's Studies Journal (Special Issue: Girl trouble? Feminist inquiry into the lives of young women)*, 12(2), 99–113.

Quinlivan, K.A. (2002a), 'On dangerous ground: Working to affirming representations of sexual diversity for students in two New Zealand secondary schools', Doctoral dissertation, University of Canterbury, Christchurch.

Quinlivan, K. (2002b), 'Whose problem is this? Queerying the framing of gay and lesbian students within "at risk" discourses', in K. Robinson, J. Irwin & T. Ferfolja (eds), *From Here to Diversity: The social impact of lesbian and gay issues in New Zealand and Australia* (17–32), New York: Haworth.

Quinlivan, K. (2013), 'Disrupting heteronormativity: A high-school queer–straight alliance?', in N. Higgins & C. Freeman (eds), *Childhoods: Growing up in Aotearoa New Zealand* (249–61), Dunedin: Otago University Press.

Rasmussen, M.L. (2004a), 'Safety and subversion: The production of sexualities and genders in school spaces', in S. Talburt, E. Rofes & M.L. Rasmussen (eds), *Youth and Sexualities* (131–52), New York: Palgrave and MacMillan.

Sedgwick, E. (1990), *Epistemology of the Closet*, Los Angeles: University of California.

Silin, J.G. (1997), 'The pervert in the classroom', in J. Tobin (ed.), *Making a Place for Pleasure in Early Childhood Education*, (214–34), Hew Haven: Yale University Press.

Sinkinson, M. & Burrows, L. (2011), 'Reframing health education in New Zealand/Aotearoa schools', *Asia-Pacific Journal of Health, Sport and Physical Education*, 2(3–4), 53–69.

Smith, L. (2006), 'Un/silencing lesbian and bisexual students: Some women's experiences of how their high schools met their needs', Master's dissertation, University of Otago, Dunedin.

Smith, L. (2012), 'Gender and the formal', Doctoral dissertation, University of Otago, Dunedin.

Smith, L., Nairn. K. & Sandretto, S. (2015). 'Complicating heteronormative spaces at school formals in New Zealand', *Gender, Place and Culture*. DOI: 10.1080/0966369X.2015.1034245

Stapp, A-M. (1991), 'Coming out as a young lesbian: A study of the effects of secondary school environments on young women being able to identify as lesbian: A proposal for change', Master's dissertation, Victoria University, Wellington.

Surtees, N. (2008), 'Teachers following children?: Heteronormative responses within a discourse of child-centredness and the emergent curriculum', *Australian Journal of Early Childhood*, 33(3), 10–17.

Surtees, N. (2012), Families and kinship: Reframing forms of intimacy and care in inclusionary early childhood education settings', in D. Gordon-Burns, A.C. Gunn, K. Purdue & N. Surtees (eds), *Te Aotūroa Tātaki: Inclusive Early Childhood Education: Perspectives on inclusion, social justice and equity from Aotearoa New Zealand* (39–56), Wellington: NZCER Press.

Surtees, N. & Gunn, A.C. (2010), '(Re)marking heteronormativity: Resisting practices in early childhood education contexts', *Australasian Journal of Early Childhood*, 35(1), 42–47.

Sykes, H. (2011), *Queer Bodies: Sexualities, genders and fatness in physical education*, New York: Peter Lang.

Terreni, L., Gunn, A., Kelly, J. & Surtees, N. (2010), 'In and out of the closet: Successes and challenges experienced by gay- and lesbian-headed families in their interactions with the education system in New Zealand', in V. Green & S. Cherrington (eds), *Delving into Diversity: An international exploration of issues of diversity in education* (151–61), New York: Nova Science.

Thrupp, M. & White, M. (2013), 'Research, Analysis and Insight into National Standards (RAINS) Project: Final report: The damage done': www.waikato.ac.nz/_data/assets/pdf_file/0010/179407/RAINS-Final-report_2013-11-22.pdf AFQjCNFLPMywOO4 zhD7h-rDGt_dIKjDakg&sig2=Q388yq0NulwHlfbQb 1ce7w&bvm=bv. 80120444,d. dGY

Town, S. (1999), 'Queer(y)ing masculinities in schools: Faggots, fairies and the first fifteen', in R. Law, H. Campbell & J. Dolan (eds), *Masculinities in Aotearoa/New Zealand* (135–52), Palmerston North: Dunmore.

Town, S. (2002), 'Playing with fire: (Homo)sexuality and schooling in New Zealand', in K. Robinson, J. Irwin & T. Ferfolja (eds), *From Here to Diversity: The social impact of lesbian and gay issues in New Zealand and Australia* (1–15), New York: Haworth.

Vincent, K. & Ballard, K. (1997), 'Living on the margins: Lesbian experience in secondary school', *New Zealand Journal of Educational Studies, 32*(2), 147–61.

# Appendix
Additional resources

Queer organisations such as Rainbow Youth (Auckland) and Queer Support (University of Otago) run groups for queer and trans* students. They also provide workshops on sexual and gender diversity for teachers and students in tertiary and high school settings.

The Human Rights Commission online report *Trans People: Facts and information* (www.hrc.co.nz/human-rights-environment/action-on-the-transgender-inquiry/resources/trans-people-facts-information/) provides practical advice for schools about such things as trans* students and the wearing of sports uniforms; what should happen during swimming lessons; information on changing areas and toilets; and what schools should do when a student undergoes the process of transitioning.

*Educating for Diversity* (Burford, Lucassen, Penniket & Hamilton, 2013, Rainbow Youth Inc), which evaluates Rainbow Youth's sexuality and gender diversity workshops, also provides a number of suggestions for how schools can provide more supportive and inclusive environments for trans* students. These include teacher education on gender and sexual diversity issues, policy reviews, and the forming of Queer–Straight Alliances.

In *Affirming Diversity of Sexualities and Gender Identities in the School Community: Guidelines for boards of trustees and principals*, the NZPPTA (2012) provides a number of case studies that can be used by boards of trustees and school management to discuss sexual and gender diversity with staff and address gaps in current school policy.

In *Safety in Our Schools*, the New Zealand AIDS Foundation, Rainbow Youth and Out There (2004) provide a number of recommendations for how schools can address heteronormativity and create a safe and supportive learning environment. Some of these include school management taking a lead in supporting queer students, including material on gender and sexual diversities in the curriculum, and displaying posters that affirm diversity.

Many of the practices suggested for schools can be readily adapted to initial teacher education and early childhood education.

# Author biographies

**Louisa Allen** is an associate professor in the faculty of education at the University of Auckland. She specialises in research in the areas of sexualities, young people and schooling, and innovative research methodologies that seek to engage hard-to-reach research populations. Most recently she has been examining these through the lens of queer and feminist new materialist theoretical frameworks. She has written four books; the latest, co-edited with Mary Lou Rasmussen and Kathleen Quinlivan, is entitled *The Politics of Pleasure in Sexuality Education: Pleasure bound* (Routledge, 2014).

**James Burford** is a lecturer at the faculty of learning sciences and education at Thammasat University, Thailand. He has a background in teaching, youth work and community development. His primary research area is higher education studies, where he has used queer concepts to explore the affective–political dimensions of doctoral education. James has also researched and published in several other areas, including LGBT diversity education, gender/sexuality in international development, and the cultural politics of fat and transgender embodiment.

**Vicki Carpenter** is a primary school teacher who has also worked extensively in initial and postgraduate teacher education. Her research interests centre on schooling in low socioeconomic sector (urban) communities, and teacher education and sexual orientation. She recently co-edited *Twelve Thousand Hours: Education and poverty in Aotearoa New Zealand* (Dunmore Press, 2014). Vicki has a strong interest in Freirean pedagogy and matters of social justice.

**Katie Fitzpatrick** is an associate professor of health and physical education at the University of Auckland. She has a background in teaching in schools in South Auckland. She has also worked on policy documents, including the health and physical education sections of *The New Zealand Curriculum* and, most recently, as the lead writer on the sexuality education guidelines (2015). She is the author of *Critical Pedagogy, Physical Education and Urban Schooling* (Peter Lang, 2013) and co-editor of *Health Education:*

*Critical perspectives* (Routledge, 2014). Her current teaching and research interests include critical approaches to health and physical education, sexuality education, diversity and research methodology, including critical ethnography, poetry and narrative.

**Debi Futter-Puati** teaches and researches in health and physical education, Pacific education and teacher education. Debi's interests include resiliency, youth voice, social justice and celebrating diversity, especially within health and education contexts. She is currently completing her doctorate, which explores sexuality education in the Cook Islands through the lens of youth desires narrative.

**Alexandra Gunn** teaches and researches in early childhood, inclusion, assessment and teacher education. Formerly an early childhood teacher, her work centres on social justice, teachers' beliefs and practices, and the production and disruption of taken-for-granted norms. She co-edited *Te Aotūroa Tātaki – Inclusive Early Childhood Education: Perspectives on inclusion, social justice and equity from Aotearoa New Zealand* (NZCER Press, 2012).

**Ann Hardie** teaches in initial teacher education programmes at Victoria University of Wellington and previously at Te Whare Wānanga o Awanuiārangi. Formerly a primary and intermediate teacher, her work is predominantly in primary pedagogy with an emphasis on inclusive and equitable practice. Ann's research is focused on issues of social justice for children of queer families. She strives to engage teachers in inclusive practices that facilitate respect and visibility.

**Rebeccah Hibbert** is an independent researcher with a Masters in education from the University of Canterbury. She is passionate about practical education solutions that advantage learners and their diverse needs. Rebeccah has worked with teen parents and a community action group focused on reducing drug-related harm. She takes a strengths-based approach to her work and research.

**Jenny Hindin-Miller** has worked with young people for most of her life: as a teacher, a probation officer and, from 1994 to 2008, as co-founder and director of Karanga Mai Young Parents College, one of New Zealand's 22 Teen Parent

Units. Jenny is passionate about the transformative potential of education. In 2013 she completed her PhD research into the lives of 10 teenage mothers: 'Re-storying identities: Young women's narratives of teenage parenthood and educational support'. Today she works voluntarily, coordinating youth and adult volunteers and supporting a range of community-based initiatives working with youth, junior youth and children.

**Janette Kelly** is a lecturer in early childhood initial teacher education at the University of Waikato. Her teaching and research have focused on young children and pedagogy: the arts and visual methods, education outside the classroom including sustainability, and issues related to diversity and difference, particularly gender and sexualities. She is currently researching for her doctorate, investigating adults' provocations and responses to children's working theories and meaning making about diversity and difference in the social world.

**Debora Lee** works as a student success advisor, using her background in early childhood teaching and initial teacher education to promote positive outcomes for students from diverse communities. Her research interests focus on social justice issues in education. Her previous research includes investigating the experiences of gay women and their families in early childhood education, and student teacher opportunities for learning during practicum placements.

**lisahunter** teaches and researches at Te Whare Wananga O Waikato The University of Waikato, in pedagogy, embodied subjectivities, sex/uality and gender, physical culture and movement studies, health and physical education, and teacher education. Her current interests include sensory, digital and narrative research methods, ethnography, public pedagogies and sexuality education. lisahunter recently co-edited *Pierre Bourdieu and Physical Culture* (Routledge, 2015).

**Joe MacDonald** is interested in the overlaps between community development, social justice and health services. They[1] currently work in mental health as the Affinity Services Rainbow Liaison. Joe completed a

---

1 The use of the singular pronoun 'they' is an emerging convention that allows people to use a term that respects the diversity of gender beyond the traditional gender binary

Masters degree in gender studies, sociology and social work, and enjoys running workshops and training about self-determination, respect, and diversity of sexes/genders/sexualities for staff working in mental health and addiction services.

**Samuel Orchard** is an artist, youth worker, activist and queer trans man. He creates stories about and for queer and trans people that move beyond the common narratives that are propagated by mainstream commercial media.

**Kathleen Quinlivan** is a senior lecturer in the College of Education, Health and Human Development at the University of Canterbury, and has published widely in the area of sexualities, genders and schooling. Recent co-edited books include *The Politics of Pleasure in Sexuality Education: Pleasure bound* (Routledge, 2014) and *Educational Enactments in a Globalised World: Intercultural conversations* (Sense, 2009). A monograph, *Contemporary Issues in Sexuality Education For Young People: Learning and teaching with theory* (Palgrave MacMillan, 2016) is forthcoming.

**Susan Sandretto** works at the University of Otago where she contributes to education studies at the undergraduate level, and teacher education programmes at the undergraduate and postgraduate levels. She also teaches qualitative research and supervises at the postgraduate level. Her research interests include critical multiliteracies, critical literacy, gender issues in education, second language acquisition and practitioner research. Her book, *Planting Seeds: Embedding critical literacy into your classroom programme* (NZCER Press, 2011) was the result of three years of research with primary and secondary teachers. Susan is a former primary school teacher.

**Steven Sexton** is a primary school teacher who now works for the University of Otago's College of Education. Steven is the programme coordinator for the Master of Teaching and Learning and both teaches and supervises undergraduate primary education student teachers. His research interests are in teacher cognition, science education and heteronormativity in schools.

**Lee Smith** is an assistant research fellow at the University of Otago's College of Education and School of Dentistry. Her work involves studying young people in educational and other community settings, using qualitative methods. Her personal research focuses include young people, genders and sexualities, with a specific interest in queer theory and post-structural theory.

**Philip Wills** (Kai Tahu, Pākehā) studied to be a primary school teacher, but was flummoxed in his attempts to respond agentically to the transphobia and homophobia he encountered in schools. Philip is interested in the design and facilitation of educational spaces, particularly those dedicated to revolutionary change. He cares about the survival and autonomous development of indigenous ways of understanding bodies and relationships.

# Index

*Acting Out* research project 210–11
adolescence: normative trajectories 176–77; *see also* teenage pregnancy and parenthood
*Affirming Diversity of Sexualities and Gender Identities in the School Community* (NZPPTA) 240
age-and-stage theory 13, 68
agency: of children, to disrupt gender norms and standards 223; material 103–04; in relation to space 103, 104
American Psychological Association, definition of sexual orientation 191
*And Tango Makes Three* (Richardson & Parnell) 40
androgynous 158, 159
aporia (double bind) 137, 138, 139–41, 142–46, 147
arts, as challenge to social and cultural norms 144–45
asexuals 14, 156
Auckland College of Education (ACE): initial teacher education research study, 2002 192–200; merger with University of Auckland 193–94

Bailey, Martin, *My Favourite Places* 40
biculturalism 126
bigendered 158, 159
binary thinking 21, 24, 28, 49, 50–51, 91, 92
bisexuals 14, 15, 99, 155, 156, 213; *see also* both-sex attraction
boards of trustees, New Zealand schools 164
body: body subjects lower status than academic subjects 119; Christian discourses 119–20; and sexuality education 119, 120; *see also* embodiment
books *see* picture books
both-sex attraction: and curriculum 228–29; secondary school students 11, 68; *see also* bisexuals
Bourdieu, Pierre 19, 118–19, 129, 211, 212–16, 222–23

Brannen, Sarah, *Uncle Bobby's Wedding* 41
Bryan, Jennifer, *The Different Dragon* 40
bullying 8; in school playground, in performance of 'tough' masculinity 102; secondary schools 11, 68, 69–70, 78, 83, 84, 88, 89, 93, 111, 166
Burford, Jamie 205
Butler, Judith 19, 27, 50, 63, 83, 100, 124

Calvin Klein, Eternity advertisement 56–58, 63
capital: Bourdieu's concept 214, 215, 216, 218; forms of 118–19
Care of Children Act 2004 22, 228
Carlson, Urzila 89
charter schools 232–33
children: agency, to disrupt gender norms and standards 227; empowerment 27; gender 24, 29; innocence 12, 26–27, 52; play 21, 24, 29; relationships, in *Te Whāriki* 26; self-esteem 38, 46; sexuality 12–14, 26–27, 29, 190; United Nations Convention on the Rights of the Child (UNROC) 82–83; *see also* early childhood education; families/whānau; parents
Christchurch, Civic Crèche case 14, 227
Christianity: conflicts with Pasifika cultural values 127–29; and initial teacher education 197, 200; and sexuality 119–20, 121, 127–28, 217
cisgender 15, 161–62
cisnormativity 15, 161–62, 216, 227, 229; in New Zealand education settings 164–67, 168, 170, 233, 234, 235; *see also* heteronormativity
*City Life* (Ferreira) 40
Civil Union Act 2004 22, 89, 190, 204, 228
Coffey, Tamati 89
colonisation 117–18; and sexuality 119, 121–22, 132, 162–63
competition between educational institutions 231–32
contextual twist 221
couples, at secondary school 106–11, 113

247

critical ethnography 122
critical literacy 52–53, 235; analysis of popular culture texts 54–64
cross-dressers 14
cultural authorisation 222
cultural capital 119
cultural diversity 220, 227, 229
cultural lag 72
culture, and sexuality 118, 119, 126–32
culture of schools and students 68, 69, 78–79, 83, 89; boys' schools 93–94, 95; Teen Parent Units 182–85
Curious, queer youth network 135
curriculum: hidden curriculum and heteronormativity 203, 211, 214–15; implementation of current policy 227; inclusive education 36–37, 46–47, 49–50, 64, 190, 202–04, 210, 228–29, 232; initial teacher education 190, 202–04, 206, 211; materials to support gender, sexual and family diversity 234; pluralist or multicultural 192; *see also New Zealand Curriculum; Te Whāriki*

*Daddy, Papa and Me* (Newman) 39
De Haan, Linda: *King and King* 40; *King and King and Family* 44–45
decile ratings 85, 104–05, 138
dental dams 10
Derrida, Jacques 137, 138, 146, 147
difference, valuing and engaging with 137–38, 144
*Different Dragon, The* (Bryan) 40
discourse *see* language
discrimination 203–04; gender 9, 82; sexuality 9, 31, 82, 120, 142, 189–90, 191, 201
diversity: beginning teachers' work with 192; cultural and religious 220, 227, 229; gender 11, 24–25, 126, 136, 192, 228–29, 234, 235; hierarchy 203, 204, 216; in secondary schools 87, 89, 94, 95; social 19, 29, 226, 228–29, 232; *see also* family diversity; sexual diversity
*Donovan's Big Day* (Newman) 41
double binds 137–38, 139–41, 146, 147; negotiating 144–46; productive 142–44
doxa, Bourdieu's concept 213, 214, 223; (hetero)doxa of practices in relation to sex, gender and sexualities 216–22

early childhood education and care: assumptions about parents and families 10, 214; government policy 232; heteronormativity 10, 21–23, 24–32, 52, 190, 204, 219; pedagogy of relationships 30–31; support for diversity 229; in Teen Parent Units 184; *see also Te Whāriki*
economic capital 119, 215
*Educating for Diversity* (Burford, Lucassen, Penniket & Hamilton) 240
Education Act 1989 22
Education Review Office 118
Ellis, Peter 14
embodiment: cisnormativity 162; embodied and spatial elements of schooling 102–13; heteronormativity 200–01; *see also* body
empowerment, children 27
equity and inequity 36, 45, 99, 167, 179, 192, 193–94, 201, 205, 219
*Eternity* (Calvin Klein fragrance) advertisement 56–58, 63
exclusion *see* inclusion and exclusion

fa'a Samoa 127
fa'afafine 14, 126, 160, 163, 227
fag discourse 70, 72, 74, 75
families/whānau: children's drawings 57; early childhood teachers' support 23, 24–25, 30–31; inclusion in running of centres/schools 234–35; in *Te Whāriki* 26, 29; traditional nuclear family 24, 57, 60, 216; 'We're a Family' study 22; *see also* parents
*Family Book, The* (Parr) 41
family diversity: and changing roles of women 177; failure to recognise 10; and neo-liberalism 177; portrayed in picture books 35, 36, 40, 45, 46, 234; support from teachers and institutions 23, 24–25, 29–31, 228–29, 235; 'We're a Family' study 22
*Felicia's Favorite Story* (Garden) 45
femininity: emphasised (focus on pleasing men) 84, 91; expression 159; heterosexual 50, 57, 84, 88, 91–92, 100–01, 106, 120, 124, 231; more acceptable variations than masculinity 84–85, 109; non-normative 91, 179; normative gender codes 83–84; in relation to lesbianism 88

Ferreira, Jeannelle, *City Life* 40
field, Bourdieu's concept 118–19, 129, 211, 213–15, 218, 221, 223
focus group research method 72–73
Foucault, Michel 11–12, 19, 83, 125
Freud, Sigmund 13
friendship circles: regulation of masculinities in secondary schools 72–74, 75–77, 79; stability 77–78; *see also* peer groups
frigidity 12

Garden, Leslea, *Felicia's Favorite Story* 45
Garden, Nancy, *Molly's Family* 43–44
'gay': use of term 74–75, 79, 213, 230–31; using term to police gender norms 90–92
Gay and Lesbian Alliance Against Defamation (GLAAD), Media Award 55
gay discourse 70–72, 74
gay men and youth 14, 15, 27, 155, 156; as 'abnormal other' 51, 68, 69, 93, 99, 124–25, 136, 140, 142, 213; perceived femininity 93; *see also* homosexuality; queer students
gay parades 103
gay parents 22; in picture book stories 37, 38, 39, 40, 44–45, 46
gay rights 125
Gay–Straight Alliance (GSA) model 136
gender: children 24, 29; constructions 24, 50–51, 52, 83–84, 136; discrimination on basis of 9, 82; disruption of norms and standards 227; diversity 11, 24, 126, 136, 192, 228–29, 234, 235; in education settings 10, 11; identity 51, 102, 155–61; post-structural theory 25, 83–85; and sexuality 50–51, 57–58, 84, 94, 100, 110–11, 120, 124, 132, 136; stereotypes 39–40; *see also* femininity; masculinity
gender diverse people *see* trans* people
gender expression 159
gender-neutral terminology 30, 235
genderqueers 14, 154, 158, 159
*Graduating Teacher Standards* (New Zealand Teachers Council) 192
Gramsci, Antonio, theory of hegemony 51, 63

habitus, Bourdieu's concept 214, 215, 218, 220, 221, 223

health and physical education 117–18, 119, 122–23, 219–20; *see also* sexuality education
Health and Safety in Employment Act 2002 190, 204
(hetero)doxa of practices in relation to sex, gender and sexualities 216–22
(hetero)norm 22
heteronormativity 9, 21; challenging in fiction 46; and cisnormativity 161–62; critical literacy as a tool to deconstruct hegemony 52–64; destabilisation 135, 136, 137, 138, 142, 144–45, 147, 211, 222–24, 226, 227, 229; dominance 120, 213, 215; embodiment 100–01; entrenchment in society 95; heteronormative hegemony as a theoretical tool 50–52; and identity 102; jokes 90–92, 94; male domination 91, 109; in popular culture texts 49–50, 52, 54–64; power relationships 21, 28; regulatory effects 100, 101, 137; relationships between opposite genders potentially sexual 111–12; spatial practice 229; taken for granted 53–54, 63, 84, 90, 111–12, 125, 212, 213, 220; use of term 15; young women, social expectations of starting sex 173, 177, 179; *see also* cisnormativity
(hetero)normativity: concepts 209, 210, 212–16; doxa 213, 214, 216–22; field, habitus, capital and practice 213–15, 218, 220, 221, 223; as monstrous spectre 209, 224; symbolic power, capital and violence 215–16, 217, 218, 224; ways to counter 212, 222–24
heteronormativity in education settings 9–12, 120, 190, 210, 215, 226, 230, 231–32, 233–34; areas for future research 226–28; early childhood education and care 10, 21–23, 24–32, 52, 190, 204, 219; embodied and spatial elements of schooling 102–13; in initial teacher education 11, 191–93, 196–98, 199–202, 205–06, 210, 211–12, 216–22; primary schools 10, 52, 99, 100–01; secondary schools 10–11, 52, 79, 90, 93, 94, 95, 99, 100–09, 110–12, 124–27, 132, 136, 142; strategies for change 233–35; teacher challenges to 52, 218, 219–24, 231–35; Teen Parent Unit challenges to 183–85

heterosexual matrix (Butler) 50–52, 63, 84, 100, 124, 126
heterosexuality: assumption that all intimate relationships heterosexual 124, 125; Calvin Klein Eternity advertisement 56–58; compulsory 50–51, 60, 100, 124, 191; hegemonic masculinity 70; heterosexual/homosexual binary 50–51, 53, 91, 92, 100, 124–25, 126, 205, 231, 234; 'normal' sexuality 9, 12, 24, 27, 82, 84, 99, 100, 101, 105–09, 136, 197, 198, 210, 215; presumption of potentially sexual relationships 111–12; proof of not being gay 125–26; in *School Journal* 58–63; *see also* opposite-sex attraction
high schools *see* secondary schools
Hill, Tara Theresa, *What Can You Do with Two Mommies* 43, 44
*History of Sexuality, The* (Foucault) 11–12
'homohysteria' 70
homonormativity 223
homophobia 15, 43, 46; *Acting Out* research project 210–11; bullying 10, 68, 69–70, 111; definition 191–92; in early childhood education settings 23, 31, 46; in education settings 22, 99, 210; and hegemonic masculinity 70, 90; Homer Simpson 54–56, 63; in initial teacher education 191–92, 199–202, 222; jokes 90–92; language 69, 70, 71, 72, 75, 79; in secondary schools 68, 69–70, 72, 79, 87, 89, 90–91, 92–94, 95, 125, 126, 230; and sexuality education 120; use of term 15, 210; in workplace 190, 197, 198–200, 204, 222, 228
Homosexual Law Reform Act 1986 189
homosexuality: acceptance of 88–89; Freud's theory 13; heterosexual/homosexual binary 50–51, 53, 91, 92, 100, 124–25, 126, 205, 231, 234; negative views in schools with religious foundations 72; 'othered' identity 99, 124–25, 136, 140, 142, 197; use of term 'homosexual' 12; Western construct 126; *see also* gay men and youth; lesbians
Housing NZ 175
*How Safe?* (Painter) 163–65
Human Rights Act 1993 9, 22, 82, 83, 189–90

Human Rights Commission 82; *To Be Who I Am – Kia noho au ki tōku anō ao* 165; *Trans People: Facts and Information* 240
humour 109; Homer's Phobia episode of *The Simpsons* 54–56, 63; homophobic jokes 90–92
hybrid identities 121
hypersexualisation 14

identity: destabilisation by queer theory 102; gender 51, 102, 155–61; and heteronormativity 102; hybrid 121; Māori youth 128; 'othered' 99, 124–25, 136, 140, 142, 197, 210; Pasifika youth 128–29; teenage parents 180; *see also* sexual identity
identity markers 122
*In Our Mothers' House* (Polacco) 43–44, 45, 46
inclusion and exclusion: teenage parents 174, 176, 180; trans* people 153–54, 163; *see also* diversity
inclusive education 9, 19, 137; curriculum 36–37, 46–47, 49–50, 64, 190, 202–04, 228–29, 232; definition 50; early childhood 22, 25, 30, 31, 32, 232; initial teacher education 36, 193–94, 195–96, 201, 202–04, 206, 211; law and government policy 22; school and centre policies and resources to support 35, 36, 37–47, 219, 234; secondary schools 87, 137, 142; teaching for 23, 46–47, 52, 192–93, 216–22, 228–29, 230, 234–35; tertiary environments 191
inequity *see* equity and inequity
initial teacher education (ITE): curriculum 190, 202–04, 206, 210; entry standards 233; evaluation study, Faculty of Education University of Auckland 2014 204–05; heteronormativity 11, 191–93, 196–98, 199–201, 205–06, 210, 211–12, 216–22; merger of Auckland College of Education with University of Auckland 193–94; picture books to encourage inclusive practices 36, 219; policy context and sexual diversity 189–90, 229; research study, Auckland College of Education 2002 194–204; research study, Faculty

of Education University of Auckland 2009 195–204; and sexualities 191–99, 200–01, 202–06, 211, 214–15, 216–22; tertiary environments 190–91
intersex 14, 151, 157, 213
Isaacs, Susan 13
*It's Okay to be Different* (Parr) 41

Karanga Mai Young Parents' College 174
Key, John 74–75
'Kikorangi High School' study 122–32
*King and King* (De Haan and Nijland) 42
*King and King and Family* (De Haan and Nijland) 44–45
King, Truby 12–13

language: fag discourse 70, 72, 74, 75; within friendship circles 75–76; 'gay,' use of term 74–75, 79, 125–26, 213, 230–31; gay discourse 70–72, 74; homophobic 69, 70, 71, 72, 75, 79; homosexually themed 74; shifting definitions of queer language, New Zealand 72–78, 79; student rejections of traditional sexual identity categories 139, 231; 'that's so gay' 71, 72, 74–75, 79, 230–31; *see also* terminology
legislation 189–90, 206, 226, 227; *see also* names of Acts, e.g. Human Rights Act 1993
'lesbian baby boom' 10
lesbian parents 22, 23, 24–25, 31, 37, 38, 39, 40, 42–44, 45, 221–22; in picture book stories 37, 38, 39, 40, 42–44, 45, 46
lesbian students, secondary schools 10, 87–88, 110–11
lesbians 14, 15, 155, 156, 213; as 'abnormal other' 51, 99; and femininity 88; Māori 126; using term to police gender norms 90–92; Western term 126
LGBfakeT 152
LGBT (lesbian, gay, bisexual, transgender): effects of terminology 152; in tertiary education environment 190–91, 192
LGBTI (lesbian, gay, bisexual, transgender or intersex) 99
LGBTQ (lesbian, gay, bisexual, transgender or queer): texts 53; visibility on Auckland ITE campuses 194–99, 201, 204, 205, 206; youth 135

liberal tolerance 201
'logic of practice' (Bourdieu) 118, 119

Māori: effect of colonisation on approaches to sexuality 121, 162–63; equity policies 194; gender and sexuality terms 14, 126, 160, 163, 164; non-Western approaches to sexuality 14, 121, 126, 127, 151, 162–63, 164
Māori students and youth 153; fluid identity 128; future research on 227; sexuality education 118, 122–24, 131–32
marriage: heterosexual, monogamous 12, 58, 59, 60; and reproduction 57; *see also* same-sex marriage
Marriage (Definition of Marriage) Amendment Act 2013 9, 89, 190, 228
masculinity: and bullying in school playground 102; expression 159; gay masculinities 55, 70, 94; hegemonic 24, 70, 77, 84, 90, 93, 95, 109; heterosexual 50, 55, 100, 124; non-traditional 70, 84, 109; normative gender codes 83–84; regulation in secondary school friendship circles 72–74, 75–78, 79; secondary school students 68, 70, 72, 76–79, 90, 94, 106, 109
Massachusetts Safe Schools Program 136
masturbation 12
Mau, Alison 89
*Milly, Molly and Different Dads* (Pittar) 40
Ministry of Education: *Te Whāriki* 21, 25–27; Teen Parent Units 174–75; *see also* New Zealand Curriculum
*Molly's Family* (Garden) 43–44
*Mommy, Mama and Me* (Newman) 39
motherhood: average age of first-time mothers 177–78; 'ideal' 177; neo-liberal discourse 177, 181–82, 231; *see also* teenage pregnancy and parenthood
*My Favourite Places* (Bailey) 40

National Certificate of Educational Achievement (NCEA) 119, 175, 179
National-led coalition government 232–33
neo-liberalism: analysis of discourses 235; discourse of motherhood 177, 181–82, 231; and family diversity 177; initial teacher education policies 190

New Zealand AIDS Foundation 138, 164, 165, 240
*New Zealand Curriculum: Health and Physical Education* 117; inclusiveness 36, 37, 49–50, 64
New Zealand Families Commission 22
New Zealand Post Primary Teachers' Association 15, 88, 95, 165, 230; *Affirming Diversity of Sexualities and Gender Identities in the School Community* 240
New Zealand Teachers Council, *Graduating Teacher Standards* 192
Newman, Lesléa: *Daddy, Papa and Me* 39; *Mommy, Mama and Me* 39; *Donovan's Big Day* 41
Nijland, Stern: *King and King* 42; *King and King and Family* 44–45
No Outsiders Project Team 36
non-gendered 158, 159
nuclear family: nuclear gay family 42; traditional 24, 57, 60

Oelschlager, Vanita: *Tale of Two Daddies* 39; *Tale of Two Mommies* 39
omnisexuals 156
opposite-sex attraction 24, 59, 60–63, 84, 155; proof of not being gay 125–26; secondary school students 68, 88, 106–09, 111–13, 125–26; *see also* heterosexuality
oral sex 10
Otago University Students' Association, Queer Support 164–65, 167, 235, 240
'othered' identity 21, 49, 51, 57, 68, 69, 93, 99, 124–25, 136, 140, 142, 197, 210, 213
OUT THERE 164, 165, 240

Painter, Holly, *How Safe?* 164–65
pansexuals 14, 155, 156
parenthood, teenage *see* teenage pregnancy and parenthood
parents: assumptions about 10, 214; *see also* same-sex parents
Parnell, Peter, *And Tango Makes Three* 40
Parr, Todd: *The Family Book* 39; *It's Okay to be Different* 41
partnership schools 232–33
Pasifika: equity policies 194; gender and sexuality terms 14, 126, 160, 163
Pasifika students and youth: complex identities 121–22; conflict between cultural practices and Christianity 127–29; future research on 227; multiple identities 128–29; non-Western views of sexuality 14, 126, 128; sexuality education 118, 122–24, 131–32; teenage pregnancy and parenthood 129–31
pe'a (tattoo) 127–28
peer educators 235
peer groups: bullying of queer youth 11, 69; development of similar views within group 69; influence on individual members 69, 70; learning about sexuality out of school class time 105–06; reinscribing heteronormativity 93; status of couples 106–08; *see also* friendship circles; queer youth groups
peer support 136, 142–44, 147
'perversity' 12
photo-diaries, of sexuality at school 104–05; heteronormativity 105–09; lesbian students 110–11; opposite-sex couple 'just talking' 111–12
picture books: encompassing sexuality and family diversity 35, 36, 37–47, 219; tools for combating homophobia 36; traditional parent/family representations 214
Pittar, Gill, *Milly, Molly and Different Dads* 40
Plunket Society 12–13, 175
Polacco, Patricia, *In Our Mothers' House* 43–44, 45, 46
popular culture, heteronormativity in 49–50, 52, 54–64
post-structural theory: discourse 83, 100; gender and sexuality 25, 83–85
power relationships: colonial 121; and heteronormativity 21, 28, 32; and space 103; symbolic power, Bourdieu's concept 215, 218; teenage parents' experiences of school 179–80
practice, Bourdieu's concept 214
pregnancy *see* teenage pregnancy and parenthood
pride marches 103
primary schools: books and popular culture texts 36, 58–63; curriculum 228, 232; heteronormativity 10, 52, 99, 100–01; National Standards 119, 232; sexuality education 216–18
priority learners 232, 233

QSA Network Aotearoa 141
Q'topia, Christchurch 135
queer, use of term 14–15, 27–28, 72, 189
queer students: acceptance of 87–90, 94, 95, 230–31; bullying of 11, 68, 69–70, 78, 83, 84, 88, 93; deficit understandings of 140–41, 142, 143, 145; educational environments hostile and alienating 226; perceived femininity of boys 94; *Safety in our Schools* resource 164, 165; and school formal 82, 85, 86, 87–95, 230; school support 234; secondary schools 11, 67–68, 69–70, 72–79, 83, 84, 108–09, 138–41, 230–31; *see also* lesbian students
Queer Support, Otago University Students' Association 164–65, 167, 235, 240
Queer–Straight Alliances (QSAs) 135, 230, 231, 234; case study methodology 138–39; development inside and outside schools 135–37; double binds 137–38, 139–41, 142–46, 147; social justice and support role 142–44
queer theory 14, 51, 100, 101–02, 210, 222; using to practise beyond the (hetero) norm 27–29, 32
Queer/trans Visibility and Action project 205
queer youth groups 77, 78
Queers in Tertiary Education hui 205

race issues 146, 204
Rainbow Staff Group, Faculty of Education University of Auckland 195, 204–05
Rainbow Youth 135, 164, 165, 167, 235, 240; WTF campaign 169
relationships: children, in *Te Whāriki* 26; pedagogy of, in early childhood education 30–31; researcher, with subjects of study 123; *see also* power relationships
religious diversity 220, 227
Richardson, Justin, *And Tango Makes Three* 40

*Safety in our Schools – Ko te haumaru i o tatou kura* 164, 165, 240–41
same-sex attraction 10, 15, 84, 155; and curriculum 228–29; secondary school students 11, 68, 77, 83, 108–09, 110–11, 112, 230–31
same-sex marriage 9, 24, 89

same-sex parents: disclosure practices 37; and early childhood education 10, 24–25, 30–31; heteronormative assumptions about children 23, 24–25, 37; and primary schools 10; stories in picture books 35, 36, 37–41, 43–45; and teacher education 214, 221–22; *see also* gay parents; lesbian parents
same-sex relationships: acceptance of 89; invisibility in school 111; portrayal in books 46, 219; women choosing to have children 10
same-sex weddings, picture books 41–42
Samoan students and youth 127–29
school formal: discourses 83; as heteronormative social event 83, 92, 93, 214; as rite of passage 82; same-sex partners, boys 82, 85, 87, 90–94, 95; same-sex partners, girls 82, 85, 87–92, 94–95; school policies, boys' school 92–93, 95; school policies, co-educational and girls' schools 86, 87–88, 94–95; study methodology 85–86
*School Journal* 58–60, 228; cartoon: *She loves me, she loves me not* 60–63
schools: heteronormativity 120; sites of surveillance and regulation 120, 137; *see also* primary schools; secondary schools
secondary schools: boys' school culture 93–94, 95, 165; bullying 11, 68, 69–70, 78, 83, 84, 88, 89, 93, 111, 166; culture 68, 69, 78–79; diversity in 87, 89, 230; embodied and spatial elements 102–13; gay-friendly 68, 70; heteronormativity 10–11, 52, 79, 90, 93, 94, 95, 99, 100–09, 110–12, 124–26, 132, 136, 142; homophobia 68, 69–70, 72, 79, 87, 89, 90–91, 92–94, 95, 125, 126, 230; masculinity codes 68, 70, 72, 76–77, 79, 94; sexuality education 10, 105, 122–24, 131–32, 218–19; *see also* lesbian students; Māori students and youth; Pasifika students and youth; queer students; Queer–Straight Alliances (QSAs); school formal; Teen Parent Units (TPUs); trans* students
self-awareness 129
self-esteem: children 38, 46; secondary school students 67
sexual diversity: and colonisation 121, 126; in curriculum 192, 228–29,

235; and double bind 136–37; and initial teacher education 191–99, 200–01, 202–06, 211, 214–15, 216–22; Queer–Straight Alliance role 136, 140; school and centre policies and resources to address 35, 36, 37–47, 87, 89, 93, 99, 219, 234; silencing of 228; teaching 11, 24–25, 192–93; *see also* inclusion and exclusion; inclusive education; sexual orientation

sexual identity 67, 69, 70, 77, 92, 99, 155–61; destabilisation by queer theory 102; fluidity and changeability 92; student rejections of labels for traditional categories 139, 231

sexual orientation: definitions 155–56, 191; and empowerment 27; equity policies 189, 194; and heterosexual matrix 124; in initial teacher education 193, 195, 196–99, 201, 202–06, 210; legislation 189–90; presumed 125; visibility in initial teacher education 193, 195, 196–99, 201, 202–06; *see also* asexuals; bisexuals; cross-dressers; faʻafafine; gay men and youth; genderqueers; homosexuality; intersexed; lesbians; LGBT; LGBTI; LGBTQ; pansexuals; sexual diversity; takatāpui; trans* people

sexuality: children 12–14, 26–27, 29, 190; and Christianity 119–20, 121, 127–28; and colonisation 119, 121–22, 132, 161–62; constructions 52, 56, 136, 210; and culture 118, 119, 126–32; discourses based on colonial history 119–20; discrimination on basis of 9, 31, 82, 120, 142, 189–90, 191, 201; in education settings 10, 11, 14; and gender 50–51, 57–58, 64, 94, 100, 110–11, 120, 124, 132, 136; historical societal attitudes 190; Māori and Pasifika 118, 122–24, 126–31, 162–63; 'normal' 24, 84, 99, 100, 101, 105–09, 136, 197, 198, 210; in personal and private realm 52; post-structural theory 83–85; *see also* sexual diversity; sexual orientation

sexuality education 10, 105, 117, 216, 235; controversial school subject 119; and cultural values and norms 118, 119, 126; description 117; (hetero)doxa of practices in relation to sex, gender and sexualities 216–22; Māori and Pasifika students 118, 122–24, 131–32; partnership schools 233

shock and shame tactics 168–69

silence 125, 198–99

*Simpsons, The* 49; Homer's Phobia 54–56, 63

social and support networks for LGBTQ youth 135; *see also* Queer–Straight Alliances (QSAs)

social capital 119, 214

social diversity 19, 29, 226, 228–29, 232

social inclusion *see* inclusion and exclusion

social justice 9, 122; Bourdieu 212; curriculum 190, 228–29; in initial teacher education 206; and legislative changes 206; Queer–Straight Alliance role 141, 142–44, 145, 147; school policies 82, 88, 138; teaching for 19, 22, 29, 31, 32, 35, 36, 45, 46, 189, 192, 204, 219, 227

space: as backdrop for people and action 103; embodied and spatial elements of schooling 102–13; fluid meanings and functions 103, 104; and heteronormativity 229

*Spacegirl Pukes* (Watson) 40

sperm donation 10, 23

sports 70, 84

stereotypes 39, 40, 55, 145, 216, 223

straight, definition 155, 156, 213

students *see* lesbian students; Māori students and youth; Pasifika students and youth; queer students; school formal; teenage pregnancy and parenthood; trans* students

suicide, trans* students 166

support networks for LGBTQ youth 135; *see also* Queer–Straight Alliances (QSAs)

symbolic power, Bourdieu's concept 215, 218

symbolic violence, Bourdieu's concept 215–16, 217, 224

takatāpui 14, 126, 160, 163, 164, 227

*Tale of Two Daddies* (Oelschlager) 39

*Tale of Two Mommies* (Oelschlager) 39

TAMS (Text Analysis Mark up System) 86

tattoos 127–28

Te Whāriki 21; inclusiveness 37; and queer theory 28; sexuality absent from

text 26; using as a tool to practise beyond the (hetero)norm 25–27, 28–30
teacher education *see* initial teacher education
teachers: areas of future research on queer teachers 227–28; balance of worldviews 46–47; challenging heteronormativity 218, 219–24, 231–35; early childhood education settings 22, 24–27, 28–32, 45–46, 216–22; post-graduate qualifications 233; promotion of inclusion 22, 46–47, 52, 192–93, 216–22, 228–29, 230, 234–35; promotion of social justice 19, 22, 29, 31, 32, 35, 36, 45, 46, 189, 192, 204, 219, 227; workplace safety 190, 197, 198–200, 204, 222, 228
teaching resources, to support gender, sexual and family diversity 234
Teen Parent Units (TPUs) 130, 173, 178, 179, 180, 182; experiences of culture 182–85; historical overview 174–75; transformative effects 183–86
teenage pregnancy and parenthood 129–31, 173; breastfeeding 181; critique of deficit constructions 178–82; experiences of pregnancies when disengaged from school 181; experiences of school disengagement 178–80, 182; experiences of school pregnancies 180–81; pregnancy as a life 'turning point' 181–82; research studies 174; societal constructions of teenage motherhood 175–78, 185, 186, 231
television, queer characters 89
terminology 14–15, 30, 74–75, 79, 139, 154, 155–64, 213, 230–31, 235; *see also* language
'terrain of exchange' 49
tertiary education, LBGT faculty members and students 190–91
texts: critical analysis 52–64; definition 49; LGBTQ content 53; popular culture 49–51, 52, 54–64
theatre, as challenge to social and cultural norms 144–45
'thing-power' 103–04
*To Be Who I Am – Kia noho au ki tōku anō ao* (Human Rights Commission) 165

Topp Twins 88
trans* people 10, 14, 15, 150–51, 158, 159, 213; disadvantage 161–62; emerging questions for studies of education 167–70; exclusion 153–544, 163; media representation 168, 169; perspectives on education 150–52, 162, 164–67, 170–71; trans* contrasted with cisgender 161–62, 164–67, 168, 170; use of term trans* 10, 150, 154, 163; visibility 161, 166, 168–70
*Trans People: Facts and Information* (Human Rights Commission) 240
trans* students: acceptance 230; bullying 166; educational environments hostile and alienating 226; exclusion 164–66; future research on 227; mental health and suicide 166; recommendations for educators 167; *Safety in our Schools* resource 164, 165; school support 234; secondary schools 11, 164–66, 168, 218
transphobia 162, 235; bullying 10
Tui High School case study: acknowledging and working the double binds 139–41, 147; methodology 138–39; productive dissensus: negotiating double binds 144–46; productive double binds 142–44
tūpuna Māori 162–63

*Uncle Bobby's Wedding* (Brannen) 41
United Nations Convention on the Rights of the Child (UNCROC) 82–83
University of Auckland, Faculty of Education: evaluation study, 2014 204–05; from merger with Auckland College of Education 193–94; Rainbow Staff Group (RSG) 195, 203–05; research study, 2009 195–204
University of Canterbury 138

'vibrant matter' 103, 104
violence, symbolic, Bourdieu's concept 214–16
visibility: heteronormativity 99, 106–07, 109, 125, 161, 165; LGBTQ, on Auckland ITE campuses 194–99, 201, 204, 205, 206; queer identities in charter schools 233; queer

youth 135; queerness in New Zealand society 87–88; same-sex parents 31, 39, 42, 45; same-sex relationships in school 111; trans* people/students 161, 165, 166, 168–69

wāhine Māori 162
Watson, Katy, *Spacegirl Pukes* 40
'We're a Family' study 22
whānau *see* families/whānau
whāriki metaphor 28; *see also Te Whāriki*
*What Can You Do with Two Mommies?* (Hill) 43, 44

women: changing roles 177; equity policies 194; Faculty of Education staff, University of Auckland 194
Work and Income 175
workplace safety for queers 190, 197, 198–99, 204, 222, 228

youth *see* gay men and youth; lesbian students; LGBTQ – youth; Māori students and youth; Pasifika students and youth; queer students; queer youth groups
Youth'12 research group 166